Up the Down Escalator

By the Same Author

Living on Thin Air

Up the Down Escalator

Why the Global Pessimists are Wrong

CHARLES LEADBEATER

VIKING

an imprint of

PENGUIN BOOKS

VIKING

Published by the Penguin Group

Penguin Books Ltd, 80 Strand, London WC2R 0RL, England
Penguin Putnam Inc., 375 Hudson Street, New York, New York 10014, USA
Penguin Books Australia Ltd, 250 Camberwell Road,
Camberwell, Victoria 3124, Australia
Penguin Books Canada Ltd, 10 Alcorn Avenue, Toronto, Ontario, Canada M4V 3B2
Penguin Books India (P) Ltd, 11 Community Centre,
Panchsheel Park, New Delhi – 110 017, India
Penguin Books (NZ) Ltd, Cnr Rosedale and Airborne Roads,
Albany, Auckland, New Zealand
Penguin Books (South Africa) (Pty) Ltd, 24 Sturdee Avenue,
Rosebank 2196, South Africa

Penguin Books Ltd, Registered Offices: 80 Strand, London WC2R 0RL, England

www.penguin.com

First published 2002
1

Copyright © Charles Leadbeater, 2002

Set in 12/14.75pt Monotype Bembo
Typeset by Rowland Phototypesetting Ltd, Bury St Edmunds, Suffolk
Printed in Great Britain by Clays Ltd, St Ives plc

A CIP catalogue record for this book is available from the British Library

ISBN 0-670-91322-7

For the extremely fine Henrietta and Freddie

Contents

Acknowledgements   ix

Preface: Pessimism in Power   1

1. The Gathering Gloom   15
2. The Great Escape   44
3. Death Wish Nation   72
4. The Pessimists' Alliance   102
5. The Dream of Digitopia   114
6. The Terror of Technotopia   150
7. Innovation Rules   173
8. The Age of Self-rule   199
9. The End of Capitalism   220
10. The Personalized Society   252
11. Globalization Can Be Good   289
12. Militant Optimism   328

Notes   355

Bibliography   363

Acknowledgements

Many people helped me to write this book, without necessarily being aware of it, over the two years it has taken to put together.

I would particularly like to thank my publisher at Viking, Juliet Annan, who encouraged me to stick with the idea even when it was in a dreadful mess. Also at Viking I would like to thank Kate Barker and Charlotte Greig. As ever I am grateful to my agent David Godwin for shepherding the project along. Bela Cunha copyedited the manuscript with great care and patience.

I have learned a lot from the many people I have worked with on projects over the past couple of years including: John Browne and Nick Butler at BP; John Hewitt and David McNeil at the Arts Council of England; John Newbigin and Heather Rabbats at Channel 4 television and its former chief executive Michael Jackson; Tom Bentley and many others at Demos, including Kate Oakley; Chris Spray and his colleagues at Atlas Venture; Eliza Burrows and David Abraham at Discovery Networks; Fritz Gutrodt and others at Swiss Re; Philip Dodd at the Institute of Contemporary Arts and Wilf Stevenson at the Smith Institute; Colin Burns and Maura Shea at IDEO; Mathew Taylor at the Institute for Public Policy Research and the Rockefeller Foundation for inviting me to two weekend seminars at Bellagio in northern Italy; Martin Horton and Mel Ussher at the Improvement and Development Agency; Hilary Cottam at the Design Council; and Mandy Barrie, Emma Scott and Janet Evans at the Department of Culture. In addition I have learned a great deal from conversations and working with David Miliband, Ed Miliband and Geoff Mulgan. *Up the Down Escalator* is peppered with quotations from other books from which I have invariably learned a great deal more than the material directly referred to in the text.

I owe a debt to Denis Grant for keeping me fit and giving me stamina. My main debt goes to our close friends and my family, young and old, who make everything worthwhile for me, and especially to my wife Geraldine Bedell, who for six years has tolerated my working in our bedroom and without whom I would be incapable.

For further information about my work and future projects please visit www.charlesleadbeater.net

Preface: Pessimism in Power

Pessimism is in power: a chronic pessimism about the prospects for our society, families, jobs, the environment and the world at large. Pessimism that we are in the midst of creating a global dystopia is becoming deeply embedded in our culture. Pessimism is pervasive, plausible and ingrained. It is now possible, and in some circles almost mandatory, to be deeply pessimistic on virtually any subject. Globalization is blowing a gale of disorder through our lives, handing control over our economic prospects to multinational companies and frenzied financial markets. Millions live on an endless plateau of poverty and destitution in the developing world, while affluent consumers in post-industrial societies worry about which brands to buy. Mankind is in the midst of a gigantic gamble with the earth's ecosystem, which is being driven to the point of near collapse through overpopulation, consumption and industrial development. We will leave future generations to fend for themselves in a wasteland. Science and technology threaten us with further untold risks and dangers, from genetically modified foods and microscopic nano-machines that may take over our bodies and minds, to biological weapons that could soon fall into the hands of crazed terrorists. In the face of these challenges our political leaders are at best pragmatic managers of crisis and disorder, at worst corrupt agents of it. Democratic debate has been reduced to an arm of the marketing and media industries. Politicians are creations of advertising departments. They are tyrannized by opinion polls and focus groups. Government is increasingly in hock to big companies who provide many basic services and fund political parties. The role of politics is increasingly to acclimatize us to the brute fact that life is out of our control. Politics is ever less about our collectively taking control of our destiny. Western media-saturated culture is increasingly shallow and dumb: we are like zombies in front of mindless entertainment, from *Big Brother* to *Who Wants to Be a Millionaire?* We are surrounded by end-less, mindless cacophony and trivia that constantly distract us and rob us of the time for contemplation and reflection. There is no space, other than perhaps the toilet, that is beyond the reach of marketing and new technology and even that last bastion of free thought will surely soon fall. Meanwhile the traditional, nuclear family is collapsing and with it the founda-tion for most morality. We can no longer rely on basic civility and morals in an increasingly venal, self-interested society, in which common codes are collapsing. The anarchy in our everyday lives is reflected back to us in the international sphere, with the growing sense of threat posed by terrorists, rogue states and fanatics of all shapes and sizes. George Steiner remarks in *Grammars of Creation* that there is a 'core tiredness' in the spirit of the times. But in reality it is far worse than that: everything seems to be degenerating and spiralling out of control.

On all these counts we seem to have good grounds for being deeply pessimistic about our futures. We should abandon the illusion of hope and adapt to the grim reality. One of the most cogent and compelling advocates of pessimism has been the US journalist and foreign affairs commentator Robert D. Kaplan. In *Warrior Politics* Kaplan sets out the case for thinking of the future in bleak, if not nightmarish terms. The benefits of global capitalism are not distributed equally. The more dynamic the capitalist expansion the more unequal the distri-bution of wealth, he argues. Enormous disparities in wealth will feed fundamentalist terrorism that will be enabled as never before by the distribution of technology. Terrorists will use information technology to coordinate their dispersed activities, and increasingly biological weapons, to strike unseen. The spread of information technology will not lead to new social compacts and more democracy but to new disputes and divisions, as people find ever more complex issues to disagree over. Violent populism will sweep the fast growing, impoverished cities of the developing world in which perhaps three billion people will live. Never before have so many people lived in such poverty so intimately. The political consequences could be explosive. The developing world will be awash with vast populations of underpaid, underemployed, badly educated, landless labourers, disoriented by urban living and divided by ethnicity and religion. They will be looking for leaders to save and inspire them. Democratization will not provide the stability and order these populations need. It will, Kaplan maintains, create a generation of weak leaders. Authoritarian and populist leaders will be the norm. National government will increasingly be bypassed by great cities and by supranational institutions. In rich developed countries most people will live in a thin technological bubble, subsisting on mindless entertainment, drifting from one craze to the next, one relationship to the next, conditioned by global media so that they are virtually unable to think for themselves. Even the small shreds of optimism we have left should make us nervous: optimism about the potential of science and technology at the start of the twentieth century only paved the way for the horrors of warfare and authoritarianism that followed. It is scary stuff.

Kaplan is far from alone. The anti-globalization and environmental movements prey on fear of the future. They cannot survive without serving the public with a regular diet of pessimism. Those movements might be expected to be pessimistic. Yet many of the most alarming accounts of our future have come from within the establishment. One of the chief critics of global capitalism is George Soros, who made his fortune from the markets. It was Bill Joy, the co-founder of Sun Microsystems, who warned that carbon-based life forms, that is us, may well be overtaken by silicon-based life forms, that is computers and robots, in the course of this century. The next stage of evolution could be for humans to become machines, because machines will be so much smarter than us. Martin Rees, Britain's astronomer royal, raised the stakes even higher in an extraordinarily gloomy assessment of our life chances in the journal *Prospect*. Within a few years, Rees warned, thousands, even millions, of people will acquire the capability to make and disseminate weapons that could cause widespread epidemics. A crazed fanatic, with the mind-set of someone who now programmes computer viruses, could trigger a global catastrophe. The only real hope, Rees argues, is that we might in time establish more orderly communities on the moon or Mars. Rees does not explain how these communities would be technologically advanced but free from the nutters who would presumably all remain on the ravaged earth. He sums up:

This new century, on this planet, might be a defining moment for the cosmos. Our actions could initiate the irreversible spread of life beyond the solar system. Or in contrast, through malign intent or misadventure, 21st-century technology could jeopardise life's cosmic potential, when its evolution has barely begun.[1]

It would be foolish in the extreme simply to ignore such authoritative voices of pessimism. Yet the argument of this book is that we should not take this chronic, apocalyptic pessimism at face value. *Up the Down Escalator* identifies, analyses and challenges the power of pessimism: arguing against pessimism feels like walking up the down escalator, it is hard work. Yet there are strong grounds for thinking quite optimistically about what the twenty-first century might hold, not least that we might avoid and correct some of the mistakes that were made in the twentieth century. (Pessimists in general take a dim view of our ability to learn from mistakes.)

Pessimism comes at us from all directions. Not only is it possible to be pessimistic about a widening array of issues, it is also possible for people holding very different values to be pessimistic, for slightly different reasons, about the same issues. Reactionary pessimists, usually from the right, for example, bemoan technology and globalization because they threaten to wreck tradition, dissolve ancient institutions and rob us of old identities. Radical pessimists, usually from the left, believe globalization and technology are creating a diminished, corporate and anti-democratic culture in which we have all become drones in a giant commercial machine, our sense of individuality and freedom robbed from us by invasive corporate marketing. As Franz Kafka put it, in modern capitalism 'there is an abundance of hope, but none for us'. Together these radical and reactionary elements are forming an extraordinary, unspoken alliance, which is arguably the strongest force in politics in most developed countries. The meat and drink of this alliance is alarmism, anxiety and fear. These accounts from left and right, environmental activists and religious conservatives, angry anarchists and nostalgic aristocrats, feed on many of the same themes. Individualization is eating away at the social bonds that sustain community. Constant change is exhausting and disorienting us. We are slaves to fashion and novelty. Boundaries and borders, moral and national, that once provided us with a sense of stability and identity are being dissolved. We are lost. Globalization is standardizing culture around crude commercial values that leave little room for difference, diversity and dissent. Technology is increasingly driving us into the hands of global corporations, which will put us on a treadmill of largely self-defeating, shallow innovations that eliminate slow, tacit, craft and low-tech forms of knowledge and production. The market, far from providing greater choice, is an agent for cultural cleansing. As cultural differences are eliminated so are the grounds for dissent and democracy. We risk losing our connections to the soil and nature. Growing numbers of people feel unable to lead what they could call authentic lives. We feel cut off from ourselves. The citizens of western liberal democracies are suffering from a possibly terminal dose of false consciousness, unable to discern, articulate or defend their own interests. All the forces that apparently drive society forward – innovation, technology, individualism, globalization – are pulling us into a downward spiral. Far from living in a period of progress, we are gripped by a deepening, irreversible degeneration that is eating away at society from within. Pessimists do not shy from apocalyptic language and the techniques of the horror film. The key texts of pessimism are littered with talk of anarchy and apocalypse, ungovernable masses and corporations, societies that are in the grip of a death wish.

Just as pessimism can appeal across the social and political spectrum, so it can find its expression in many ways as well. Pessimism is as much, if not more, a cultural force than an overtly political one. It has two main expressions. The first tendency is to retreat from the uncontrollable world into nostalgia, domesticity and spirituality. The second tendency is to want to confront the world, often violently. One major expression of pessimism is the cult of nostalgia. In a period of accelerated technological and social change, it should be no surprise that we are also in the midst of a nostalgia boom: a yearning for a rosy past when society was simpler, calmer, more understandable and dependable. New technology, which allows us to store, retrieve and play with our memories, only feeds this appetite to sanctify an air-brushed version of how good the past used to be. Another expression is the yearning to retreat from the complex and threatening world into an inner utopia. When pessimism moves from culture into politics, from private into public, it acquires a more violent form. All too easily political pessimism feeds an inflamed, angry, populist force, whipped up into a hysteria of victimhood. This politics of blame encourages us to look for the culprits, the people who set in motion the degeneration of our society: foreigners, aliens, weirdos, avant-garde artists who transgress moral borders and scientists who transgress natural ones. This populist pessimism often emerges as endism: a fear that vital institutions and traditions upon which our lives seem to depend are about to come to an end. So we live with a daily diet of warnings that the end is nigh for reading, thinking, the family, the pound, democracy, justice and the world.

There are two fundamental reasons for resisting the appeal of chronic pessimism. The first is that chronic pessimism can all too easily become self-fulfilling. The pessimists' argument is not just that we should be realistic. The argument is not that we face an uncertain and risky future, for which we should be prepared. The pessimist argument is more apocalyptic than that: we are in the grip of irreversible, chronic forces that are leading to degeneration. Psychological studies define pessimism not as a realistic sense that things might go badly, but as a state in which people feel helpless and out of control, so much so that they cannot take action to avoid or correct mistakes. People who become severely depressed and pessimistic often fall into a state of learned helplessness: they become so accustomed to the idea that they are helpless that they believe it, even when it is not true. That is the condition we are in danger of falling into: we are learning to make ourselves helpless.

The leading authority on the psychological roots of

pessimism and optimism, the US psychologist Martin E. P. Seligman, claims that the rise of depression has much to do with the rise of individualism. Why is it, Seligman asks, in a world in which we have more money, choice, power, education, books, records and leisure, that depression should be so much more prevalent than it was when developed societies were poorer?[2] Severe depression is ten times more prevalent today than it was fifty years ago. It assaults women twice as often as men and it now strikes a decade earlier in life than it did even a generation ago, in the US at least. A large part of the explanation, Seligman says, is that much of the moral furniture upon which earlier generations could rely – faith in God, the nation, the family – have become threadbare in the last forty years. As individualism has become stronger, so we tend to take our setbacks more personally.

At the core of the psychology of pessimism is a sense of helplessness, in which nothing that someone chooses to do affects what happens to them. Pessimists learn to think of themselves as helpless victims of circumstances beyond their control. They tend to regard misfortune as their own fault, expect it to be enduring and that it will undermine everything else they try to do to correct the situation. Pessimists often become paralysed by their own, inflated, sense of helplessness. Pessimistic prophecies can be self-fulfilling. Psychological studies over many years show that pessimists achieve less, give up more easily, become depressed more readily. In contrast, the same experiments show that optimists do better at school and college, at work and in sport. There is additional evidence that optimists tend to live longer and have better health. Optimism and pessimism may both have had evolutionary value for us. One theory argues that optimistic illusions about reality helped us to evolve.[3] Why else would humans plant seeds in April, hang on through drought and harvest them in October, unless they were capable of thinking of the future?

Without optimism why would people have set off for the moon, fought Nazism, conquered Everest or unravelled DNA? Optimism lies behind creativity and innovation: hope in the face of uncertainty and doubt.

That is not an argument for naive optimism, which can be just as dangerous as chronic pessimism. There is considerable evidence that depressed people are sadder but wiser. Depressed and pessimistic people are often good judges of how much control they have in psychological tests and they have a good memory of how well they did. Optimists, on the other hand, tend to overestimate how much control they have and consistently apply a rosy gloss to past setbacks and failures. Pessimists tend to be even-handed and accurate in their assessment of the position. Optimists tend to be lopsided; they distort reality. That, however, is why optimism is so useful: it allows people to persist and seek opportunities that are not immediately obvious. Optimists tend not to give up and not to be daunted. They may sometimes, however, be foolhardy. Overoptimism can lead to hubris.

So the case for pessimism, based on psychological studies, is that it can make us more accurate in predicting events, particularly in a world of uncertainty. However, pessimism also leaves people prone to anxiety and depression; it tends to produce inertia rather than action in the face of setbacks; makes people more likely to give up when they encounter obstacles and so it becomes a self-fulfilling prophecy. When pessimists are proved right and events turn out badly, this becomes just further proof of the case for pessimism: a setback becomes a disaster, a disaster a catastrophe. Realistic pessimism, which is reflective and calculating, can be extremely useful, particularly when it is combined with a spirit of optimism that carries people forward. As the Italian Marxist Antonio Gramsci put it: optimism of the will needs to be matched by pessimism of the intellect. To put it a different way:

we need to be passionate and ambitious but hard-headed at the same time. Pessimism can pull us back from the risky exaggerations optimism encourages us to entertain, making us think twice before we make rash or foolhardy gestures. Chronic, all-engulfing pessimism is disabling. Chronic pessimism might have been warranted when two out of three children died before the age of five, when women routinely died in childbirth and when a period of cold weather led to mass starvation. But our current state hardly compares with that. It is in the optimistic moments in our lives that we make new plans and without those we would achieve nothing that involved overcoming obstacles. Without optimism the jet plane and the computer would still be on the drawing board and the four-minute mile would be unrun. Optimism is the basis for creativity and innovation, which are our main sources of hope.

The second plank of the case against chronic pessimism is that it does not add up, in part because it so heavily discounts powerful tendencies at work that could make life much better for many millions of people in the twenty-first century. Globalization has not gone too far but not far enough. Poverty in developing countries will be reduced only through more economic integration and trade. That is not a solution on its own, but it is a vital part of the solution. Millions of people have been lifted out of poverty in the last two decades in developing countries through globalization, not in spite of it. Globalization and new technology are not creating a population of mindless drones. On the contrary, they are expanding the opportunities for cultural expression and cross-fertilization of ideas. Our culture is not becoming more homogenized but in many ways more diverse and home to many hybrids. How can we be in a period of remorseless cultural decline and dumbing down when more people than ever can read, write, compose, draw, film, play and communicate? In the twentieth century we only just began the task of educating ourselves throughout life. Even in the UK a national system of secondary education is only fifty years old. In this century education will spread throughout the world, starting with basic primary education for children, and across many more ages. Until very recently learning has been an elite activity. In the twenty-first century it could become a mass activity and that in turn could have huge consequences for democracy and culture. The ideal of individual self-rule could spread around the world in the twenty-first century. With that new varieties of individualism will develop which stress the creative and productive aspects of individualism as well as mere consumerism. Different kinds of market society will develop that blend the market with different cultural and religious values. In many countries the role of the state and public services will be enhanced. Collaboration will be as much part of the modern culture of leisure and work as individualism. Young people who have grown up with the technology and culture of the networked society seem to be both more individualistic and more collaborative, more private and more social. This generation is not in the grip of moral decay, far from it; teenagers seem highly morally aware especially of egalitarian issues of racism and sexism, as well as global issues such as the environment. Technology, for good and ill, will deliver abundance to us, in communications and computing, which could transform how we organize our lives economically and socially, in politics and government. There is every prospect that millions more people will live longer, better-quality lives in this century. Improvements in technology, for instance the fuel cell and the use of hydrogen as a fuel source, will help us deliver economic growth but with less environmental damage. It should soon be possible for millions of people in large cities to use cars that create very little pollution. Hope that we might solve our environmental problems rests on our ability to innovate.

Innovation and creativity will be the most potent forces for improvement in our lives. Technology will open up ways to transform our world far more than politics. That, combined with greater pragmatism in politics, will be no bad thing. At the start of the twentieth century mass utopian dreams were focused on projects for rational, large-scale planning and top down experiments in social mobilization: fascism, communism, nationalism, city planning, mass production industries. Given the largely disastrous track record of these grand utopias in the last century, we may be better off investing our hopes not in sweeping utopian visions provided by leaders but in the social process of innovation and creativity. Technology is flowing out of the control of institutions and experts and into the hands of people. That will carry risks, but it will also create a huge distributed capacity for creativity. It will be increasingly difficult for tyrants to hold on to power simply by keeping populations in a state of ignorance. Democratic culture and the scrutiny of those in power should be enhanced. Abuses of power will be uncovered and challenged in this century more easily and more often than in the last. About seventy million people in Europe died in the twentieth century through warfare, starvation, deportation and murder in the name of utopias. That is extremely unlikely to happen in the twenty-first. There will not be another gulag nor for that matter a Cultural Revolution on the scale that was possible in the twentieth century. The dynamics of globalization, democracy and communications will not allow it.

The arch-pessimists share with utopians a desire to close off the future, to see it as the inevitable product of irreversible trends. But innovation and creativity, unlike utopian visions, have to be open to change, improvement, criticism and new ideas. Innovation is a constant process: it is never closed and finished. Its appeal, on the contrary, is the way it constantly throws the world open to new possibilities and interpretations.

That is why innovation, expressed through culture, science and technology, can provide us with a powerful non-utopian source of hope for the future.

Hope depends on life being more than a mere lottery. A sense of hope for the future is possible only based on a structured account of how the world might get better, perhaps in part through our own actions. There is not much room for hope in a world that seems irrational, chaotic and anarchic. For pessimists that is how the world seems to be and will be perhaps for evermore. The case against pessimism is that powerful forces at work in technology, science, politics and culture will this century give many millions more people more control, choice and reason for hope about their lives.

1. The Gathering Gloom

We are haunted by pessimism. Our world seems so out of control, driven by dynamics we can barely comprehend let alone shape. The forces that so carelessly uproot our lives – the arrival of a new technology, the gyrations of a distant stock market – are far removed from us and yet their destructive consequences penetrate deep into our lives. It is not simply that the combined forces of global capital and trade, innovation in science and technology, make us seem insignificant. These forces seem so unintelligible, beyond our grasp. We live out our lives in the intimacy of our homes, families and friendships, at a level of emotional detail that these global forces could not seem to care about. Ours is an increasingly complex world in which our lives depend upon technologies we barely understand and people we never meet. Our lives seem to be built not on knowledge but on foundations of our own ignorance. It seems increasingly difficult to work out the why and how of our society changes. Events that seemed so huge at the time – the death of Princess Diana, the Internet boom of the late 1990s – turn out to have been passing bubbles. The world is all the more threatening to most people because of our global connectedness. Far distant events that may seem insignificant – a child killed in a refugee camp, the collapse of a small country's currency – can suddenly have a huge impact on us. Yet small, largely unknown events and organizations can set off avalanches: a dedicated team of suicidal hijackers can throw the world into a tailspin. A loose, networked organization based in the mountains of one of the world's most backward countries can take on the world's superpower and, for a time at least, win. For many people, from different vantage points, the world has become unfathomable socially and morally, as they count the toll of family breakdown and rising crime; individualism and hedonism; a loss of respect for authority and the unravelling of bonds of community. Everything is becoming unbundled. People can no longer rely on their neighbours, fellow citizens and, *in extremis*, some children can no longer rely on their parents. Common moral codes and cultures, the basis for our ability to trust strangers, seem to be falling apart. In short, things look bleak, as bleak as most of us have ever experienced.

This rising tide of pessimism is not just prompted by the sense that western societies have been destabilized from without by the dreadful events of 11 September 2001. Nor is it simply that we fear economic recession, a recurrent worry across generations. This deep-seated sense of pessimism in modern society cannot be explained as an hysterical moral panic of the kind that comes around with new technologies and lifestyles. The gloom blanketing many western liberal societies stems from a deeper fear that our societies are eating away at themselves, from within. We are not so much in decline, as degenerating. We are so fatigued, bedazzled and confused by choice, innovation and novelty, that we are exhausted morally and socially. We have lost our bearings, as we grow disillusioned with the shallow world that markets, technology and progress seem to have delivered to us. The 1990s were meant to be the decade of western liberal triumphalism after the fall of the Berlin Wall and the collapse of communism. Far from it. In retrospect the late 1990s at least were accompanied by an outpouring of self-doubt and even self-loathing, from the intelligentsia of developed liberal societies.

Fear that western society is in serious, if not terminal, decline is far from new. Oswald Spengler's *Decline of the West*, published in German in 1918, maintained that all civilizations go through cycles of decline.[1] In the 1940s Max Horkheimer and Theodor Adorno, the leading lights of the Frankfurt School of German refugee social theorists, argued in *The Dialectic of the Enlightenment* that the pursuit of science, rationality and technology, to rid us of faith in religion and superstition, had simply delivered us into the hands of more sophisticated forms of oppression and mythology. Many of these twentieth-century arguments that the pursuit of progress leads to inevitable and irreversible decline, drew on nineteenth-century accounts of how industrialism sets in train a process of social, moral and mental degeneration. So is there anything new and distinctive about the current wave of pessimism?

September 11th

One part of that answer lies in the events of September 11th, the war that followed and what these reveal about our world. Just as it was difficult not to watch the horror unfolding in New York, so too it was difficult not to see those events in part as a judgement upon our age. We look back on the just departed 1990s with a sense of bewilderment that things could have gone so badly wrong, so fast. The nineties were a decade of optimism, hedonism, individual expression and infectious enthusiasm. We skated, blissfully and perhaps wilfully, ignorant of how thin was the ice below us. The nineties seemed a time when some of the big issues that had troubled earlier times were settled, if not sorted. In politics, the battle between the market and the planned economy was decisively resolved in favour of the market. The Cold War came to an end. Democracy seemed to be spreading around the world. Peace of a kind eventually came to Bosnia and seemed possible in Northern Ireland and the Middle East. It was a decade of

creativity, invention, entrepreneurship and new beginnings –
the new economy, New Labour, new Britain, the new world
order – that declared a decisive break with the past. We could
free ourselves from the shackles of history to think afresh about
the future. Attitudes towards the nineties will vary. Some will
look back with regret at the loss of that optimism, the hope
invested in the Internet and new technology, the sense that
the world was changing for the better. Others will regard
the nineties as a shallow, feckless, self-obsessed era in which
fashion, novelty, trivia and celebrity transfixed us. To its
critics, the decade was at best complacent, at worst arrogant.
Whatever your view, the roaring nineties came to an end with
the terrorist attacks of 11 September 2001. The last decade
of the twentieth century was marked by a sense of gilded
innocence. The first decade of this century is more troubled,
but also more forgetful and distracted.

In the 1990s we became used to the idea that 'reality' could
be managed, kept at arms' length, made virtual by computers,
packaged for a special strand of television programmes or
'spun' by PR men so that it became what was seen in the eye
of the beholder. The events on September 11th, for a while
at least, made the 1990s seem a self-aggrandizing era in which
challenges and achievements were inflated out of all proportion so we could flatter ourselves.

The September 11th attacks were in part a parable about
our faith in new technology. America was attacked because
its technology was humbled. A small group of highly professional and disciplined men evaded surveillance and security
technology to hijack planes stuffed with computers; they were
armed with little more than a few small knives. They employed
Bronze Age technology to bring down computer age planes
and buildings. Our faith in technology means we increasingly
look for technological threats: armed with hammers we look
for nails. The September 11th conspiracy evaded this by going

underneath the high-tech radar. Yet the kind of technology that proved so feeble in preventing the attacks proved just as potent in amplifying its terror. After catastrophes in bygone times – bombs, rail crashes, natural disasters – people would have used their imaginations to piece together events relayed to them in words. The September 11th attacks became a global, collective experience of terror and shock because we could see it from every angle, as it unfolded. Across the world, telecommunications networks jammed as people shared their shock. It was virtually impossible to remain cut off from what was happening. The imagination had very little work left to do. This was an attack designed for the always on, available everywhere, new media world. The hijackers may have hated the West but they understood completely how it worked: its strengths and its weaknesses. The attacks may have been orchestrated from a society in which the media was state controlled but the planners had read the dean of media theorists, Marshal McLuhan; they designed their attacks for the 24/7 television age. The impact was all the more upsetting because mobile telephones and voice mail gave us access to the most intimate details: final messages of love from people who knew they were about to die. The technology took us, almost indecently, into the most harrowing details of the most terrifying moments anyone can face. Modern telecommunications technology became a tool for the word-of-mouth marketing of terror.

That is one reason why the attacks had such an impact on so many of us, far distant from New York: we had been cast in the role of audience, a role we could not help but perform. Time and again it was remarked that the events of September 11th seemed to follow the script of a disaster movie. The attacks were said to have brought terror to the streets of America. Don DeLillo, writing in *Harper's Magazine*, went further and announced that after the attacks 'the world narrative belongs to terrorists'. Yet terror plays as much of a role in art and culture as it does in politics and warfare. Terror is big business. It is an everyday part of modern life in films and novels. Millions of us, paradoxically perhaps, choose to engage with forms of art that terrify us. We do not run from terror, most of the time we seem to enjoy it. The leading instigator of terror in America is not Osama bin Laden but Stephen King. As he once put it: 'I recognize terror as the finest emotion and so I will try to terrorize the reader.'

The September 11th attacks underlined what a complex, risky world we live in; a world in which borders are open, communications are cheap, information plentiful, knowledge easy to acquire and as a result risks and threats can come from unusual sources. Take an example from business: Napster, the renegade start-up, created by a twenty-something college drop-out, that managed to threaten the foundations of the pop music industry. Despite the employment of armies of consultants and strategists, no one in the large music and media companies predicted that this threat would come from Shawn Fanning, working with a borrowed laptop and employing techniques used by computer hackers. Similarly, despite all the technology and manpower at the disposal of the CIA and the FBI, a nation planning to erect a high-tech defensive shield around itself could not stop a small group of fanatics intent on mass destruction. Bureaucratic large organizations, multinational corporations included, are very powerful but also extremely vulnerable. They tend to look for threats and opportunities that operate on the same scale as they do. They find it hard to recognize threats that seem insignificant. In contrast to the bureaucracy of large organizations, Osama bin Laden orchestrated not an army, nor even a formal organization but a network of self-organizing terrorist cells, which were coordinated without requiring a hierarchy or formal institution. As these networks appear to have little formal structure and leadership it is difficult to work out when they have been extinguished.

Even more worrying is the realization that the source of our pessimism, in this case terrorism, is not 'out there' in Afghanistan but may well be 'in here'. Among the harbours for this terrorism are our large and anonymous urban centres, just as much as the steep valleys of Afghanistan. The conflict that the 'war on terrorism' most resembles is not military conflict but the 'war on drugs' which is drawn out, conducted at home as much as abroad and involves legal, financial and cultural warfare as much as military might. In an open, borderless, complex world it is increasingly difficult to predict, using tried and tested techniques, where threats will come from and how challenges will unfold. We seem to be operating in a fog. The terrorists were completely at ease with this borderless world, moving easily between Pakistan, Germany, Spain, Switzerland, Canada and the US. They were well educated and spoke many languages. The terrorists had the advantage because they had made the intellectual and imaginative leap into the borderless world. Technology and scientific research flows freely across borders. This exchange of ideas is the driving force for innovation. Yet all too easily this could involve the trade in the technology of nuclear and biological warfare. In the knowledge economy, small groups armed with the right know-how and skills – how to fly large planes – can inflict huge damage without needing access to vast physical resources. The attacks underline just how difficult it is to draw borders between states, and boundaries between benign and evil uses for a technology.

The fact that our enemies could be camouflaged in our midst, living next door to us, eating in the same restaurants, is one of the most troubling legacies of the affair. What has become of the notion of 'our' society or 'our' nation if it provides such ready cover for sworn enemies? The September

11th attacks suggest that the great strengths of our societies
– their freedom, tolerance of difference, internationalism –
qualities that make our societies creative, diverse and dynamic,
are also the source of our vulnerabilities. The freedoms that
drive the market economy and liberal democracy seem to
imperil our security. The terrorists did not just oppose our
values of freedom and individualism; they cynically exploited
them. The suicide hijackers were not mad clerics. They lived
the American lifestyle quite plausibly, soaking in the Florida
sun, relaxing in bars and driving smart cars. Yet the appeals
of that lifestyle left them untouched. The hijackers enjoyed
American hospitality while despising it. America is the easiest
place in the world to set up a business. The al Qaeda terrorists
exploited that freedom to the full.

The new economy boom of the 1990s was fuelled in part
by liberal US immigration laws to attract people with brains
and big ideas from all over the world. They were brought
together from China and India, Asia and Europe in the
common pursuit of riches and entrepreneurial success in places
like Silicon Valley. The idea perhaps was that the common
currency of the market, McDonald's and MTV, stock options
and computer software, would glue them together. September
11th seemed to show that this swirling anonymity was unsustainable. To hold together, society needs stronger glue and
more commitment from its citizens to a common code of
values and beliefs. Society is more than a platform for economic activity. Liberal societies may decide to police their
membership far more carefully in future. The danger of that
is that we start to see the enemy within wherever we turn,
even if the supposed enemies are law-abiding, peaceable,
hard-working people who just happen to be different from
'us'. The danger is not just that freedom might be imperilled
by greater surveillance but that trust and tolerance will be
eroded as well. The immediate aftermath of the New York

tragedy saw an outpouring of civic spirit, but in the long run it raises questions about the basis for civic solidarity in highly diverse, open, cosmopolitan societies.

The new economy boom was perhaps the high point of the utopian faith in globalization in the 1990s. The idea seemed to be that the Internet, the World Wide Web and communications technology would combine almost effortlessly to spread markets, consumer goods and US brands around the world. The September attacks only added to a sense of pessimism that globalization was a complex, messy process, which was more likely to produce conflict and downsides than benefits. Many outside the US, for good or ill, see globalization as a cloak for the spread of US corporate power and values. Many inside the US see globalization on the contrary as a source of US vulnerability, an unwanted burden at best and at worst a source of new threats. Anti-globalization campaigners complain that the world is becoming an economic and cultural clone of the US, which is increasingly providing the financial, military, economic and cultural platform for our lives. It often does not look that way in the US where many people are fearful of being exposed to a wider world. Far from the US arrogantly using its power, time and again, it seems to vacillate. It is not so much lumbering as uncertain and hesitant. Either way America acts can be seen as grounds for pessimism. Either we face a world dominated by an overweeningly powerful single superpower that throws its weight around, or we could have a hesitant giant, unwilling to engage with an outside world that unaccountably it finds threatening.

The September 11th attacks set off a train of events which spread gloom, foreboding and dread around the world: hundreds of thousands of people lost jobs in tourism, travel and leisure industries; anthrax scares spread through the US, closing down Congress for days; Muslims in western countries suffered abuse and violence; in the war in Afghanistan thousands lost their lives; the Middle East became an even more volatile place. Yet the September 11th attacks do not completely explain the depth of our gloom. The sense of dread had been building up for some time. Globalization, the creation of a single market system integrating the world's major economies, had seemed a *fait accompli* by the mid 1990s. Even before the September 11th attacks it was clear globalization was a fraught and deeply contested process. The New York financial district was already suffering from the collapse of the high-tech stock market bubble. The 1990s were a technotopian era in which many came to believe that scientists and technology could provide solutions to complex problems: biotechnology could dramatically increase food production; genetics would eliminate many diseases; communications technology could overcome social dislocation and cultural differences. As Don DeLillo put it: 'The dramatic climb of the Dow and the speed of the internet summoned us all to live permanently in the future, in the utopian glow of cyber capital, because there is no memory there and this is where markets are uncontrolled and investment potential has no limit.'[2]

Foreboding

By the time the September 11th suicide bombers attacked, that technotopian faith had already given way to a sense of disillusion and doubt. Technology invariably failed to deliver on the overstated claims made for it. The unravelling of the human genome turned out to be just the start of a long process that might eventually lead to new genetics cures. New generations of mobile telephone technologies, it transpired, would not deliver the high-quality video on demand claimed for them and for which telecommunications companies paid so handsomely. New technology promised us abundance but too often seemed only to deliver cacophony. The Internet appeared to have created a digital Babel.

That fading faith in technotopia reflects a deeper, nagging distrust of science. Our era is more dependent and at ease with the products of science than any other. The products of science are threaded through our lives, from the cars we drive, to the pills we take and the fuel we burn. Yet we are as troubled as we are inspired by what science offers. Science has transformed how we can see and understand the world. We can see into the deepest reaches of the universe, across millions of years and into the most intimate recesses of our own bodies. Science has expanded what we can make from the physical world around us, for example, by expanding the life of finite resources such as oil and gas. Science also helps us to create new resources. Science is our best bet for shaping the future. Yet as scientific knowledge grows it also seems to fracture. No sooner has a scientific claim been made than it is contested and disputed. The future, once clear, becomes clouded by uncertainty. Scientific knowledge advances by becoming yet more arcane and specialized and so increasingly beyond the reach of the man or woman in the street. In the great scheme of things science may be a tool for human advancement but for most people it seems way beyond their comprehension and control. It is another abstract, huge force driving on our lives but over which we feel we have little influence. Every advance brings with it new risks and dangers, for example that biotechnology will create Frankenstein foods. These risks, especially when articulated by the popular press, terrorize us.

We have overinvested hope and expectation in science and technology in part because other sources of inspiration seem so exhausted. Politics is not just enfeebled by a lack of vision. Worse than that, politicians frequently turn out to be corrupt. Political power has increasingly become a commodity to be bought and sold. Even if political leaders are not corrupt they seem in our eyes diminished compared with leaders from earlier eras. Modern politics, it turns out, is often no more than a highly specialized branch of the media and marketing industries, and one that attracts low ratings even on its biggest nights on television. Political debate has become a managed spectacle, a series of soundbites rather than open, disputatious democratic debate. As politics has been thrown into disrepute, so our faith in our ability collectively to shape our future has been undermined. Politics is increasingly about how we adjust to and accommodate change, rather than initiate it ourselves, together. Politics is no longer about society taking charge of its own destiny but about managing a society that is being made to change by forces outside its control. The state and public sector, which in many countries were vital to modern- ization and improved living standards after the Second World War now seem bedraggled, cumbersome, slow and uninspir- ing, at least in the UK. Firemen and other public servants may have been the heroes in New York on September 11th and after, but that does not alter the fact that in the UK at least large parts of the public sector seem to be falling apart: the railways are in a state of collapse; children are sent home from school for lack of teachers; patients wait months for routine operations. As these civic aspects of society, once dynamos of change, give us so few grounds for hope it is little wonder that commerce and science have filled the gap.

Even modern culture is for many a source of pessimism, further proof that the world is falling to bits. We live in an age when more people than ever can read, write, communicate, draw, design, perform and play. We have greater access than ever to books, films, paintings and other cultural artefacts and experiences. Yet this democratization of culture is for many a source of deep anxiety. To pessimists mass culture is nothing more than endless pap and trivia. Rather than lifting people up and challenging them, it is designed to 'dumb them down' and reduce them. This despair with the state of modern culture is not confined to popular culture; it also applies to high culture. To many people, modern art seems to veer between being trivial and deviant, insulting and irrelevant, grotesque and disfigured. Modern art often seems to be no more than a giant joke played out by the avant-garde elite on a bemused public. It is no longer angry and impassioned but ironic and knowing. This narcissistic shallowness of modern culture speaks of a society that has lost its way.

Many people seem to feel the bonds of connection that hold society together, bonds of obligation, loyalty, affiliation and faith are withering and fraying to a dangerous degree. The economic growth of the 1990s masked a deepening social recession. In the 1970s it was commonplace to think that new technology would deliver to us a leisure society, in which we worked fewer hours in less arduous jobs. Our most difficult dilemma would be how to spend our leisure time. Instead modern work seems anecdotally to have become more anxious, stressful and demanding. Thanks to technology we can work longer hours, in the office and at home.[3] The pressures of work, combined with a culture of excessive individualism and choice, have helped to sanction divorce and family breakdown. Too many children are badly behaved and brought up in a culture that teaches them to assert their rights before they meet their obligations. Our societies are increasingly cosmopolitan and heterogeneous: they seem to lack the common core of values and history they once had. The elites of our society no longer feel connected to the people in its provincial and suburban core. The elites are metropolitan and international. They are more at home in an airport lounge than a local pub. The officer class no longer recognizes its responsibilities to the ranks. No wonder then that respect for tradition and authority is in terminal decline.

But that is not the end of it. We are not just eating away at the social foundations of life but their environmental and biological foundations as well. Progress measured as an orgy of consumerism is in truth a degenerative process. The grounds for environmental pessimism are legion. The human species, growing to an unprecedented scale, threatens to wreck the planet, extinguish other species in record numbers and imperil the prospects for future generations. Pollution is depleting the ozone layer, poisoning habitats and changing the climate with dreadful consequences. Non-renewable resources are being exhausted at an unparalleled rate while much of humanity starves because food production cannot keep pace with population growth. Species and ecologies that have taken millions of years to evolve have been changed irrevocably within a few generations. The modern lives we lead are built on environmental ruination that threatens our children and grandchildren.

The September 11th attacks and their aftermath gave us good reason to feel pessimistic. But by then pessimism was already established as the most powerful ideology of our age. Pessimistic accounts of our future make sense of the central fact that most troubles people: the world seems out of control, falling to bits, eating away at its own core. Modern society might give us occasional reasons to feel optimistic – a new car, a holiday, a slightly faster Internet connection – but these provide localized, specific and individualized sources of hope. They do not give us grounds for believing that society as a whole will be a better place. It is no coincidence that pessimism has arisen so powerfully, in so many areas of life, from politics to culture, from the state of the environment to fear of crime. In all these areas the same themes are at work. The forces which appear to offer progress – an expansion of choice, constant innovation, the dismantling of boundaries that keep people hemmed in – seem to be turning sour. Expanded choice leads to irresponsibility. Constant change leads to exhaustion and a cult of novelty. The dismantling of boundaries robs us of a sense of identity and order.

Choice

Pessimism arises most commonly when people feel a lack of control over their lives: they feel helpless.[4] Yet most people in western liberal democracies live with a degree of choice and control that previous generations would have found unimaginable.

Our material wealth and the workings of the market give us an unbelievable array of choices whenever we visit a supermarket. We can buy milk with lactose or without, and with varying degrees of fat and flavourings. In most large cities food from all over the world can be delivered to your door or taken out of a freezer to be microwaved in a few minutes. Even basic aspects of our lives, such as controlling the temperature and light in our houses, we take for granted in a way that previous generations could not. We expect choice and control not just as consumers but in many other aspects of our lives. We want careers that express our talents and we are prepared to move job, town and even continent to find the right job. A majority of young people now go on to some form of higher education with a dizzying array of courses and curricula to choose from. In our personal lives traditional constraints on mate selection based on age, gender, class, background, race and ethnicity are breaking down. We do not marry people chosen for us by our parents. Increasingly we can choose when and how to have children. In future we will have some choice over what mix of genes they will have. Family arrangements can be selected from a widening menu and marriages that turn sour can be ended. Most of us live in democracies which, however imperfect, give us far more choice than people a century ago had over their rulers.

We are living in a far less collective, more democratic, less deferential culture, in which people will make up their own rules. It is the end of mass society, when there was little choice but to do what everyone else did. Nowhere is this more marked than in modern television. In the UK television started its life under state patronage and control in the shape of the BBC. It was used as a tool of education and social improvement. Viewers had limited choice about what they could watch and when. The people in charge of BBC television were known as 'controllers'. But a combination of deregulation, new technology and globalization has brought not just a swathe of new digital channels but also 24/7 television. The old world in which a cultural priesthood could determine what we watched has gone for good. Television has become more commercial and yet more democratic; more diverse and bawdier, at the same time. Across a wide range of industries passengers, viewers, visitors, students, savers and patients have become customers to be acquired, served, managed and retained. Consumers are the arbiters of value.

This expansion of choice has been driven by globalization that has opened up established industries to new sources of competition, many of them from the developing world. Deregulation in industries such as banking and telecommunications has allowed new competitors to challenge incumbents. Both these have provided consumers with more choice, a process which the Internet has amplified.[5] Globalization, deregulation and information technologies should be creating a consumer cornucopia in which more information can be more easily acquired about a wider range of products and translated into demands that companies have to respond to more rapidly.

For the first time in human history very large numbers of people should feel they are sovereign: they control their lives to a far greater extent than previous generations. They can credibly aspire to live the kind of lives they want to live, unconstrained by material, economic or cultural factors. We can even choose to fight death. As a result, surely we should expect pessimism, and the depression associated with it, to be in long-term decline. Yet quite the opposite appears to be the case, at least as far as the US is concerned. For women born around the time of the First World War, now likely to be grandmothers, the lifetime prevalence of depression was about 1 per cent. Among women born around the Second World War lifetime prevalence of depression was 3.5 per cent. Those born in the 1950s had a 7 per cent chance of becoming depressed. By the time the current generation of US school-children leave school their chances of suffering a major depressive episode in their lives will be between 12 per cent and 15 per cent. The chances of becoming depressed appear to have increased tenfold over the past century, just as choice and control over our lives expanded.[6] Why?

One explanation is that the degree of choice we have is illusory in part because brands play an increasingly important role in orchestrating our desires.[7] People everywhere increasingly want the same products that are badges of success: McDonald's, Calvin Klein, Giorgio Armani, BMW, Nokia. Critics argue that globalization and deregulation is the enemy of diversity because it drives out small local producers in favour of global conglomerates such as Wal-Mart which exert growing power over producers scattered around the world. The power of global corporations may be one reason why we experience growing wealth as a lack of control. Far from choice leading to fragmentation, the fear of conservatives and communitarians, actually globalization is leading to standardiz-ation, according to critics from the left: our lives are hemmed

in by the marketing strategies of global corporations. The
world is not out of control: it is too much under control, of
the wrong people: giant corporations.

Another explanation for the growth of depression is that
we are far more aware of its symptoms because we live in a
far more self-aware age. Since the late 1950s hundreds of
thousands of academic articles have been published in psychology journals dealing with depression, neurosis and anxiety. Very few are concerned with joy and pleasure. As we live
in a more individualized culture, we have been brought up to
expect satisfaction. When we do not get it, we are more
attuned to our sense of failure. We are more likely to see
failure as a personal judgement upon us, rather than as a
product of external factors beyond our control. We want to
be successful on our own terms. But as a result we run the risk
of failing on our own terms as well. As we are more self-aware
than previous generations, we are more likely to be aware
of our successes and more likely to articulate our sense of
disappointment at our failings.[8]

This is not just an individual problem. The growth of
individualism seems to contribute to a sense of collective
despair. A culture of extreme individualism can make it far
more difficult to solve collective problems, for example mass
transport and pollution control, which leave us feeling rich
but out of control and frustrated at the same time: we sit in
traffic jams in fantastically high-tech cars. Individualism can
corrode the affective and emotional bonds of community that
sustain people as well as ties of obligation and trust. Many
large-scale studies by social scientists and economists have
shown that the quality of our relationships, family life and
community are far more important to our sense of happiness
and well-being than additional material wealth.

It is not just that individual desire can have negative side-
effects, such as corroding community. A life in pursuit of

consumer satisfaction is by definition hollow. Desire, the motive force of the consumer life, can be self-defeating. As W. B. Yeats put it, satisfaction of one desire merely becomes the grounds for a new desire. For every wish that is satisfied, there arise ten that are not. As soon as we possess what we desired, we learn how little worth desiring it was. A life driven by desire creates a culture of obsessive expansion, restless movement and constant agitation. Pessimistic accounts of modern individualism, from communitarians and ecologists, nostalgists and downshifters, argue that satisfaction comes from a sense of origin and rootedness: knowing your place in a settled order. Fulfilment arises not from chasing desire but from learning how to renounce shallow novelty and fashion. Communitarians blame excessive individualism for rotting the bonds of obligation and attachment that cement society. They recommend a return to a world in which duty, obligation and deferment of pleasure play a larger role. Environmentalists argue excessive consumerism is at the root of ecological catastrophe. Learning how to go without will be the critical skill in future. Moderation and self-control will be the foundations for the good life rather than getting what you want. Nostalgists want to protect old methods and communities of production that are threatened by blanket consumerism and the global market. Moralizers of left and right fear young people are ensnared by a hedonistic, senseless, raucous culture of drugs and consumerism. They recommend tighter regulation of culture and entertainment by state and parents. For pessimists choice and individual realization are not constitutive of the modern world, they threaten to disintegrate it.

Change

If pursuit of greater choice, self-control and individual expression is one mark of modern society, then a closely linked
feature is our insatiable appetite for change and innovation in
science and popular culture. No one wants to be good and
dutiful any more or merely a face in the crowd; everyone
wants to be cool.[9] In the 1950s being cool might have been
confined to a self-styled cultural elite. Now it is a mass aspiration. Everyone is desperately fleeing the middle-aged main-
stream, in a state of permanent, private cultural rebellion
against being boring and predictable. Our societies invest more
in change, through scientific discovery, industrial innovation
and the search for novelty and fashion, than previous societies.
Older societies disdained change and prized stability. We live
in societies of permanent and systematic change. That is why
they are so unsettling and provide such fertile grounds for
pessimism alongside hope for an improved future.

We devote huge resources to changing ourselves: the way
we work, the products we use, the way we live and communicate, even our genetic make-up. Everything now seems to be
malleable, in Marx's phrase, to melt into thin air. Producing
change has become a systematic and organized activity in
research labs, business incubators, universities, hospitals and
science parks. In the year 1900 eight out of every ten US
patents were granted to lone inventors, working as amateurs
often in their back rooms. These days most important patents
are awarded to companies, universities and research institutes.
A growing share of the workforce is engaged in the generation
of innovation. In the year 1900 US industry employed perhaps
20,000 scientists and technicians. These days it employs 1.5
million. Designers, programmers, researchers, scientists and
technicians are all architects of innovation in different fields.

We are doing more scientific research, more productively than previous generations and translating the results more quickly into commercial products. The gap between scientific discovery and commercial exploitation is collapsing. New technologies are reaching global markets ever more quickly. The mobile phone has become a mass product in less than a decade. The Aids virus was discovered only in 1984 but within six years the functions of its seven genes were largely understood, by 1995 the entire genetic structure had been mapped and only a year later drugs designed to interfere with one of the genes were already in use. All that was due to the science of genetics, which sprang from the decoding of DNA in 1953. The impact of innovation is greater because science is woven through our society more intimately than ever before. According to the OECD, perhaps half the growth of the twentieth-century global economy has been due to innovation and invention, rather than simply improvements in pro-ductivity and the processing of more resources. Change has become so essential because innovation is the driving force of economic growth. Increasingly we rely on finding creative solutions to problems – new ways to organize ourselves and make use of resources – rather than mainly distributive sol-utions: new ways to share out a finite set of resources. That does not mean the distribution of resources does not matter on grounds of fairness or economic efficiency. But it does mean that most of the significant gains in terms of living standards and well-being will come from innovation and crea-tivity rather than redistribution.

Yet while our capacity for change drives innovation, its outcomes have become more uncertain and unpredictable. It is difficult to predict how pervasive technologies such as ubiquitous computing, nanotechnology and genetics will be taken up and used. Technology is increasingly migrating out of large institutions towards consumers and users. This is a world in which many people are players, adapters and contributors in innovation. Change does not come down the pipeline from the laboratory to a passive, waiting audience. These days consumers, patients, viewers, citizens, and for that matter terrorists, are protagonists in the process of spreading new software, entertainment formats, fashions and military technologies. In democratic, open and educated societies, in which consumers and citizens are armed with technology, information and choice, change will be more raucous, less predictable and more tumultuous. Those who were once in charge – the priesthood, the officer class, the patrons of culture – no longer exert such control. Social change does not come about by instruction from on high, nor by technocrats 'pulling levers' on a giant machine; it is ever more like a virus or a forest fire.

As a result our own mass distributed capacity for change makes our societies seem chaotic, turbulent, disordered and unmanageable. According to Robert Axelrod and Michael Cohen in *Harnessing Complexity*, modern society resembles the complex, mutually adaptive systems in nature – for example the rich ecology of a rainforest – where many participants are interacting in intricate ways to reshape their collective futures. These systems are not completely chaotic but they cannot be managed from on high. No one is in control of them. Order emerges out of mutually adaptive changes made by many different participants, combined with some simple rules for success and failure. Ours is a world in which change has become constant, powerful and liberating but as a result it is perhaps more bewildering, frightening and alarming. While optimists argue that change is increasingly democratic and participative, pessimists focus on the sense of loss that change brings, as it sweeps away the past. Valuable organizations, skills, cultures seem to be in danger of being written off simply because they are slow or old. Progress seems to require the elimination of the past.

Boundaries

To understand why boundaries, and their destruction, matter so much to us, think for a moment about the simple act of eating. It is utterly familiar that we bring food to our mouths to chew and swallow.[10] The food is broken down in our digestive systems into simple, small molecules, which we absorb into our body. Then we build them up again into complex molecules. Why do we have this slightly convoluted way of ingesting energy? Why don't we simply take up some food, rub it on our skins and merge with it, to get the energy directly to the cells that need it? Our digestive system is a permeable barrier that allows us to take in food from the world around us, while screening out threats and risks. If we took in food by simply rubbing against it, we might find ourselves taking in energy when we did not want it, for example by accidentally rubbing against a bar of chocolate, or conversely allowing it to disperse from us without control. Without the boundary of a digestive system, we would be in constant danger of merging with the environment around us.

We rely on boundaries and borders, such as our digestive system, to impose order on the world. Our lives are defined by boundaries and walls, from dykes and ditches, to hedges and fences, city walls and national borders, gates and turnstiles, prisons and monasteries, bouncers on the doors to private clubs and passwords to computer systems. Borders and boundaries help define who we are, what we can do and where we can go. In the last two decades innovation and change, globalization and deregulation have brought down many of the borders we are familiar with. The modern world has become more exciting and threatening because it seems so boundaryless.

Information and communication technologies have helped

to overcome boundaries of space and time. In Calcutta you can visit the Citibank call centre, next to one operated by British Airways, which answers calls from customers all over the US. The staff have American names, watch American television, eat American food in the canteen and come to work late in the evening to coincide with the US working day. Channel 4 television runs an online homework service for school kids, where the questions are often answered by maths graduates in Delhi. The national borders of countries are more open than ever to trade and finance and increasingly people. The line between left and right has blurred to the point of becoming indistinguishable as many parties of the left have adapted to economic reality, fiscal discipline and the power of the market. Companies have been bringing down demarcation lines that separate people into different disciplines, departments and occupations. The goal of modern managers is to overcome and dismantle the boundaries that their predecessors erected in the name of specialization, focus and efficiency. Jack Welch, the legendary leader of General Electric, stated in his annual report for 1994: 'Boundaryless behaviour is the soul of today's GE. Simply put, people seem compelled to build layers and walls between themselves and others and that human tendency tends to cramp people.' Companies are increasingly embedded in complex networks of relationships rather than being neatly bounded organizations. That is one reason why careers have become increasingly boundaryless. The traditional career unfolded in a single organization or within a discipline with clear rules, skills and structure.[11] Modern careers increasingly lack that clarity. In Silicon Valley, and other high-tech clusters, people increasingly build their careers by hopping from company to company. Careers are becoming a succession of projects and tasks, rather than a steady acquisition of skills to do a well-defined job. In culture, the lines between high, fine-art culture and popular culture are increasingly blurred. Science progresses by transgressing boundaries: animal organs are used in humans; genetic engineering alters how plants and animals grow; miniature machines can enhance human bodies.

Why have we witnessed such a bonfire of boundaries in the last two decades? A complex, mutually adaptive system – such as a highly networked market economy – thrives on interaction. The more interactions in a network, the more powerful the network becomes. Barriers, boundaries and borders block these interactions. They create inflexibility because they prevent resources and people moving to where the need is greatest, the returns are highest, the audience interest most intense, the consumers most eager, the costs lowest. Inflexibility is bad for efficiency because it locks up resources. Boundaries can also be bad for creativity and problem solving, which invariably involves people from different backgrounds, disciplines and organizations coming together to address a shared problem, lending their different skills and perspectives to solve a common problem. Bounded organizations, professions and disciplines create fixed ways of seeing the world. To be creative often means moving beyond the boundaries of your discipline or world view.

The implication is that the people, organizations and nations most at ease with boundary crossing will be the most successful in future because they will be able to adjust more rapidly to changing circumstances and to combine their talents most productively to come up with new ideas. Those people who are happy only within the protection of secure borders will tend to get left behind. As Los Angeles-based writer Joel Kotkin put it in his 1993 book *Tribes*:

These global tribes are today's quintessential cosmopolitans, in sharp contrast to narrow provincials. As the conventional barriers of nation-state and regions become less meaningful under the weight of global economic forces, it is likely such dispersed peoples – and their worldwide business and cultural networks – will increasingly shape the economic destiny of mankind.

Provincials, locals and isolates, cut off from the international flow of ideas and opportunities, fear change, mobility and outsiders, Kotkin claimed. Pascal Zachary in *The Global Me* maintains that cosmopolitanism is essential for success in business, politics and culture in a more global and mobile world:

Diversity defines the health and wealth of nations in a new century. Mighty is the mongrel. The mixing of races, ethnic groups and nationalities – at home and abroad – is at a record level. The hybrid is hip. In a world of deepening connections, individuals and corporations and entire nations draw strength and personality from as near as their local neighbourhood and as far away as a distant continent. The impure, the melange, the adulterated, the blemished, the rough, the mix and match – these people are inheriting the earth. Mixing is the new norm . . . Mixing trumps isolation. It spawns creativity, nourishes the human spirit, spurs economic growth and empowers nations. Racial, ethnic and national categories no longer impose fixed barriers.

Boundaries and borders play a valuable role in our lives. That is why their loss troubles us. Boundaries provide people with a sense of belonging, attachment and identity. They help to define the limits of community: who is inside and who outside. The political controversy over how we should treat asylum seekers and economic migrants is all about how we can enforce borders in an increasingly porous world and how we should frame our obligations to poor people seeking a better way of life. The debate over the future of the welfare state is now framed in how we can impose boundaries on our obligations as taxpayers by limiting entitlements to those who cannot work, train or learn. Boundaries help impose stability on systems that might otherwise tend to chaos. A society without boundaries is like an organism without a digestive system: it is in danger of collapsing into its environment. On the other hand, societies and economic systems with too many of the wrong kinds of borders become sclerotic. Those with too few borders and boundaries might become dangerously unstable. One reason we feel our society is out of control is that old boundaries between classes, nations and cultures have collapsed, leaving us feeling exposed, while new sources of order and stability are yet to be established.

Living in a borderless world poses immense demands on people. Not only does it require flexibility and agility, openness and tolerance, it seems to throw in doubt the value of people who see themselves as rooted and provincial. There is a tendency to value the hybrid and the marginal at the expense of the dull core. Cosmopolitan elites in world cities set the agenda in fashion, culture and the media, while most people live in provincial towns and suburbs. William Leach in *Country of Exiles*, a polemic against mobility and cosmopolitanism in the US, makes an impassioned, communitarian plea for a strong sense of place, along with the boundaries that give it meaning. A sense of place fosters creativity, loyalty, passion, Leach argues:

Without a sense of boundaried place, there can be no citizenship, no basis for common bonds to others, no willingness to give to the commonweal or to be taxed, even lightly, in behalf of the welfare of others . . . A living sense of boundaried place, a patriotism beyond love of abstract principles, is the main condition of citizenship.

Leach's argument is that while metropolitan elites might sneer at the provincial, in reality provincialism is the heart of any

society. Excessive cosmopolitanism, like excessive individualism, will eat away that solid core.

This decaying sense of place has already infected architecture. Places are increasingly losing their sense of distinctiveness
and meaning for us. In a more mobile and fluid world the
places where we spend most of our time are increasingly
functional, transactional and interchangeable: gyms, airports,
supermarkets, car parks, modern open-plan offices, executive
housing estates, shopping malls, multiplex cinemas. They
merge into one another. Modern office blocks are built not
to last but to be folded down again in a couple of decades.
Too many of the places we inhabit are temporary, functional
sheds, pods and warehouses, bled dry of their social and
civic significance.[12] To give but one example: the largest
two buildings in the 'historic' Hampshire market town of
Petersfield are now the Waitrose supermarket and its car park,
and the new Tesco supermarket just up the road. The other
most visited building in town seems to be a recently opened
drive-thru McDonald's.

Borders can be rigid boundaries or sites of exchange and
transit, where people from different cultures mingle and share.
The reaction against the boundaryless world could create
a backlash: more gated communities and more barriers to
migrants, more regulation of science and constraints on creativity. That would spell stagnation. To avoid that we need to
learn how better to establish boundaries through negotiation,
to make them semi-permeable and adaptive. Providing people
with a sense of stability in a less bounded world will be a vital
political task in the decades to come.

Pessimism has become the most powerful and pervasive ideology of our times, and apparently for good reason. Politics is at
best timid and at worst corrupt. Government is stumbling
and ineffective. Democracy is outflanked by global corporate

power. Community is unravelling and unreliable. Our culture is dumbing us down and reducing art to a joke. Science is beyond our comprehension so we can only stand, powerless and in awe, as it creates huge risks for us just as it opens up new knowledge. Distinctive and historic cultures and languages are crushed by the standardizing power of global brands. Globalization offers most people few opportunities but rather less control and more insecurity. Individualism, the holy grail of modern society, is highly corrosive of other vital values such as community, duty and loyalty, as well as the environment. Our appetite for novelty and change exhausts and bewilders us. The borderless world leaves us dizzy and disoriented because all the familiar signposts have been removed. The world seems rich and exciting but dangerously out of control. Reactions to the sense of helplessness come out in all sorts of different ways, obvious and unexpected, as pessimism feeds into our culture and politics.

2. The Great Escape

There once was a place where neighbours greeted neighbours in the quiet of summer twilight. Where children chased fireflies. And porch swings provided easy refuge from the care of the day. The movie house showed cartoons on Saturday. The grocery store delivered. And there was one teacher who always knew you, who had that 'special something'. Remember that place? Perhaps from your childhood. Or maybe just from stories. It held a magic all of its own. The special magic of an American home town. Now, the people at Disney – itself an American family tradition – are creating a place that celebrates this legacy. A place that recalls the timeless traditions and boundless spirit that are the best parts of who we are . . .

There is a place that takes you back to that time of innocence. A place of caramel apples and cotton candy, secret forests and hopscotch on the street. That place is here again, in a new town called Celebration . . . A new American town of block parties and Fourth of July parades. Of spaghetti dinners and school bake sales, lollipops and fireflies in a jar. And while we can't return to these times we can arrive at a place that embraces all of these things.

That is how Disney sold the idea behind its model Florida town, Celebration. A place planned so that harassed and disenchanted adults could feel they were going back to the home of their childhood, or at least the home of the movies of their childhood: a town where instead of crime on every corner there would be lemonade stands.[1] But Celebration was not created just out of a sentimental longing for a bygone age. These model towns – Poundbury, the retro town developed by Prince Charles in the mid 1990s on the edge of Dorchester, is another example — embody a very modern belief in the power of design and planning to create a better environment and through that better people. Prince Charles is backing another utopian village of about 140 homes in St Austell, where people will be encouraged to do without cars and work from homes built in Victorian or Edwardian styles. Celebration and Poundbury are examples of utopian nostalgia: places where everything is freshly minted to look old. Their rallying cry is that the best hope for our future is to use new technology to return us to the past. They are a cross between a social experiment and a theme park.

Celebration stands in a long tradition of utopian settlements, places with names like Harmony, Eden and Amity. Like them Celebration is a commentary on what its designers and inhabitants think is wrong with the world around it: depersonalized, ugly, suburban sprawl, freeways connecting homes to malls and factory outlets, in which mothers in particular become full-time drivers. Disney created Celebration in part to exploit 10,000 acres of prime real estate next to its Florida theme park, a social extension of the quarantined dream zone, protected from the disappointment and mayhem around it. Celebration accounts for nearly 4,890 acres of Disney property. The planned development includes 2,034 acres for residential space, 350 acres for offices, a similar amount for retail and 210 acres for industry.[2] This, along with a state of the art school and medical centres, golf course, 5,000-seater performance centre, 810-room hotel and 1,290 acres of public space, is Celebration. Despite the costs and complexity of the project, the town is meant to appeal to an ideal of simplicity, to recreate the elusive sense of place missing from the lives of middle-income Americans. The town is perhaps the most extreme expression of the neo-traditionalist, New Urbanist architectural movement that has swept America in the last decade. The New Urbanists reject the subtopian, suburban vacuum at the heart of American life.[3] The authors of the essay which is counted as the intellectual launch pad of the New Urbanist movement declared: 'Americans need to be reacquainted with their small town heritage and to be persuaded of the importance of protecting the human habitat every bit as rigorously as the natural habitat.'[4]

This rejection of both large-scale city life and the suburbs is at the heart of Celebration's appeal. The town's 'Downtown Celebration Architectural Walking Tour' issued in 1997 explained:

Celebration is designed to offer a return to a more sociable and civic minded way of life. It is a walking town. The town plan places special emphasis on restoring streets and sidewalks to the public realm on the assumption that streets should belong to people, not cars. In the Celebration Village you can pick up a quart of milk or step out for a quick cup of coffee without getting into a car. The town centre (not the mall) is intended as the primary focus for community life.

Celebration offered its residents a perfectly ordered world of traditional architecture, open spaces, a state of the art school, first-class health care and total safety. It was an attempt to create community as a consumer experience. The reality turned out to be far more complex. As the residents found out, Disney's brand could only take so much trouble. Citizens of its model community proved far less compliant than its workforce. A tangible sense of community comes only through developing a public space, no matter how provisional and limited, to allow debate on issues that affect the whole community. In Celebration, the focus of that became the model progressive school, which had been designed by a team including most of the leaders of progressive education in the US. It was a bold attempt to create the school of the future, quite unlike the factories for learning that still dominate state education. It was at this point that the conflict between Celebration's offer of a return to a nostalgic Arcadian past ran headlong into its parallel offer of a utopian future. The model school, which promoted individualized learning styles, child-centred assessment, group work, flexible use of space and lots of computer time, was the utopian future. The parents wanted the educational equivalents of porches, swings and homemade lemonade: rigorous testing and attention to the 3Rs.

Disney described the utopian and nostalgic community of Celebration in a language of hope. Yet its backdrop, and the main reason for its appeal was a deep pessimism about the state of the world and the diminished prospects for reform and improvement. That is why nostalgia, going back to a rosy past, seems such an attractive option.

Pessimism is so powerful because there are so many different ways for people to be pessimistic about so many different things, from the state of the family to the state of the planet. Pessimism expresses itself most powerfully in our culture and social life rather than directly in politics and public life. Pessimism is not an ideology but a cultural tide: a doubtful, even depressive attitude towards the future that often simultaneously elevates a rosy, nostalgic view of the past. The dominant culture of pessimism expresses itself in two main ways. One is an urge to escape from the modern world with its multiple, intractable sources of worry. Just as modern technology and commerce create these worries, so our culture creates escape hatches for us to disappear down. The other main reaction is an urge to confront and resist the forces of progress, technology and modernity which are to blame for our degeneration. This confrontation can come from two main sources, either on the conservative grounds of defending tradition against the ravages of modernity, or on the radical and rebellious grounds that progress simply cloaks corporate power and oppression. This chapter is about how pessimism breeds a desire to escape the modern world; the next chapter examines how pessimism can turn nasty and violent.

Nostalgia

The idea of escape from work, stress, congestion, crime, anxiety, chaos and complexity seems increasingly attractive. That desire may take physical forms: a desire to escape from the city to the country, to leave the office and work from home, to flee Britain to a homestead in France. But it is equally likely that the desire for escape will find spiritual and emotional expression: an escape into ourselves, our home or an imaginary past. This desire for the great escape is wrapped up with nostalgia.

Nostalgia is literally a longing for home.[5] It stems not just from a sense that the past has been displaced or even lost but from a romantic fantasy that it can be recovered, like a long-lost love, at least for a moment. Nostalgia can be a longing for a place, a homeland or a neighbourhood. But even then, nostalgia is more a yearning for a feeling: the feeling of being at home, safe, warm, protected, looked after; the thrill of a crowd experience on a strike, march, war; the excitement of a journey. Nostalgia is a yearning for a time and experience as much as a place, and it is as much part of the modern world as new technology. As the pace of change accelerates, and dislocations of communities, identities and occupations become more common and more profound, so the scope for nostalgia for our origins in the lost, simpler past becomes more alluring.

When nostalgia was first recognized in the seventeenth century it was thought to be an individual affliction, often accompanied by physical symptoms. The mania of longing was first diagnosed by a Swiss doctor Johannes Hofer, working in wartime with Swiss soldiers who yearned obsessively to return to their villages and hallucinated about their homeland. By the nineteenth century nostalgia had become less an individual medical condition and more public and cultural in the form of romantic nationalism and anti-industrialism. At the end of the twentieth century nostalgia had become a staple diet in our culture. The more rapidly we are propelled into an uncertain future the more we yearn for the imagined security of the past.

Advocates of nostalgia might yearn for a golden era of clear boundaries and values. But in conjuring up this imagined past, we also mourn the passing of our hopes for the future. In my memories of my childhood in the sixties in Shrewsbury, I do not just feel nostalgic about aspects of life in a small provincial town, the sense of community among families on our street. I also feel nostalgic for the sense of naive excitement that people had about a future in which everyone would have cars, televisions, record players and chances to go to university. We feel nostalgic about the past not just for what we imagine it was, but for how hopeful we used to feel about the future. That is one reason we invest so much hope in our children, and worry so much about the quality of their childhood. We want them to have a childhood they can feel nostalgic about when they are adults. That is one reason why the family is one of the most potent objects of nostalgia.

The Family Album

Nostalgia for our lost family life has become a way to explain all sorts of social phenomena, from teenager violence to drug abuse and wider social decay. The dissolution of the traditional family, gathered around its hearth in cosy harmony, explains why we feel so much is going wrong, when we are so materially wealthy. The case for feeling nostalgic about the nuclear family of the 1950s and early 1960s is strong, particularly in the US, on the surface at least.[6]

Rates of divorce were then half those of today. The postwar baby boom made America a child-centred society. Gang warfare among teenagers did not lead to drive-by shootings. Crack had not become an epidemic. Discipline problems in schools were minor. Children did not turn up toting guns. Home ownership exploded, spawning new suburbs where nuclear families could find a togetherness and privacy not possible for earlier generations that grew up in extended families or in apartment buildings. Many working-class families grew more affluent thanks to steady, white collar jobs. In the 1950s much of the increase in US gross national product was oriented towards consumer durables, household goods and new homes. The family house, with a car parked out front, became the realizable ideal. The world so scorned by the planners at Celebration, at least for a time, was the best hope many millions of people had for a better life.

Yet our nostalgia for this safer, more placid and dependable time is only possible with extremely selective editing. The nuclear family, far from being traditional, was a creation of the postwar era. The family of the 1950s was not the expression of tradition but the creation of that decade of expanding male employment, motorcars and home appliances. The eighteenth- and nineteenth-century family household was likely to comprise not just parents and children, but quite possibly grandparents, relatives, servants and paying guests, not to mention the odd working animal. In the 'traditional' extended family, the home was not a perfect refuge from the world of work but usually a place of production and a harsh one at that. In working-class homes, parents did not look after young children, who were often cared for by older siblings. In the eighteenth and nineteenth centuries the family and the home were not a zone for personal fulfilment, either for women or for men. The nuclear family of the 1950s is an invented tradition.

The appeal of that tradition, in contrast to the chaotic families we live in today, rests on editing out many of its downsides. Critics allege that hypermobility is eating away at the family. Yet people born in the early twenty-first century are far more likely to live near their birthplaces than people born in the nineteenth, large swathes of whom emigrated across vast distances or moved from country to town. Another myth is that modern Americans have lost touch with older generations, who might live a long way away. Yet more Americans have grandparents alive than any previous generation and are more likely to see them. In earlier generations you lost touch with your grandparents because they died about the age of fifty-five. In Britain grandparents play a critical role in the childcare arrangements of working families. In the 1940s one in ten American children did not live with either parent, in part because of ill health, compared with one in twenty-five today.

The nuclear family of the 1950s was built on the economic foundations of the time, which provided job security for most male workers and rising living standards. That allowed millions of people to feel optimistic about their own lives and the society around them after years of war and depression. The modern family is in crisis because those economic and social conditions seem to have passed away. Rising job insecurity and stagnant real wages, along with women's aspirations for careers, have encouraged more two-earner households, which in turn creates more stress in family life. The American Dream and the ideal of the nuclear family are increasingly at odds. Our nostalgic romantic account of the past prevents us from coming to terms with the adjustments we need to make to adapt our families, networks and social institutions to these new challenges. Nostalgia far from providing a solution or even an escape, becomes an obstacle to adjustment and innovation in the present.

As Stephanie Coontz puts it:

We must abandon any illusion that we can or should revive some largely mythical traditional family. We need to invent new family traditions and find ways of reviving older community ones, not wallow in nostalgia for the past or heap contempt on people whose family values do not live up to ours. There are good grounds for hope that we can develop such traditions, but only if we discard simplistic solutions based on romanticisation of the past.[7]

The Nostalgia Boom

The family is just one object of the nostalgia that pervades our culture. The tendency to wallow in nostalgia is not confined to a particular section of society, nor to a particular political faction or period of history. Nostalgia can thrive on left and right, among new age environmentalists and aristocrats.[8] In the UK the nostalgia wave comes from many sources: it is so flexible and adaptive.

One is a pervasive sense of national decline. Thus the growth of the heritage industry in the 1980s was greeted as a cultural endorsement of the Thatcher government's nationalistic policies, which were seen by some as an attempt to hand over the interpretation of the nation's history to an anti-democratic elite.[9] Heritage and nostalgia were associated with stately homes and the monarchy. Britain, in the midst of savage industrial decline, was more likely to manufacture heritage than goods. The Prime Minister's job was to become curator-in-chief of a country that was rapidly turning into a demeaning historical theme park. History and learning, that used to require respect, sobriety and effort, were reduced to little more than leisure, theatre and shopping by the bogus history of heritage, critics such as Robert Hewison and Patrick Wright claimed. Nostalgia was part and parcel of the climate of decline that had settled upon Britain in the postwar years and refused to budge. In John Wyndham's 1957 novel *The Midwich Cuckoos* alien children (the bearers of modernity, pop culture and science) take over a village of 'simple ordinariness' turning its world upside down. Midwich could have had signs at its entrance, Wyndham wrote, bearing a notice: 'Midwich/ Do Not Disturb'. Apostles of nostalgia, such as Prince Charles, would like to do something similar for Britain: hang a large 'Do Not Disturb' sign on the door.

But the nostalgia boom is not driven by politics nor by the faded aristocracy. Nostalgia can take many different forms, at turns commercial, democratic, local, participative and populist as well as conservative. The late Raphael Samuel located nostalgia as part of the growth of popular DIY history during the 1970s. Not only have we become more interested in history but the scale, richness and diversity of the history we are interested in has expanded enormously in the past thirty years. History used to be about stately homes, battles and kings and queens. Now it can be about everything from pencils to mustard, toys to matches, the kitchen to the brick.[10] In 1882 there were 268 historic monuments in the UK; now there are more than 13,000. New museums and heritage sites are opening all the time. More than half of Britain's museums have opened in the last thirty years. Britain, which only a few decades ago was in the grip of a slum-clearance and modernization programme, now has over 500,000 historic buildings. There are more than 5,500 conservation areas. Nostalgia is pronounced in the UK because in part it is an economic necessity. In the global tourism business the UK specializes in holidays that provide 'quaintness' just as the Swiss provide snow and clocks. Yet the growth of historical sites is marked in other societies as well: in the US the number of sites in the National Registry of Historical Places has grown from 1,200 in 1968 to almost 40,000 today.[11]

The scope for history and nostalgia has expanded. New agers and organic farmers, for example, claim a material and spiritual kinship with the earliest inhabitants of the British Isles. They can feel nostalgic for an Arcadian landscape that disappeared 7,000 years ago. Long-distance tourist walks, such as the South Downs Way, guide walkers from pubs to bed and breakfast accommodation, following ancient pathways. Ancient woodlands, which seemed on the verge of extinction in the 1960s, are now protected as if they were historic monuments in their own right. By the late 1990s, thanks to the interest taken by local and national woodland conservation trusts, allied to the resurrection of the ancient art of coppicing, we had more ancient woodland than we did in 1975. Preservation of historic town buildings has replaced modernization and streamlining as the great object of municipal idealism and civic pride. Here, as in the US, historic sites are the foundation stone for civic, downtown renewal.[12] Progress is about carrying the past around with us.

This participative culture of nostalgia has been driven by an appetite for do-it-yourself history and scholarship, often as a direct response to social dislocation. Compiling family history started as a mass activity in the 1970s, precisely at a time when social mobility was felt to be rising markedly. The very popular website Friends Reunited is a high-tech version of this collective and participatory form of nostalgia. By contacting long-lost school mates we can recapture a sense, however dim, of what it was like to be young, perhaps through contacting our first love. Labour and industrial history became popular in the

1970s just as traditional class politics began to wane and industry started to contract. The heritage theme parks that dot the country are like socially owned souvenirs, which like all souvenirs carry with them traces of an authentic experience. When we travel we collect souvenirs – pictures, posters, tea towels, mugs – to serve as reminders of the experience we had, the place we had been to, to show that we really had 'been there'. Heritage parks serve the same function for social history. We have mining and shipbuilding museums manned by real miners and welders. What until very recently was productive work and craft, is now tourism and spectacle. Nostalgia, alongside terror and excitement, are among the staples of the entertainment, experience economy.

Nostalgia has become more pervasive because what we count as 'historic' has expanded so much. In the process, nostalgia has become more democratic, less elitist and more commercial. Museums do not just carry sacred objects for scholarly study; they provide visitors with experiences of what life would have been like.[13] The 'past' has become more and more recent. Anything before 1980 is now regarded as 'period'. Our history is less and less about the continuities of national institutions, Parliament or monarchy. It is more about the lived experience, work and leisure, of the little platoons of society: thus the popularity of the series of television programmes, *1900 House* and *1940s House*, in which modern families attempted to live out the lives of earlier generations. Thirty years ago popular history was about visiting stately homes. These days popular history, and with it opportunities for nostalgia, are multiplying and we can be players in the process. Nostalgia has become more commercial and regressive, but at the same time more democratic, participative and diverse. These days we are far less likely to feel the pull of a grand nostalgia, for a distant past of 'the' nation. Instead we are attracted by the far more intimate nostalgia of histories of work, family life, leisure and entertainment. That is why nostalgia embraces us so warmly.

New-tech Nostalgia

Progress and nostalgia are like identical twins that do not recognize one another: bound together and yet completely uncomprehending. The dislocations created by innovation in turn create the conditions in which nostalgia breeds. Globaliz-ation promotes a yearning for local roots and identities. Our immersion in the digital and virtual world creates a demand for tactile and tangible skills at home: cooking, gardening and decorating. The growth of individualism makes us yearn for a time when we lived in real communities, with a sense of shared memory and moral commitment. Divorce, separation and the rise of the flexible family make us yearn for the idealized nuclear family of the past, gathered around the black and white tele-vision. Fear of modern crime makes us nostalgic for an era when criminals were rough diamonds, hard but decent like the Kray gang in the East End, pitted against the likes of Dixon of Dock Green. With money from television, British football stadia become modern sites of entertainment but that promotes a wave of nostalgia for standing on the terraces.

Modern culture has dramatically expanded the range of experiences we can feel nostalgic about and accelerated the rate at which we can manufacture nostalgia. The modern economy is propelled by the search for the next new thing. Whatever is currently fashionable, or state of the art, can quickly pass out of fashion to be replaced by the new model. No sooner has that happened than the displaced music, clothes, style or look can become a candidate for nostalgia. Fashions and styles are not discarded but stored, ready to be reused. In the past, antiques played a privileged role in nostalgia. Houses had prized pieces of furniture, heirlooms, which linked us to a distant way of life in an industry or a village. But we have become much more creative in manufacturing nostalgia.

It took 300 years for the English Civil War Battle of Naseby to be re-enacted by members of the Sealed Knot Society. The Battle of Orgreave, a confrontation between police and mass pickets during the 1984–5 miners' strike, was re-enacted for television in 2001, just sixteen years later, with former, now unemployed, miners playing themselves for the cameras. No sooner had Volkswagen announced the end of production of the original Beetle than a new Beetle, echoing the design and style of the original, was on the market. BMW brought production of the original Mini to an end to allow themselves to produce a nostalgic remix. Modern cultural products can keep going round and round, remixed and reused, as if on a giant spool. Rock bands do not die, they keep coming back to life to bring a tear to our eye and to make us wonder at the physical fitness of the modern sixty-year-old. The Rolling Stones celebrated their fortieth anniversary as a band in 2002. Those of us brought up in the 1970s need never leave our childhoods behind because the clothes, music and television programmes from that era are so freely available. We can go back in time with seventies nights at clubs and pubs. We need never say goodbye to our history: thanks to digital technology it can always be with us.

Nostalgia is central to the modern, always in flux, cultural capitalism of entertainment and leisure. Take the cinema as an example. *Jurassic Park* is a classic techno fairy tale, in which the very latest in new genetics technology is used to recreate a lost, idyllic, pre-human world. Modern technology is valued not for creating a futuristic landscape but to bring back a lost past. In *Titanic* and *Gladiator* computer-generated special effects allow us to see inside the experience as it must have been for those present. But nostalgia is the enemy of accurate historical recollection. On the contrary, the point of nostalgia is that it allows us to mix things up, to forget inconvenient details about the past while remembering only what we want. Nostalgia is consumer-driven history that depends on our wilful toleration of inaccuracy.

New technology has played a critical role in making nostalgia so pervasive and accessible. The explosion of digital storage capacity in computers, cameras, video recorders and music machines means no event, action or creation need go unrecorded. Not only can all of us capture more of our own private histories, but we can touch them up and manipulate them. Old sepia photographs can be brought back to life and made better than new. Cine film of family holidays can be put on to video. While new technology dramatically expands our capacity to distribute what we write, draw, design, paint or film, it does not necessarily make it easier to create entirely new kinds of products. Partly as a result we have an explosion of television channels in which digital technology is being used to provide endless re-runs of *Dad's Army*, *Birds of a Feather* and other classic television programmes from the 1970s and 1980s. We can listen to digitally remastered recordings and watch digitally remastered films that are far better than the originals. New technology mainly gives us improved versions of experiences we have already had. The nostalgia boom is not just a reaction against the pace of innovation; it is made possible by new technology. We are using new technology to propel us into the past.

The digitopianism of the 1990s has provoked a yearning to retreat from the future into a cosy version of the past. Perhaps that is why in 2001, in an economy which makes its living mainly from services, finance, media and creative industries, the debate about Britain's future was dominated by the fate of two of the oldest industries: farming and the railways, both of which exert a powerful nostalgic pull on the nation's emotions.

Rural Rides

Farming provides an urban society, largely ignorant of how food is produced, with an imagined link to a pastoral, rural idyll of the green and pleasant land. It is that image, and the psychological comfort it provides, that we want to protect, not farming per se. The railways, similarly, matter to us not just because they are a vital part of the transport system but because they are part of the nation's romantic life: a reminder of an era when Britain was a nation that could justly claim to be at the forefront of modernity. As Britain increasingly makes its living from services and technology, media and finance, so the fate of these old, foundational industries proves troubling to us. In the year 2000 Britain was mainly known abroad for its rail crashes and the diseases – BSE and foot and mouth – which disabled its farming industry. Nostalgia for a time when trains were safe and the countryside was not the source of disease cannot quite hide the fact that both industries appear to be in desperate straits.

British images of the rural economy have long been deeply contested. Modern agriculture was created by improvements to techniques for land use, sowing, reaping and breeding that in their time were revolutionary. Two centuries ago agriculture was the leading edge of innovation, producing rapid productivity gains and dislocation. Britain could not have become the nineteenth-century power it did unless it had been home to agricultural modernization and creativity. The settled era many feel nostalgia for was in fact a time of revolutionary upheaval in farming techniques, land use and social relations. Our agricultural industry is a creation of that past period of innovation. More recently, the demands of the Second World War promoted another wave of modernization, a dramatic increase in state involvement and a new emphasis on planning to improve an industry that was fragmented, poorly managed and by default largely organic. Bodies such as the Council for the Protection of Rural England argued that farmers had to embrace new techniques and fertilizers to save the countryside from suburban sprawl. The Blair government is the inheritor of this vision of agriculture saved by modernization.[14]

Yet most people, and perhaps especially those living in suburbs and cities, hold on to a sentimental, melancholic and nostalgic view of the countryside as the home to idealized rural life. The language of Stanley Baldwin, the pre-war Conservative leader, borrowing from George Orwell, still echoes loudly in our culture today: 'To me England is the country, and the country is England. And when I ask myself what I mean by England . . . England comes to me through my various senses.'

Baldwin went on to conjure up hammer on anvil, corncrakes and scythes, the sight of the plough team and the smell of wood smoke. 'These things strike down into the very depths of our nature,' he said. That vein of nostalgia still runs through our society. Soon after John Major came to power in 1992, he talked of Englishness in similarly elegiac and nostalgic terms, of warm beer and cricket.

We value the countryside not just for its land and animals but for the kind of behaviour it encourages. We like to imagine that people in the countryside are not drunk, rude or violent but polite, neighbourly and thoughtful. They are not stressed, greedy, rushed and overworked but have time for a chat, to muse and wonder. They are not on the treadmill of consumer demands but happy with a simpler life. Drugs and poverty are urban blights that we like to imagine do not touch the country. Middle-class families in their droves would like to leave the city in search of this idyll. They are surprised to discover it disappeared several decades ago and that many of the blights of modern life afflict the countryside as deeply as the towns.

For urbanites, the countryside provides a cultural set-aside. We are paying farmers vast subsidies not just to set-aside land but to set-aside values and a way of life, which we fondly hope can be maintained in pockets even as we acknowledge it has been lost for most of us. The modern advocates of this intimate link between the soil, culture, health and moral values are writers such as George Monbiot, who advocates a modern peasant economy, based on organic food and local markets, bypassing the supermarkets and disavowing the false claims of modern science. But all too easily this intriguing account of what an innovative, local and organic future might hold becomes co-opted into the elegiac, melancholy and hopeless battle in which the doughty and honest countryside is pitted against the much greater forces of modernity, science, commerce and rationalism. One of the most articulate exponents of this rural melancholy was W.G. Hoskins, the father of local history, who became a television celebrity in the 1970s thanks to a series about the English landscape. In 1963 his proposal for the future of Rutland, then England's smallest county, sums up the nostalgic tendency:

Rutland should be set aside at once as England's first Human Conservancy. We have Nature Reserves of various kinds for the protection of rare animals, birds and plants. Only the human being is not protected against incessant noise, speech and all the other acids of modernity. Rutland is still largely untouched . . . still a picture of a human, peaceful, slow-moving, pre-industrial England . . . One would like to think that one day soon at each entrance to this little county, beside a glancing willow-fringed stream, there will stand a notice saying *Human Conservancy: Abandon the Rat Race at this Point.*[15]

Hoskins had no doubt that local history was a kind of social therapy to provide people with a sense of roots and belonging:

Some shallow brained theorists would doubtless call this 'escapism', but the fact is that we are not born internationalists . . . We belong to a particular place and the bigger and more incomprehensible the world grows the more people will turn to study something of which they can grasp the scale and in which they can find a personal and individual meaning.[16]

The battle over the countryside then is about the slow against the fast, the old against the novel, the local against the national, the deep and rooted against the shallow and impressionable, tradition and evolution against innovation and design, local knowledge against the specialists and theorists. These deep reservoirs of nostalgia lie dormant in our culture, waiting to be deployed, whenever the future of the countryside comes up for debate. Even now many urbanites have their images of the English countryside filtered by John Constable's painting *The Cornfield*. Corn spills down an embankment through grass and ferns to a stream. Giant trees reach up to the clouds. A small boy lies on his front drinking from a stream so clear it will not harm him. People are working in the fields.[17] The debate over the countryside is about far more than farmers, fields and animals. It is about our imagined relationship with a past that we feel separated from and which we hope was simpler and better. If we lose 'the countryside' we lose that link which we believe is morally and culturally sustaining. The further we travel from the rural origins of that myth the more vital and fantastical it becomes.

The railways were one of the few modern technologies that Hoskins was prepared to allow into rural life because they opened up new vistas of rural tranquillity. This was the railway England of the *Titchfield Thunderbolt*, the 1952 Ealing comedy in which local residents fight the closure of a branch line by running the railway themselves with an ancient steam engine brought out of retirement from the local museum. There is no better slogan for this still powerful account of our nation's historic identity than 'Branch Line Britain': an amateur service, operating locally, back and forth, never connecting to a wider network, always happier to turn back from the mainline to modernity, and disappear back into history. There are 127 steam railways and museums in Britain; ninety-one in England alone. Hundreds of thousands of people visit them each year, to go nowhere. These railways invariably interweave fantasy and reality. You can, for example, catch *Thomas the Tank Engine* to Haworth to get the Brontë experience. These steam railways represent the dream face of British trains: an authentic reminder of how good things once were, in our imaginations at least. The visits made to these railways are a homage being paid to the past, in which children are inducted as a rite of passage, so they too can connect with the feeling of melancholy our railways induce. Britain's once proud railways set the standard for the world. The British gauge was the operating system of the worldwide expansion of railways, just as Windows has been for computers. But now British railways are a cruel joke: British rail travellers pay some of the highest fares in the world, for some of the most crowded trains, with aged rolling stock and a disturbingly poor safety record. The truth seems to be that the only railways in Britain that are consistently first class are those steam railways preserved for tourists that go nowhere.

Not a Lovely War

Of course, it is not a one-way ticket. Nostalgia does not infect all our culture, especially youth culture. A good example of nostalgia in retreat is our attitude towards warfare. War has often provided communities with a shared sense of meaning and purpose, which artists were often enlisted to express. No more so than in Britain. As Linda Colley pointed out in her history of Britain: war was the midwife of national unity. Great Britain was forged by war, especially wars of religious significance in the 100 years up to Waterloo, which pitted a plucky, little Protestant island against the world's largest Catholic power, France. That national unity was impossible without its cultural representations. In the nineteenth century warfare became a vital part of Britain's cultural life. Popular images in painting, poetry and literature painted a romanticized picture of war and the warrior as younger generations were prepared to fight for Empire and justice. Even as recently as the 1950s heroic and idealized depictions of real wars were still big box office. In 1950 the films *Odette* and *The Wooden Horse* were among the top ten at the British box office. *The Cruel Sea* was the top film in 1953, the *Dam Busters* in 1955, *Reach for the Sky* in 1956 and in 1960, as Britain was little more than a decade away from joining the Common Market, the biggest film in Britain was *Sink the Bismarck*.[18]

Yet after the 1950s, Britain's real wars in colonial outposts and in the Falklands and Bosnia, the Gulf and Afghanistan, have not provided nostalgic material for glorifying heroism. They have conspicuously failed to connect with nostalgia for the Blitz and the Second World War. Modern wars, which often involve the indiscriminate killing of defenceless civilians, are recognized as morally ambiguous. The modern always on, always there, global media brings us both sides of the story at the same time. As we come to know more about war so we are unwilling to accept romanticized versions of it. These days far from concentrating on the heroes of battle, artists are far more likely to focus on innocent victims.

The English have a huge capacity to invoke an entirely invented sense of past for which they feel genuine affection. England is an old country; the opportunities for nostalgia are legion. Yet the withdrawal into nostalgia, the yearning for a sense of authenticity, origins and roots, is near universal, especially in an era of such dislocation and discontinuity. Those who seek solace in nostalgia do not campaign on the streets at G8 summits. They do not want to argue with the system. They just want to escape from it. This desire to escape, withdraw and go missing is perhaps the most powerful response to the rise of the global high-tech economy. Nostalgia is one, social version of that desire to escape. Domesticity, downshifting and self-help are personalized expressions of the same tendency.

Inner Escape

If escaping into the rose-tinted past proves impossible, then escaping into yourself is a more realistic goal: to retreat into a world in which you are in control of what is going on. This desire to assert personal control over a small space in a world that seems chaotic is all around us. As an example, take the burgeoning cult of domesticity. The retreat into domesticity as an antidote to innovation and change is far from new. In the sixteenth century animals were an unsentimental part of the working household for most people. They only became pets – objects of sentiment – in the nineteenth and twentieth centuries when agriculture became more industrialized. Now we wax nostalgic about farm animals imagining they were better treated in days gone by, when in fact they were regarded far less sentimentally.[19]

In the 1990s domestic guides and goddesses took on a central role in people's lives, telling us how to live satisfied, trendy and happy lives at home. The world around you may be mayhem, but with the right guides you can turn your home into a reflection not just of your tastes but of your creative capacities as well. The more our working lives seem to involve screens, computers and ephemera, the more we seem to like to engage in physical and manual labour at home, redesigning gardens, changing our rooms and cooking. Or perhaps it is simply that we like the *idea* of doing all these things and so we celebrate the possibility with glossy television programmes. It is so rare these days for anyone to have the time to cook a proper meal that we like to watch it being done on television to remind us of what it is like. Television cooking programmes in part instruct us on how to cook and in part feed us with nostalgia for the days of proper food, before cook-chilled ready meals and microwaves. During the last five years, in which cookery programmes on television and books have boomed, the amount of pre-cooked food sold in supermarkets has increased by 35 per cent.

Thus in the last decade domesticity, creative labour in the home, has become a cult. Television programmes about gardening, home decoration and cooking fill our living rooms and the books associated with the programmes occupy the bestseller lists. They provide not just information and recipes but guidance, confidence and intimacy. They make us feel supported and cared for, as if we are part of a giant social movement to paint our rooms bright colours. They do not just offer us the finished product – the great meal, the scented garden, the stylish room – but the therapeutic process of getting there. For Nigel Slater, resident chef at the *Observer*: 'Cooking can be as passionate, creative, life-enhancing, uplifting, satisfying and exhilarating as anything else you do with your life.'[20] Lose yourself, transcend your worries, by getting involved in the process of mixing, cutting, chopping and flavouring. In the process the architects of our domestic utopias become celebrities and models, their own lives the subjects of television commercials. In a world of computers and mobile phones we hope to find ourselves in the domestic and physical satisfactions of painting, sawing, digging, planting, baking and roasting. All of which requires us to build up our personal skills and knowledge to set against a world in which we are increasingly made to feel feeble by the explosion of complex technical and scientific know-how. We now go to the gym to expend physical energy that our grandfathers expended at work in manual labour. It may be stretching the point slightly to say the careers of Jamie Oliver, Carole Smillie and Charlie Dimmock and their ilk are all products of our reactions against the globalized high-tech economy, but it is no accident that domesticity has become such a cult in such a fractured world. This is a familiar, nostalgic theme. The cult of gardening developed in towns in the eighteenth century as more people became detached from direct working on the land. One response to that growing dislocation was the creation of a small piece of rural paradise in your own backyard. Flower gardens became a way for humble men to show respectability. Care for a garden was taken as a sign of sobriety, industry and tidiness. Gardens were then, and are now, a sign of social contentment, a source of spiritual and emotional release: a little bit of paradise at home. The garden has always been an escape, a source of renewed vitality. No matter how battered by the world a gardener feels he or she can always retreat into their garden to order, arrange and manipulate it.

Taken a step further this cult of domesticity becomes about more leisure time at home, but recreating home as a space for work, through downshifting. People who consciously decided to extract themselves from the rat race were once an oddity. These days it is rapidly becoming a mass aspiration for the harassed, professional middle classes. A new modesty towards consumption is the precondition for a new more rewarding working life. With fewer, simpler needs, you have to work less hard and so engage less with the high-pressure, commercial world. More of what you need – whether that be food or education – can be met by your own labour or that of those around you. Working at home, among neighbours who are doing the same, allows one to rebuild relationships, see more of the kids, tap into inner sources of creativity. This return to a pre-industrial mode of work and family life is made possible by new technology that allows people to create home offices. Once again, we are using new technology to go back to a version of the past.

For some people, however, downshifting is just the first step on the road to a more far-reaching spiritual transformation. The inner utopia of self-help and spiritual renewal has become almost a religion. Its priests and prophets are celebrities; their books sell millions of copies around the world. Sarah Ban Breathnach tells us in the introduction to *Simple Abundance* that she set out to write a lifestyle management book about how to work from home and eliminate clutter in her life and ended up writing a guide to a 'spiritual Safari' which would show readers how to live in a 'state of grace' having 'spun straw into gold'.

It is perhaps going too far to call this search for simplicity and inner calm an ideology, but it invariably combines several core beliefs in its view of the world. All these self-help books get going against a deeply pessimistic backdrop. As Duane Elgin puts it in *Voluntary Simplicity*: 'Many persons in developed nations find life to be psychologically and spiritually hollow – living in massive urban environments of alienating scale and complexity, divorced from the natural environment and working in jobs that are unsatisfying.' Elgin goes on to develop this into a theory of civilizational growth, decline and crisis: debt-burdened and stagnating economies; the loss of a compelling sense of social purpose; bureaucratic complexity and political gridlock. The dream of material abundance gives way to a nightmare of unexpected problems. Institutions falter under the weight of expectations upon them and their inability to solve complex problems. Leaders become managers with little time to focus on the larger forces at work and issues at stake. Discontent leads to ever more rapid turnover of leaders with less power. Society becomes chaotic and incomprehensible. Only brute force and authoritarian use of power achieves results. We turn to technology to solve our problems – biotechnology to create new sources of food – only to find these just create more trouble.

The first step to salvation, according to most of these gospels of self-help, is not to confront this disordered world with the aim of reforming it, but instead to renounce it and turn away. In the entry for 5 February on her year-long journey to Simple Abundance Sarah Ban Breathnach says: 'Today deliberately turn away from the world. Don't read the newspaper or watch the nightly news for a week. Shun the glossy magazines featuring expensive suits designed for success . . . Absorb the shock of becoming aware that many of your preferences and opinions are not truly your own.' The more we consume, the more we become merely a function of our desires. Our identities become so wrapped up with our possessions that they in turn come to possess us. To find salvation we need not more material goods but less, we must turn away and renounce the lure of the material world.

The next step is to simplify your life by reducing your demands. Focus only on what little you need – mainly your relationships and the creative inner core of your person – to make yourself happy. We should not struggle to acquire more but accept just what we have. This simplification is possible only if you can focus on your true needs and purpose in life to eliminate all the unnecessary distractions and clutter. The capacity to simplify your life and renounce trivia comes only from finding your true, inner, authentic self: the inner utopia. According to *Simple Abundance* this authentic self is always with us and just waiting for us to reconnect with us. The entry for 3 February reads: 'One of the surprises that comes when you catch glimpses of your authentic self is the discovery that she's such a positive, upbeat woman. She's always smiling. She's always calm. She's always reassuring. She exudes confidence.' The authentic self can be discovered only after a prolonged inner journey, employing a wide range of techniques for meditation, contemplation and self analysis. For Duane Elgin, to live more voluntarily is to live more deliberately, intentionally and purposefully, by focusing on what really matters to us rather than on distractions foisted upon us. The outcome of this process is a life that is wholesome and balanced.

This stuff is a cocktail of new age therapies and common sense advice on time management; ecological apocalypse and communitarian social commentary; hippyish faith and personal therapy and alarmist warnings of the accumulating crises of modern capitalism. Unconventional but popular and powerful.

The growth of chronic pessimism about our future leads many people to seek an escape down one of the many hatches provided for the purpose. One very large hatch is nostalgia, a social and collective version of the desire to escape. Our capacity to produce and consume nostalgia has increased dramatically since the 1970s. In the last thirty years nostalgia has become more open, diverse, democratic, participative, commercial and embracing. Being nostalgic does not mean endorsing a patrician, establishment view of history. There are as many histories and so possible nostalgias as there are communities and industries. New technology has helped propel this nostalgia boom not just because the pace of innovation threatens to rupture our relationship with the past. New technology is a tool for nostalgia. Armed with new technology we can carry around more of our history, with sharper pictures and better sound. Self-help, domesticity, downshifting and inner utopia are individualized forms of escape. Everyday life can contain the seeds of soft-core personal utopias: the perfect curry, a new shrub, a carpet. For those who want to go hard core, the full self-help religion is at hand. You too will be able to find such a simple, surrendered balance to your life that you will be able to ignore the Yardies shooting one another in the local restaurant.

3. Death Wish Nation

Society is in a state of near catastrophic collapse. Everything is falling apart. Nothing can be relied upon. We are being overrun and undermined by foreign and unfamiliar influences. Worse, the moral and cultural core of our society is being eaten away from within. Individualism, hedonism, fashion and cosmopolitanism are spreading a moral contagion that has overrun society's badly weakened immune system. That account of how society is degenerating is the stock in trade on Britain's most successful daily newspaper the *Daily Mail*. Fear of degeneration is the currency of moralists and social commentators, from left communitarians to right-wing fundamentalists, deep-green environmentalists to aristocratic nationalists. These apostles of degeneration come from different points on the political spectrum. They have different values and ambitions. But their account of what is wrong with the world shares a common code: something is rotten in a society that is enacting a collective death wish.

The rise of the global high-tech economy has prompted many responses, among them ambitious hopes for a new world order, resistance and protest from many young people in western democracies, as well as a desire to escape into nostalgia, domesticity and inner calm. Among the most powerful and emotive reactions is the rising fear of degeneration, which when combined with political populism can lead to violence and an ugly search for scapegoats. Apostles of degeneration neither seek to escape from the world, nor renounce it: they want to confront the forces reshaping society with extreme measures.

The common theme to all accounts of degeneration, from left and right, environmentalists and cultural conservatives, is that modern society is in the grip of an uncontrollable death wish. The sources of modern society's greatest vitality also threaten to kill it. It is not just that some bad things are happening in the world; modern society has set off a deadly chain reaction, in which its lust for choice, freedom, pleasure or democracy has unleashed a degenerative decay at its core. For environmentalists and many opponents of global capitalism that death wish is the way our consumer culture leads us to embrace the market and acquiesce in corporate power. For communitarians, of left and right, the death wish is our love affair with individualism and rights, which leads us to unravel families, communities and neighbours, destroying the social capital on which society rests. For cultural and social conservatives the death wish is the urge to innovate and change, which threatens to cut us off from our life support system of history and tradition. In each of these accounts, despite coming from different political starting points, many of the same themes reoccur: a direct and vital connection to 'nature' or 'tradition', which provide people with a sense of balance and identity, is being lost; people feel increasingly unable to live an 'authentic life' because they are duped to become drones of corporate culture; spaces for democratic protest and debate in which people can express their right to be different are being closed down; every aspect of life from education to museums is being covered with a cloying conformity, forced upon us by the marketing industry.

This account of society bent on self-destruction is far from new. Ours is not the first era in which accelerated social and economic change has prompted extreme fears of degeneration.

A Brief History of Degeneration

The end of the nineteenth century is regarded as an age of reform, progress and utopian hope. Faith in progress, led by enlightened men in pursuit of scientific truth, was the religion of the day. Progress would lead society from ignorance to knowledge, superstition to science, barbarism to civilization and from worse to better. It was a period of remorseless technological triumph as one spectacular discovery followed another, transforming the quality of life for several millions of people. Death rates halved in many countries between 1880 and 1914 as west European societies moved from an age-old pattern of mass morbidity, caused by infectious diseases, poor nutrition and heavy labour, to the twentieth-century pattern of viral disease, cancer and decay through old age. It was not just that people's lives were extended. The quality of those lives improved as well. In 1895 the novelist Henry James acquired electric lighting, in 1896 he rode a bicycle, in 1897 he wrote on a typewriter and in 1898 he saw a film. Had Henry James lived a few more years, he could have travelled by aircraft, indulged in Freudian analysis and seen a scaled drawing of a working jet engine. Yet faith in the power of innovation to deliver progress bred its own reaction: a fear of degeneration. Then, as now, faith in technical progress and fear of social degeneration were reactions to the same process.

The tug of war between utopian hope and fear of degeneration was captured in 1880 by the French novelist Flaubert in notes he made for the conclusion to his unfinished novel *Bouvard and Pecuchet*. Bouvard takes an optimistic view that progress would in time give Europeans submarines to travel in, with windows to see aquatic life in perfectly clear and calm seas. The Seine would be warm and filtered. Precious stones would be abundant and houses painted with a phosphorescent substance to light the streets at night. In time evil, want and even man would disappear from the face of the earth as the human race escaped an exhausted world for more fertile planets. Pecuchet, however, is intensely pessimistic. To him modern man has been diminished to the condition of a machine. A mixture of individualism and innovation allows what he sees as anarchy and barbarity. A universal cultural vulgarity, Americanism, rules.

The nineteenth century, an age of progress and optimism, political reform and social improvement, was also the breeding ground for fears and theories of degeneration, decay, decline and regression. The dislocation brought by change, the degenerationists argued, would create a grotesque and malformed culture. Occasionally fear of degeneration prompted proposals for radical political reform. Robert Tressell's *The Ragged Trousered Philanthropist*, published posthumously in 1914, argued that degeneration was caused by the poor living conditions of the industrial working class, which required a revolutionary transformation: 'A nation of ignorant, unintelligent, half-starved, broken-spirited degenerates cannot hope to lead humanity in its never ceasing march to conquer the future.'

Mostly fear of degeneration fed racism, nationalism, eugenics and ethnic cleansing. The idea of degeneration is so powerful precisely because it is so plastic. It is not an ideology such as socialism, with a body of theory. Nor is it a political value, like liberty or equality. It is not a scientific theory, although it calls science to its aid when it suits. Fear of degeneration is a vague, shifting anxiety. Daniel Pick argues that fear of degeneration was a response to a 'felt crisis in history'.[1] In the late nineteenth century the degenerationists saw evidence for their fears in cretinism, alcoholism, inbreeding, the low morals of the urban working class, madness and crime. The industrial age was creating mass mental disorders. The nineteenth-century Italian criminal psychologist Enrico Ferri proposed that:

While contagious diseases have gradually diminished, we see on the other hand that moral diseases are growing more numerous in our so-called civilisation. While typhoid fever, smallpox, cholera and diphtheria retreated before the remedies which enlightened science applied . . . we see on the other hand that insanity, suicide and crime, that painful trinity are growing apace.[2]

Rather than propose grand schemes for social reform, the degenerationists argued the solutions lay in reinstalling a respect for the natural order, a sense of continuity and hierarchy legitimated by tradition. The most powerful expression of this argument was Max Nordau's *Degeneration*. Published in German in 1892, and in English three years later, *Degeneration* was a runaway European bestseller. In the UK it was reprinted several times within six months of its first publication. Nordau painted a picture of a society mentally and morally fatigued by the incessant pace of change. The force of innovation, driving change from within, also produced grotesque side-effects, scars and blemishes: 'We stand in the midst of a severe mental epidemic, a sort of Black Death of degeneration and hysteria.' The degenerates, in Nordau's view, encompassed the decadent and narcissistic elite, who were disconnected from, and no longer cared about, the fate of the masses, as well as many among the masses themselves, whom he compared to vermin.

Jonathan Dollimore points out in his brilliant book *Death, Desire and Loss in Western Culture*, fear that change would lead to degeneration, chaos and disorder has been a recurrent theme in literature over many periods. Nordau helped show how fear of degeneration could become a political rather than merely a cultural force. In Nordau's hands, degeneration was not a lament for a lost world, but an obsessive and demonizing ideology, which explained crime, ill health, poor education and low morals. Degeneration, brought on by urbanization, immigration and above all rapid change, left society so exhausted it was unable to prevent its own disintegration. Nordau conjectured that by the end of the twentieth century a generation might have evolved that was adapted to the conditions of modern life so that it 'would not find it injurious to read a dozen square yards of newspaper daily, to constantly be called to the telephone, to think simultaneously of five continents, to live half their time in a flying machine and to find ease in a city inhabited by millions of strangers'.

Nordau argued that as society became more complex so it became more essential, and yet more difficult, to maintain a sense of order. Hierarchy was being eaten away. Nordau combined that with a crude genetic theory: social malfunctions were being internalized and transmitted genetically through families. Nordau warned that for a complex organism: 'Anarchy in its interior is a disease that rapidly leads to death.' Nordau argued that society's organization and health were more precarious than we imagined. That order could only be maintained with effort. When that effort becomes too great, as it does in periods of upheaval and change, then we are threatened by a moral, psychic and cultural collapse. In the closing pages of *Degeneration* Nordau warned that 'Whoever looks upon civilisation as a good, having value and deserving to be defended must mercilessly crush under his thumb the anti-social vermin, i.e. the degenerates.'

In the decades after Nordau's *Degeneration* was published others would call for similar remedies, including Friedrich Nietzsche, who, in *Ecce Homo*, advocated 'the remorseless destruction of all degenerate and parasitic elements' in the name of a 'tremendous purification of mankind'. In time the threat of degeneration and desire for purification would license genocide and war. In our more democratic age, degeneration politics may not become so destructive. Nevertheless it is a powerful current in our politics and culture, on left and right. The danger of that current is very great.

The Enemy Within

Degenerationists follow the same basic argument: society has become a danger to itself because it is unable to cope with the innovation and change it has set off. The accelerating pace of change may be exciting but it is also bewildering and confusing. Society is dizzy and fatigued. Worse, the bonds of connection that hold society together are fraying and snapping. They are being eaten away by external forces – economic dislocation, immigration, the growing power of multinational institutions – but also by our moral weaknesses – excessive individualism, lack of respect for authority, the decline in duty and the rise in divorce. We are not the beneficiaries of progress but witnesses to a potentially catastrophic unbundling of civilization.

A world that has become too complex for its own good needs to be brought down to earth, back to basics, with a dose of common sense. A world that moves too fast needs to have the brakes applied. A generation obsessed with the shallow appeal of fashion, celebrity and novelty needs to be reminded of the value of tradition. A naturally independent nation needs to assert itself in a world in which it has been forced into alliances and agreements with its once sworn enemies. Defences that have been lowered to foreign influence need to be rebuilt. According to degenerationists we need constantly to keep watch over our national purity and reassert our threatened historic identity. When the desire to hold at bay a threatening and complex world is combined with the power of populism, then it can easily turn to aggression and violence. Then people search for scapegoats to vent their frustration and anger upon.

The modern appeal of degeneration politics is very powerful. The idea that society faces a threat of degeneration is not something that can be easily tested or disproved, once someone believes it. The threat of degeneration does not come from a single source. Once one starts looking for signs that society is degenerating from a presumed natural order, then the evidence is not hard to find, whether in the growth of asylum seekers flooding the country by taking advantage of our lax border controls, the low morals of the hedonistic drug-crazed young, the rampant consumerism of global branded capitalism, the feckless morals of the underclass or modern art's fascination with the obscene, grotesque and irrelevant. Although modern apostles of moral degeneration do not ascribe to Nordau's simplistic genetics, the family plays a vital role in many accounts. The collapse of the traditional family marks the degeneration of society from within. Modern dysfunctional families are the breeding grounds for the degenerates of tomorrow.

The appeal of degeneration, like nostalgia, is not confined to the moral or religious right. Degeneration comes in several different flavours from the left of politics as well. Common to all is an attack on economic growth and consumerism as the prime source of social improvement. According to degenerationists, society does not need more material wealth but stronger values to guide it. There is no more powerful version of this than the image of ecological degeneration.

Ecological Degeneration

Prophets of ecological apocalypse provide a powerful account of how society is eating away at its own foundation, through selfishness, over-consumption and shortsightedness. To 'deep greens' environmental decay is a symptom of a society that is morally enfeebled, not just unable to meet its obligations to the future but worse, consuming its future life support. The pollution generated by the unprecedented growth of the human species is poisoning the planet, depleting the ozone layer and changing the world's climate. Reckless consumption, the overdevelopment of industry and technological innovation that is out of control threaten to exhaust natural resources while also creating new risks to the global environment.

We are in the midst of a giant, uncontrolled and unrepeatable gamble with the earth, according to John McNeil in *Something New Under the Sun*, his environmental history of the twentieth century. In time the environmental impact of a century of unprecedented economic growth, industrialization and population growth will come to be seen as far more significant than even fascism and communism, world wars, famine and disease, McNeil argues. In the last century we have conspired to refashion the earth's air, water and soil to an unprecedented degree, allowing us to break through constraints that held back previous generations. But in breaking through these constraints on food production, energy and health, we have simply run into other constraints in the earth's capacity to cope with our waste by-products and pollution which threaten to destabilize the eco-systems on which we depend. We have become used to relatively stable climates, cheap energy and near constant economic growth. But our use of fossil fuels in particular threatens to undermine these conditions. Now we face global constraints on economic growth. Our negotiation with these constraints – or indeed whether we just run into them at high speed – will determine our future, McNeil argues:

This is the first time in human history that we have altered eco-systems with such intensity, on such a scale and with such speed . . . in the twentieth century humankind has begun to play dice with the planet without knowing all the rules.

The general policy until now has been to hope that a combination of human ingenuity, luck and abundant natural resources will allow continued growth to deliver hope of a better life to its growing population. In the twentieth century world population increased by a factor of four; urban population by a factor of thirteen; industrial output increased fortyfold while air pollution worsened fivefold, carbon dioxide emissions went up seventeen fold and the marine catch went up by a factor of thirty-five. Our apparent contentment is haunted by the possibility of ecological collapse. Many of the ecological buffers on which we have relied in the past – open land, clean natural water, unpolluted spaces, large areas of forest – have gone. The future may well involve wrenching upheavals to cope with the myriad impacts of warmer climate, lack of clean water and markedly reduced biodiversity.

The biologist Edward O. Wilson maintains in *The Diversity of Life* that we are going through an unprecedented period of species extinction. Demographic historians estimate that about eighty billion people have been born in the last four million years and between them these people have lived about 2.16 trillion years. Although the twentieth century accounts for just 0.00025 of human history, it has hosted about a fifth of all human years. But this demographic success has brought the world to a crisis of biodiversity, Wilson maintains. Humans have become a hundred times more numerous than any land animal of comparable size in history. As Wilson puts it:

By every conceivable measure humanity is ecologically abnormal. Our species appropriates between 20 and 40 per cent of the solar energy captured in organic material . . . There is no way we can draw upon the resources of the planet to such a degree without drastically reducing the state of most other species.

Wilson predicts that the destruction of the rainforest at the current rate – 142,000 square kilometres a year – will doom to extinction half a per cent of the forest's species each year. If deforestation continues at the current rate for a further thirty years up to a quarter of rainforest species will disappear. Wilson estimates, on the basis of conservative assumptions, that the number of species doomed to extinction each year is 27,000, each day seventy-four and each hour three. Human activity has increased extinction rates between 1,000 and 10,000 times in the rainforest alone. We are in the midst of one of the great extinction spasms of geological history, from which nature is unlikely to recover. After previous mass extinctions, tens of millions of years ago, biodiversity eventually recovered and surpassed the level it had previously reached. But Wilson calculates that recovery invariably took at least five million years.

The twentieth century, far from being a triumph for human progress, could be regarded as a giant miscalculation, a dangerous deviation from anything that could be considered natural: it has set civilization on a steep descent into global degeneracy. The sense of foreboding does not stem just from the fact that the environment is getting worse. The problem is that we seem so out of control: our ability to create new risks and dangers in the name of innovation far outstrips our ability to identify and deal with them. Ozone depleting CFCs were first synthesized in 1928. They were on the market for forty years before concerns about their impact on the ozone layer were first voiced. Agreement to phase them out was reached in 1987. What other unknown pollutants might there be in our environment eating away at the quality of our lives?

Communitarian Collapse

The social philosophy communitarianism offers a softer version of the degeneration story. Communitarians, most famously the American social theorist Amitai Etzioni, share with environmentalists a profound doubt about the values of economic growth and consumerism. One aspect of communitarianism is a growing concern for the value of social capital: the bonds of community that underpin civility, sharing, public services and trust, on which a healthy society and strong economy ultimately rest. Yet as markets have gone global, people and capital have become mobile, entertainment electronic and virtual, values more diverse and individualistic, so the market pulls apart the bonds of community upon which it rests. As September 11th showed, the financial centres of our world ultimately depend for their safety on firefighters, police officers and medics, paid for by taxes. But all too often these civic underpinnings of capitalism are neglected.

One of the most persuasive accounts of the collapse of social capital has been provided by Harvard Professor Robert Putnam in *Bowling Alone*. Putnam argues that the quality of our social bonds, not income and consumption, are the best predictors of our quality of life. Marriage and a good social life make people far happier than additional money. As we have become disconnected from family, friends, neighbours, churches, associations, clubs and community groups, so we have restricted access to the social capital that is vital for personal well-being, public health and long-term economic success, Putnam argues. People with low social capital are likely to be less happy than people whose lives are embedded in a network of family and friends. Communities with low social capital are impoverished in all sorts of ways: lower educational achievement, higher crime rates, more teenage pregnancy, poverty and drugs. We notice social capital only when it is in critically short supply. Unless we urgently devise ways to recreate social capital, Putnam maintains, we will watch the lifeblood drain from communities. We will live technologically enriched but socially impoverished lives.

David Myers writes in similar vein in *The American Paradox: Spiritual Hunger in an Age of Plenty*, noting that American society went through a steep social and emotional recession in the 1990s even as its economy boomed. Far from delivering contentment, materialism and radical individualism imperil our future, Myers argues. As the economy has expanded since the 1960s, Myers claims, the divorce rate has doubled, teen suicide tripled, violent crime quadrupled, the prison population quintupled, babies born out of wedlock sextupled and cohabitation, a predictor of divorce, has risen sevenfold. Rich western society is being eaten away from within by individualism and moral relativism, which are undermining civic engagement and social responsibility.

These arguments are worth listening to, but with caution. Putnam's gloomy assessment of the state of community in America is not shared by all. He measures traditional sources of social capital – churches, bowling leagues – but not potential new sources of social capital created by the Internet, single-issue politics or youth culture. Estimates of the decay of social capital vary, as do estimates of its connection to happiness. A recent international study of social capital, conducted by the OECD, found no evidence that it was declining dramatically, other than in the US. Communitarianism is like a political version of the UK Gold television channel: it feeds off a powerful sense of nostalgia for lost communities, civility and manners. The golden era communities of the 1950s were places of intolerance and prejudice, in which opportunities for women and blacks were far more limited. The challenge, as Putnam acknowledges, is not to go back to a lost idyll, but to create new forms of community and civic engagement, tailored to the needs of a more fluid, open, democratic and diverse society.

The Radical Left and the Conservative Right

Fear of degeneration is as much the rallying cry for much of the American new left and cultural critics of global capitalism as it is for social conservatives who want to defend a traditional order.

A prime recent example of the fear of degeneration from the left is Morris Berman, who in *The Twilight of American Culture* argues that American civilization, far from being vital and confident, is in a twilight phase, rapidly approaching the point of social and cultural bankruptcy. America's mass illiteracy and ignorance make it an international joke, according to Berman. The nation's spiritual life has been all but extinguished by corporate marketing. The gap between rich and poor has never been greater and the government's ability to narrow that gap has never been weaker. America, Berman concludes, is a moral and cultural shambles, not an economic superpower. This is a spiritual death of a particularly energetic kind of course, because the merry go round of innovation in science, technology and commerce masks the inner emptiness of a nation which is morally adrift. As Don DeLillo describes it in *White Noise*, the noise of modern culture is not a sign of life but a harbinger of death. Drawing on Joseph Tainter's analysis in *The Collapse of Complex Societies* Berman maintains that America is increasingly unable to understand and address its mounting problems, let alone do anything about them. The core of his argument is that modern society is very like the one depicted in Ray Bradbury's novel *Fahrenheit 451*. People's lives are increasingly run by screens, reading is confined to a minority and mass culture breeds ignorance and stupidity: 42 per cent of American adults cannot locate Japan on a map; 70 per cent believe in angels and 40 per cent did not know that Germany was the US's enemy in the Second World War.[3] This goes beyond dumbing down, claims Berman, it amounts to 'spiritual death' in which Americans no longer have the psychological strength to form real friendships, as he laments:

One further aspect of our current spiritual collapse is our increasing inability to relate to one another with a minimum of courtesy or even awareness . . . We have stopped holding doors for one another; don't bother to answer messages; disappear from each other's lives without explanation or regret; betray one another and then refuse to discuss it. Rudeness is now acceptable because I am the only one who inhabits my solipsistic world.

This spiritual death is the product of culture that is constantly assaulting the senses with trivia. Berman urges a small, monastic elite to form a cultural guerrilla army of intellectuals, whose goal in life is to renounce television, café latte, designer clothes, computers and the other distractions of modernity and choose instead a life of reflection and argument, based on a diet of Shakespeare and Picasso, Flaubert and Homer, organic food and simple living. After you, Morris.

Kalle Lasn, one of the media-savvy leaders of the anti-globalization movement and founder of *Adbusters*, the Canadian magazine, argues in *Culture Jam* that most people lead essentially futile lives in a world in which politicians bend at the knee to corporate power. Our stories, that Lasn claims were once passed from generation to generation, presumably around log fires, are now generated by corporate brands, Lasn says. They manipulate our desires to such an extent that it becomes impossible to live an 'authentic life'. The human spirit, which was once proudly contrary, has been tamed into a media-induced coma. Lasn claims: 'American cool is a global pandemic. Communities, traditions, cultural heritages, sovereignties, whole histories are being replaced by a barren American monoculture.'

These are voices from the self-styled radical left. Yet it is striking how much their critique of modern society shares with aristocratic and cultural conservatives on both sides of the Atlantic. As an example, take Roger Scruton, the conservative philosopher who set out his account of national degeneration in *England: An Elegy*. To caricature Scruton only slightly, modern England is a place where ladies no longer cycle to church on Sunday, past a village green where men in white flannels play cricket, in front of the friendly village pub, because if ladies did venture out they would almost certainly be knocked off their cycles by louts, the cricket field will have been turned into a development of tacky executive homes, the church will have closed long ago and the pub will be offering Thai food. England has all but gone. Scruton writes in the tradition of Philip Larkin. In his 1972 poem 'Going, Going' – first published as a prologue to a government report on the environment – Larkin gathered up pollution, rowdy mass leisure, property speculators and towniness to suggest a country sold off for profit and pleasure. Englishness would be located in meadows, lanes, choirs, guildhalls but these will be preserved only in the 'tourist' parts, as mythic memories of times gone by, Larkin predicted. Cricket, for Scruton, is the essence of Englishness because it 'displayed the reticent and understated character of the English ideal: white flannels too clean and pure to suggest physical exertion, long moments of silence and stillness, stifled murmurs of emotion should anything out of the ordinary occur and the occasional burst of subdued applause'.

For Scruton England is not an ideal, not even a nation, so much as a 'home': a place where everything is domesticated and in time even invented traditions, such as the modern monarchy, become part of the furniture. No one can quite remember how a particular piece of furniture got there, nor what its original use may have been, but it still sits there in the hallway, welcoming us back. In Scruton's familiar, homely England, things do not have to be explained nor justified, they just 'are' by virtue of being part of custom and tradition, from colliery bands to the Boy Scouts, from the Women's Institute to the guilds and trade unions. The feeling the English have of being safe in their home allows people greater freedom to be themselves: this is the root of the tradition of English eccentrics, amateurs and cranks who queue patiently, and in public, to collect stamps and proudly grow vegetables so large they could never be eaten.

This England is being scrubbed away, Scruton claims. All the qualities of the generation that fought the Second World War, gentleness, firmness, quiet courage, service to others, honesty, tolerance, grit, the spirit of fair play and the stiff upper lip, are derided and denied by mass culture and a liberal elite obsessed with intellectual fashion. Having been famous for their stoicism, decorum and sexual abstinence, the English now subsist almost as a lower form of life in a society in which long-term loyalties are regarded with cynicism and where the general response to misfortune is to search for someone else to blame. Sport, once a rehearsal for imperial virtue, has become a battleground for commerce and a theatre for over-rated celebrity. Sex, freed from its taboos, has become a mass obsession. The English regard marriage as a bore, complains Scruton, and 'litter the country with their illegitimate, uncared for and state subsidised offspring'.

Everything about the old virtuous England is going or gone: congregations and little platoons; children's games and parlour songs, proverbs and sayings. The global economy, the demo-cratization of taste, the fashionable thinking of the liberal elite and television have helped to 'erase the sense of spiritual identity in every place where piety shored up the old forms of knowledge and local custom fortified the moral sense'. The English who felt they were at home only fifty years ago, now feel they are living nowhere.

Hard Core

Putnam's communitarianism and Scruton's elegiac lament for a long-gone social idyll are degeneration in a soft-core format. If that were all that the degenerationist argument amounted to, it might be little more than a passing intellectual and cultural fashion. Yet degenerationist arguments are taking on an increasingly strident, angry and intolerant tone in the hands of their hard-core political exponents, especially conservative fundamentalists on both sides of the Atlantic. These apostles of degeneration have acquired their own followers, who want to turn rhetoric into action. Jean-Marie Le Pen's success in the first round of France's 2002 presidential election was just one example of this tendency at work.

Hard-core degeneration is not an elegiac lament; it stems from a wounded sense of betrayal. Community and tradition have not been lost, as if we mislaid them; they have been stolen from us. Our national culture is not ebbing away; it is being plundered. This is not an abstract social process; it is a struggle for power and freedom. The heroes of this struggle are the hard-working, long-suffering, down-to-earth organic core of the nation. Middle Britain, Middle America and now Middle France are not descriptions of places. They are metaphors for a state of mind that binds this hard-pressed organic core together. The unassuming, middle-income, middle-class core is being let down by the metropolitan elites, overrun by aliens and foreigners and taken for a ride by a morally decrepit underclass, which is unwilling to take responsibility for itself. This is a call to engage in a moral crusade to reclaim and cleanse society.

Nowhere is this crusading account of degeneration more powerful in the UK than in the pages of Britain's award-winning newspaper, the *Daily Mail*. For the *Mail* degeneration starts with the decadent hypocrisy and selfishness of the metropolitan elites, the chattering classes whose allegiance is to a fashionable and cosmopolitan view of the world. The elite despises the suburbs and the provinces. They travel abroad more frequently than they go anywhere outside the M25 lest they have to eat bad food. They like only places that serve cranberry juice and café latte. Economically the elite is increasingly detached from the national economy. These are the 'fat cat' lawyers, consultants, executives and media types who prosper from the winner-take-all culture of global markets. The *Daily Mail* is a pro-market paper only to the extent that the market benefits the hard-working and underpaid middle classes, who are fascinated and sometimes enraged by what other people earn. The overpaid elite are not leaders of society but parasites, leeching the hard-working middle class. The hierarchy of society is breaking down primarily because of desertions from the top.

The elite's lack of backbone is revealed by its love affair with modern art and culture: self-indulgent and liberal, fancy and intellectual, and completely out of touch with the down-to-earth expectations of suburbia. Max Nordau criticized the elite at the end of the nineteenth century for their obsession with 'inordinately erotic' modern art and their rejection of organic national culture in favour of the shallow attractions of the avant-garde. In the same vein a century later, the *Daily Mail* loves to attack Damien Hirst and Tracey Emin, elevating them to the status of national villains. (The irony is that the young British artists associated with Cool Britannia have more in common with the *Daily Mail* than one might at first think: the main themes of their work are decay and death.)

Modern culture is not soothing, pleasing and calming. It does not celebrate its links to the past but instead the chaos, disorder and disfigurements of the modern. This echoes the late nineteenth century when theories of degeneration over-lapped with interest in the idea of the grotesque.[4] The *Daily Mail* regards modern art as grotesque because it promotes perversions and transgressions – animals in tanks, art works made of bricks and bedclothes, performance art of all kinds. Modern art is a celebration of incoherent energy, chaos and intensity, it dissolves ancient unities, abolishes hierarchies of respect, overturns the order that people rely upon, implodes structures which support their lives. Modern art, for these critics, is not merely a self-centred indulgence: it is the product of a manic and diseased vitality. The *Daily Mail*'s attack on the perversions of innovation is not confined to modern art, however, it extends to science. Genetics, like modern art, is evil because it transgresses natural boundaries, creating devi-ants and mutants. That is why in parallel with attacks on modern artists, the *Daily Mail* is consumed by stories of Frankenstein foods, the grotesque monsters being created by genetic engineering and cloning.

The fickle elite are not the only parasites eating at the nation. As the elite creams off the top, the feckless, lawless underclass is draining resources from the bottom. This underclass has no work ethic and makes its money from petty crime, either by fraudulently claiming state benefits or from drugs and car theft. This underclass, the modern equivalent of Nordau's vermin, is almost beyond redemption. It breeds a culture in which there is little respect for the law, work, parents, other people or any source of authority. Finally, our national immune system is beset by parasites and infections coming from abroad. These viruses might arrive in the form of bureaucratic interventions from the European Commission in our traditions and culture or in the form of desperate asylum seekers hanging on for dear life underneath a lorry coming through the port of Dover. Foreigners are everywhere taking us for a ride. They have to be stopped!

The honest, hard-working, law-abiding middle class is endangered. It needs to stand up for itself. This account of national degeneration is not a recipe for melancholic nostalgia nor for wistful remembrance of days gone by. This politics of degeneration mobilizes people through their fear of the unknown, the immigrant and the future. Under the wrong conditions degeneration can become a highly unstable, nasty political force. Those conditions include two other features of modern political culture: endism and populism. Endism is people's fear that important features of their world are in danger of coming to an abrupt and imminent end, unless or even if they take action to protect themselves. Populism is when this protest sees the political process as the enemy and so the protest takes on direct, mass and popular form. In both cases violence is likely because people feel they have nothing to lose and no option but to resist.

Endism

Endists come in all shapes and sizes, from left and right, revolutionaries and reactionaries, religious cultists and cultural commentators. Endism is a natural reaction to the advocacy of the 'new'. The advocates of the new – the new economy, new Britain, new technology, the new world order – encourage endism as a response. Something can be genuinely new only by displacing the old. As radicals and innovators announce the arrival of the all new, they also announce the end of the old and thus encourage others into a desperate defence of what is in danger. In the last few years an entire industry has grown up to announce the end of everything from history, time, the future, architecture, reading, books, print, design, culture, the family, race, science and the world. In the UK our politics is dominated by debates over the end of things: the pound, the monarchy, Britain, the family, jobs for life, childhood, the railways and so on.

Predicting that the end was nigh used to be a minority pastime for sad men pacing West End streets in sandwich boards, palm readers in fairgrounds and evangelists with a crazed glint in their eye. Now it is a global media industry, employing latter-day priests: management consultants, futurologists, philosophers, scientists and gurus of all shapes and sizes. Endism, like terror, has a bizarre appeal: we feel attracted and fascinated by something that spreads panic and anxiety. To predict the definite end of something is to be confident, assured and armed with special insight. To predict the end of something as vital to our lives as work or the family is threatening, terrifying and upsetting. The modern fashion for endism probably started with Francis Fukuyama's *The End of History*, published in 1992, and still one of the best endist tracts. The end of the millennium may also have played a role in the surge of interest in things that appear to be coming to an end. But as Damian Thompson points out in his *The End of Time*, a useful survey of apocalyptic thought through the ages, endism needs more than a convenient date to get going: 'Apocalyptic belief in the End of Time appeals most to people who are disoriented, whose identity is under threat.' Most 'end of' tracts are based on the central claim that modernity is taking revenge upon itself. Progress, and technological progress especially, is moving so fast and opening up so many opportunities to do things differently that it is generating a destabilizing level of uncertainty and anxiety. At least we knew where we were in the old world. But the new world is full of risks and uncertainties. Social conservatives put a particularly enraged slant on endism.

A fine exponent of this creed is Melanie Phillips, now a commentator of the *Daily Mail*. In 'Sleepwalking to Tyranny' Phillips starts with the introduction of metric weights and measures and ends with the destruction of western civilization. Imperial measures of inches and pounds which, Phillips claims, flow from the British character are being abolished by EU directives which means we are sleepwalking into a tyranny from Brussels. The explanation, for Phillips, is not that using the same system of weights and measures as our main trading partners might be useful, but that our political leaders are intent on a revolutionary assault on the country's ethos and traditions. She concludes:

This attack on our history and culture goes much further still. Like the mythological pelican, the West has been pecking away at its own flesh for decades. The therapy culture undermined morality by transferring authority from 'what's right' to 'what's right for me.' Above all, the two parent family, the crucible of the sturdy individualism which underpins our democracy is under relentless attack. Put that together with multiculturalism and the European super state and you have a recipe for the destruction of Western democracy.[5]

And all because we weigh our oranges in kilograms.

Another leading advocate is Peter Hitchens, the political commentator at the *Mail on Sunday*. In his book *The Abolition of Britain* Hitchens complains that in little more than a generation an irreversible change in morals, values, customs, taboos, language, humour, art and even eating habits has been 'inflicted' upon Britain. (This has come about as a result of an external force over which we have no control and for which we take no responsibility: we are just forced to eat curry.) The way was cleared for radical change in our lives because Britain has been hoodwinked into abandoning so many life-giving traditions, among them a complex coinage system of half crowns and florins, which required a decent education system to master it; and a distinctive system of weights and measures. Britain is not unnaturally obsessed with its past, as many people suppose. According to Hitchens, on the contrary the nation is suffering from the 'end of memory': 'A nation is the sum of its memories and when those memories are allowed to die it is less of a nation . . . it is hard to see why any nation should have tried as hard as Britain has done in the past three decades to wipe out its memory.'

What is ironic is how much Hitchens is echoing writers from the radical left. Herbert Marcuse, the Marxist philosopher most beloved by the student revolutionaries of 1968, remarked in *One Dimensional Man* that he feared capitalism was creating 'man without memory'. Hitchens's remarks remind one of Milan Kundera in the *Book of Laughter and Forgetting*, who notes the words of Milan Huble, one of the 145 historians sacked in the wake of the suppressed Prague Spring: 'The first step in liquidating a people is to erase its memory. Destroy its books, its culture, its history.' Or the party slogan in Orwell's *Nineteen Eighty Four*: 'Who controls the past controls the future; who controls the present, controls the past.'

According to Hitchens, a weakened and disoriented Britain, cut off from the life support system of tradition, has been powerless to prevent from being concreted over the customs and values which made it great. So, according to Hitchens, we have had, or are about to suffer, a long series of end points: the end of parliamentary democracy, the end of union with Scotland, the end of a higher education system founded on elite institutions such as Oxford and Cambridge, the end of free thought and dissent and even, thanks to television, the end of imagination. As a result we live in a country populated by empty shells, old institutions that no longer have a proper purpose but cling to life: fertile fields that are set-aside; old rectories which are second homes for rich businessmen; warehouses that have become flats for yuppies; churches which have become arts centres. Change has become the new orthodoxy: the conservatives who attempt to resist, by staying the same, are the rebels.

Hitchens closes his tirade with a warning eerily reminiscent of Max Nordau's rallying cry to cleanse the world: 'If the decay of obligation, duty and morality continues, danger and misery will soon be hammering at the front doors of all of us . . . the longer we leave it, the more illiberal, costly and nasty the ultimate solution will have to be.'

This is not just pessimistic but apocalyptic. When deep distrust of politics is added to the mix, then the panic of endism can quickly turn into popular protest. Ironically, politics has become more populist largely thanks to new technology. Once again we see new technology used to go back to the past: to organize the oldest form of political protest, street demonstrations.

Populism

We are living in an age of electronic populism. New technology is creating more personalized services. But in parallel we
are also becoming a more 'herd like' society. The communications technology of the Internet and mobile telephones
allows new forms of collective, self-orchestrated behaviour,
including the networks described by US-based sociologist
Manuel Castells. But these networks can turn into bubbles,
crowds, clans, raves and herds. These unstructured movements, built around a passion, an issue or an interest can appear
almost overnight, their long gestation hidden from sight, and
then explode. Like the political equivalent of a financial bubble
their sudden growth makes them seem larger and more powerful than perhaps they are. These political bubbles can deflate
and disappear as quickly as they emerged, leaving perhaps a
lasting mark but probably no lasting organization: the protests
against fuel price rises in the autumn of 2000 in the UK which
almost brought the government to its knees; the anti-
paedophile protests in Portsmouth which took control of a
sprawling estate; the rolling anti-globalization and anti-road
protests which are organized using techniques employed to
orchestrate raves.

We are becoming a society of networks, clans and herds.
The financial markets appear to move in herds, shifting their
attention en masse from one currency to another, one fashionable investment to another. The popular media seems to move
like a herd, swinging from a mass attack on a football manager
who has spoken out of turn, to a moral issue and on to a
controversial television programme. For a while everyone
talks about the same issue – paedophiles, the performance of a
Cabinet minister, a controversial vaccine, railways – whipping
themselves into an overspun frenzy. Then the issue is dropped

and no one mentions it for weeks. Politicians are both victims and protagonists in this process. Increasingly political leadership is about calming media panics and influencing people through direct communication, bypassing normal political channels.

The difference these days is that the people can bite back: increasingly people want to use new technology to ask their question, make their point, have their say and if necessary organize to take to the streets. The most potent example in the UK was the eruption of anger among farmers and road hauliers over fuel prices in the autumn of 2000 in the UK. Using mobile telephones and the Internet, building on a group of people who had been involved in long-running campaigns over the support for rural communities, the fuel protesters used new technology to coordinate the oldest of protests: pickets and street demonstrations. As supplies ran short, emergency measures were put in place and panic spread. This protest did not have an organization and there were no official leaders to negotiate with. The government dealt with it through the media and eventually bought the protesters off with a package of measures. A campaign that brought the country to a standstill collapsed like a deflated balloon: it had appeared to be big but turned out to be hollow. Barely a year later it was almost completely forgotten, its leaders, who had commanded the airwaves, had returned to anonymity. One of the best guides to political behaviour in the media-saturated, connected society is the behaviour of crowds. Elias Canetti in *Crowds and Power*, a reflection on the nature of populism in the era of fascism and communism, first published in 1960, wrote:

Just as suddenly as it originates, the crowd disintegrates. In its spontaneous form it is a sensitive thing. The openness which enables it to grow is, at the same time, its danger. A foreboding of threatening disintegration is always alive in the crowd. It seeks through rapid increase, to avoid this for as long as it can; it absorbs everyone and because it does, it must ultimately fall to pieces.

We live in a world of distributed communications, in which technology is migrating to people and out of institutions that can control it. As a result people can increasingly coordinate themselves without needing a formal institution or organization to do it for them. They can produce their own information and ideas, without needing to rely on newspapers, radios and magazines. These electronic crowds are often given their purpose by the media, which inflames them and drives them on. No longer do newspapers or television companies simply deliver content to passive consumers. The consumers want to do something with the content. The audience does not just watch *Big Brother*, they talk about it and vote electronically. Why watch a programme like *Juke Box Jury* when people can vote in their millions to create their own Pop Idol? How long will politics be able to resist the encroachment of *Pop Idol* culture?

The same principle applies to populist campaigning journalism: the aim is not simply to provide people with information – for example about paedophiles – but to whip them into action – to take to the streets in protest – which then takes the story to a new level. This is a process which thrives on gossip: sourceless information, which is difficult to verify and impossible to resist. Gossip floats in the electronic ether, often with no clear point of origin and no one who need take responsibility for its instigation. In the past the reach of gossip was confined to family, friends, offices, streets – local places where eventually it could be checked. But these days rumour travels far and wide and fast. The new communications media has created a huge gossip machine, unleashing the very natural human desire for gossip on to a much larger and more potent stage. When all these ingredients combine, we have a recipe for populist protest and direct action, in which new technology organizes the most traditional and old-fashioned kind of protest: taking to the streets.

We should expect more violence, protest and direct action. The first ingredient in this recipe for violence is the multiplying accounts of how society is degenerating, eating away at itself from within. The second is the contribution of hard-core degenerationists who go a step further. For them the country is not falling to bits, it is being dismantled by parasites from above and below. We are being betrayed. Third is the call to arms to protect central features of our way of life that are in danger of being abolished, brought to an abrupt, irreversible and definitive end. It is both alarming and exhilarating. Finally, to exorcize the terror, to defend what is endangered, people take to direct action, especially when they feel the odds are so stacked against them that they have no option but to fight.

According to the apostles of degeneration, from right and left, modern society suffers from a variety of death wishes: individualism, consumerism and loss of respect for tradition, which eat away at society from within. Unwittingly we cut ourselves off from the wellsprings of vitality and authenticity in our lives, from community, nature, tradition or imagination. It is because we are cut off from these sources of stability that we grow deluded and disoriented, we lose the sense of perspective and value. We become complicit collaborators in the very degenerative processes that threatens us. We can only be awoken from this descent into chaos at moments of grave crisis. Starting from different places modern prophets of doom reach the same conclusion: globalization and modernity are degenerative processes that will eventually lead to violent conflagration. Pessimism is powerful, plausible and pervasive, whether in the soft-core form of nostalgia for a long-lost past or in the hard-core version of anger at the prospect of degeneration. It is impossible to ignore the appeal of this spreading culture of pessimism because it speaks to widely felt anxieties and fears. Yet this culture of pessimism has long passed the point of realism. It has become a chronic condition, invariably overdone, morally self-righteous and often just wrong. Far from preparing us for an uncertain future, chronic pessimism makes us feel endangered, powerless and disabled.

4. The Pessimists' Alliance

Pessimism is used as a recruiting tool by both radicals and reactionaries to rally people to their cause. This alliance of pessimists is arguably the most potent force in global politics. Radicals in the shape of anti-globalizers and environmentalists, reactionaries in the form of cultural and social conservatives share a common political home defined by their pessimism. They may differ in their values, goals, tactics, dress and sexual habits. Radicals such as Lasn argue they want to go beyond the current economic system to one that is built on non-commercial values. Reactionaries in contrast do not want to go beyond but before: back to a lost historic sense of order. Yet despite their differences they share a commitment to a pessimistic view of the world. Central to that is the common enemy of 'globalization' which stands for many different evils. For the radical pessimists, globalization is creating a world of unchecked corporate power, in which the market promotes blanket consumerism and inequality hand in hand. The reactionary pessimists bemoan the way that innovation, modernization and foreign influences threaten cherished traditions, customs and practices.

It is a sign of how politics is being reorganized into new forms that radicals and reactionaries can share so many assumptions about the world. Indeed radicals and reactionaries are increasingly just different wings of a larger political force: the Pessimists' Alliance. Central to that alliance are six central themes. It is worth spelling out these common themes, not just to show how much common ground there is but also to outline the terrain of the battle that optimists face. These are the central themes which any credible optimism will have to take on.

First, homogeneity. To the pessimists globalization is a standardizing force that is sweeping all before it, thereby eliminating the means to be different. Cultural niches might be preserved at great cost, but surrounded by an ocean of consumerism. For reactionary pessimists, such as Hitchens and Scruton, the spread of commercial culture is eliminating the space to be slow, eccentric, curmudgeonly and not part of the modern world. For the radicals, consumer culture, the spread of global brands and supply chains, is rooting out cultural differences, smashing local producers and crushing indigenous culture. Everything gets valued by the same yardsticks of MTV, Disney, McDonald's and Gap.

Second, globalization is anti-democratic. The elimination of space to be different is the fundamental reason why pessimists see globalization as anti-democratic. For radicals globalization is anti-democratic because giant corporations, spin doctors, PR companies and the media are silently taking over the institutions of representative democracy.[1] Social conservatives such as Melanie Phillips see a political class that is no longer willing to stand up for common sense and instead have become the purveyors of an artificial political correctness which sweeps before it all traditional forms of life. As that sense of cultural and political heritage is destroyed so is the basis for the UK being different. For the reactionaries, skilful and untrustworthy politicians are using the excuse of 'global competition' to force unnatural reforms on the country.

Third, human scale values. We are drawn towards the false allure of fashion, speed and novelty by marketing and gadgetry. For reactionaries human values are embodied by the older generations and communities – the stiff upper lip, decency and good manners – protected by hierarchy, decency and order, with stable, 'normal' families at their heart. For radicals, human values are likely to be more spiritual and new age. Radicals such as Lasn appear to want people to live at peace with one another, in a kind of collective consciousness, in which people share instinctively and are able to see through the false allure of material wealth.

Fourth, distrust of technology. Both radicals and reactionaries aspire to be intelligent and selective luddites, often upholding low-tech solutions and older forms of craft work, non-formal sources of knowledge and small-scale production: the farmer in his field; the herbal remedies bought from a new age boutique; the sanctification of the insight and intuitive knowledge of indigenous peoples.

Fifth, organicism. Our connections to nature, the land and soil have a primeval value. For both wings of the Pessimists' Alliance, nature, soil and land help provide a sense of balance and rootedness, timescales and values that stretch beyond the fleeting attractions of the footloose modern world. This cult of the organic can lead in quite different directions, of course. Love of the organic soil has been a vital component of rabidly nationalist politics and ethnic cleansing. For new age hippies, organicism is the basis for a new way of life in which people are more at one with their inner self as a result of being more in harmony with nature.

Sixth, authenticity. Most importantly, the alliance's members agree that modern culture makes it impossible for people to live authentic lives, in which they can be true to themselves. For the reactionaries authenticity arises from a sense of rootedness in tradition and custom. For Roger Scruton, for example, something is authentic if it has been around a long time and so can be relied upon. A building, institution, custom or product is made authentic only by being weathered by time (a message jeans manufacturers endorse). The more these traditions and communities are eliminated by the combine harvester of modern culture, so the more we are cut off from the cultural resources we need to be truly ourselves. For conservatives, the authentic is wrinkled, weathered and therefore likely to be slightly oddly shaped: it will not fit into the standardizing demands of agribusiness, supermarkets and branding. For conservatives, authentic identities – what it means to be British, male, a farmer – are embedded in history. We do not create our authentic selves, we find him or her waiting for us in our history.

The radical pessimists employ a different notion of authenticity. Many endorse an aspect of this view that authentic customs and traditions – herbal remedies for illnesses for example – emerge from a pre-commercial, pre-technological world, in which cures were not invented by scientists but developed over very many hundreds of years of communal know-how. Radical new age authenticity is a celebration of the pre-modern. But for radical melancholics the idea of authenticity also has a modern dimension. For radicals, people live lives true to themselves only when they are really free to reflect upon and make their own choices, free from the insidious pressures of advertising, the media and marketing. It is not just that modern commercial culture is shallow. The problem is far worse than that: society is suffering from a form of what Karl Marx called 'false consciousness': a widespread and systematic inability of people to understand their true needs and interests.

This idea that we are suffering from false consciousness is endorsed not just by the radicals, whom one might expect to draw on the Marxist tradition, but also by the conservatives. The conservative account, set out by the likes of Hitchens, is that Britain has become so bewildered by the fashionable thinking of the liberal elite that we are being conned into giving up precious symbols of the national way of life that make us who we are. Most famously, we are being persuaded to see ourselves as 'European' when actually we are British.

For Britons to see themselves as European is a form of false consciousness, a misunderstanding of our true nature and destiny, according to the conservatives. For the radical pessimists the kind of false consciousness we are suffering from comes squarely out of the Marxist tradition.[2] The cultural industries of advertising, pop music, media and marketing so beloved of modern politicians are nothing more than tools to manufacture our consent to remain powerless in the face of dreadful circumstances. The cultural industries, far from exciting our imagination, are designed to stop us thinking other than in the terms that are convenient for those already in power.

This critique of the media and cultural industries advanced by the likes of Thomas Frank, Morris Berman and Naomi Klein is delivered in the language and categories of Theodor Adorno, one of the leading members of the Frankfurt School. Adorno's account of the culture industries was influenced by his experience of the rise of Nazism, from which he fled, and the mass culture industry of his adopted home in Los Angeles. For Adorno, the cultural industries were a form of mass deception, unifying and pacifying society in a soporific glow of short-term pleasure. Adorno, writing in the 1940s, argued that the elimination of pre-capitalist forms of production, the decline of religion, the spread of communications technology, such as the radio, and the emergence of more diverse lifestyles should in theory have led to cultural chaos and creativity. Yet far from it, never was culture more unified or integrated, Adorno wrote. Films, radio and magazines made up a system that obeyed the same rules of mass production as any other industry that produced commodities. Culture has long ceased to be a repository for reflective comprehension or a source of individuality. Anything novel, challenging or different is either ignored and marginalized or rapidly incorporated and co-opted into the system as a whole.[3]

The Pessimists' Alliance is so powerful because it can operate on the left and right of politics, at the same time. The different wings of the alliance appear to be enemies but actually they have many shared unspoken objectives. Globalization is a standardizing force around commercial values which leaves little room for difference, diversity and dissent. Technology is increasingly driving us into the hands of global corporations, which will put us on a treadmill of largely self-defeating, shallow innovations that eliminate the slow, tacit craft and low-tech forms of knowledge and production. The market, far from providing greater choice, is an agent for cultural cleansing. As cultural difference is eliminated so are the grounds for dissent and democracy. We risk losing our connections to the soil and nature. Growing numbers of people feel unable to lead what they could call authentic lives. Western liberal democracies are suffering from a possibly terminal dose of false consciousness, unable to discern, articulate or defend our own interests. All the forces which are apparently driving society forward – innovation, technology, individualism, globalization – are actually pulling us into a downward spiral.

Just as political pessimism of the left and the right follows a common formula, so it suffers from some common weaknesses. This is not to dismiss the pessimists out of hand. Far from it, some of their critiques are heavily researched, thoughtful and passionate. But they also deploy similar rhetorical devices and assumptions to make their arguments more plausible.

First, the pessimists encourage us to view the world in very stark terms. There is little room for adaptation, complexity and evolution. They leave little room for the possibility that the forces of degeneration that they describe may also have tangible benefits. Many people's experience of the world seems to be that things get better and worse at the same time.

That is why we feel so caught. In some respects we may be living in a less democratic age, because of the power and reach of global corporations. But in fundamental respects we are living in a more democratic, open society, in which a culture of self-governance is slowly spreading. Communitarians bemoan the decline of traditional forms of social capital, built on locality and neighbourhood, but often neglect to account for new forms of collaboration and community around shared interests, hobbies and knowledge. Standardization, spread by globalization, can be a bad thing but not when common standards ease the exchange of goods and ideas.

Second, the pessimists like to simplify the processes at work to exaggerate them for apocalyptic effect. For the radical pessimists English is a killer language spreading like a cultural plague around the world, eliminating distinctive voices and cultural identities. But the rise of English is the product of a long, complex and far from inevitable process, in which many varieties and hybrids of the language have emerged. The pessimists' black and white world rules out the possibility of people reaching these fruitful combinations in language, commerce and technology. But that is how people increasingly seem to cope, by creating hybrids.

Third, the argument that modern global capitalism is uniquely destructive acquires momentum only through a contrast with the unsullied, pre-commercial, pre-technological world we imagine our ancestors lived in so happily. Pessimists of all persuasions, for example, want us to get 'back to nature'. Getting several billion people 'back to nature' with the crude agricultural technologies of yesteryear would be the best way to destroy nature, of course. To listen to the pessimists it is as if we have only just left behind a rewarding life on the land for the sake of the urban nightmare most of us live in. As Raymond Williams noted, no idea is more contested, loaded and unstable than that of what is 'natural'. The nature that is often held up as a neutral, moral and environmental bench-mark against which we should measure progress is often nothing more than a product of an earlier period of social innovation.

Fourth, the idea that we are all hapless dupes, suffering from false consciousness, unable to discern our own interests, begs the question of who would decide when consciousness was false and how the decision would be made. It is not as if you can dip a piece of litmus paper into people's heads to test for false consciousness. In the past the idea that the masses were suffering from false consciousness was deployed by religious leaders and authoritarian politicians to allow them to insert their account of what people's interests should be. In our age, commercial culture might be ribald, populist, low-brow and unruly, but it is far better that people make choices about what they read, watch on television or listen to on the radio than that they should be subjected to a censorious collective political and moral leadership. In the hands of the conservatives, false consciousness elevates a particular version of national identity and history. In the hands of radical leftists, it means ordinary people are reduced to being stupid, undiscerning, hapless victims of commercial manipulation. For all its limitations, we live in a world in which people can increasingly find, create and share ideas, which in turn allow them to shape their lives and identities.

Fifth, the pessimists share with their counterparts the super-optimists a tendency to parcel history into neat periods. The super-optimists like to announce new beginnings, blank sheets and fresh starts. The pessimists are constantly drawn towards endism, to warn that traditions, customs, ways of life are about to meet their end.

My argument is that chronic pessimism is powerful, appealing and often plausible but also wrong, misplaced and self-destructive. My argument is not that the world is a happy and rosy place. On the contrary, the pessimists are right to point out that the modern world has some very bad systemic features, which demand reform, first and foremost inequality and environmental degradation. It is very sensible to be a realistic pessimist about the scale of the challenges and difficulties we face in creating a more stable, equitable, sustainable world. The pessimists help to identify what people are concerned and worried about, the issues that they want tackled. A credible optimism should not dismiss the pessimists' arguments but find answers to them. But the chronic pessimism which now engulfs us exaggerates the problems we face and encourages us to see them as an irreversible, degenerative process. That feeds a sense of helplessness and despair, that in turn encourages people either to retreat and withdraw from civic engagement or move into a reactive burst of helpless confrontation. The politics of pessimism is counter-productive and will only reinforce the downward spiral.

Alongside a realistic pessimism about the scale of some of the challenges we face, we need a credible, strategic optimism about our future. My argument is that the fundamental forces driving modern society – technology, innovation, the spread of knowledge, globalization, the growth of democratic culture and individualism – are not degenerative but largely positive and could become massively more positive in the coming century. These forces are not totally benign. They often create significant downsides that provide the material for the pessimists' argument. What matters is how we tackle and eradicate these downsides. A credible, non-utopian optimism for the future should be based upon our collective and collaborative capacity for innovation and creativity. The second half of the book attempts to set out the grounds for that optimism. I am not arguing for a naive, self-satisfied or complacent optimism. Wishful thinking is just as dangerous as chronic pessimism is disabling. My argument is that on many issues the grounds for pessimism are often far more localized and manageable than we imagine. Solutions can and are being found to seemingly intractable problems. Too often the arch-pessimists ignore, overlook or downplay these powerful counter currents which are clearly improving the well-being and quality of life of millions of people. Pessimists see the world spiralling down, beyond our control, in a one-way, degenerative process. The truth is invariably more messy and complex. There are often equally powerful grounds for optimism and hope that in the twenty-first century life could get better for many people and not just for the rich and affluent.

Science, medicine and public health are continuing to extend the human lifespan in the developed and the developing world. In this century more of the population will live beyond the age of sixty-five than ever before. A large proportion of this elderly population will be in good health and enjoy extended periods of retirement free from work and children. Even in the developed world education has only just become a mass activity and even now it is largely confined to those below the age of twenty-two. In this century learning will become a mass activity, starting earlier, lasting longer, involving more people, in many different styles of learning. In the developing world access to basic education should become near universal with far-reaching implications for women's prospects, health, incomes, social mobility and democracy. Technology and innovation will help us to make far more of our finite resources of land and energy supplies. Productivity in agriculture has far outstripped population growth and with the advent of new genetic crops, properly regulated, those advances should continue. That will help underpin economic development in fast growing developing countries such as India and China. Carbon-free, hydrogen-based fuel cells will fuel our cars in future creating the possibility of pollution-free, but highly mobile cities. Renewable energy sources such as solar power will become commercially viable. But even without those radical innovations we should still be able to do enough, by cleaning up existing technologies and fuels, to stabilize greenhouse gases at levels that do not pose a drastically worsening risk to the world's environment.

The family is not in dire crisis as the pessimists suggest in their nostalgic yearning for the nuclear family of yesteryear. In many ways it is stronger than ever: more grandparents know more grandchildren than in any previous era. The modern family is the focal point of many strains from the demands of work in the modern labour market and relationship breakdown. However, with the help of supportive public policies and enlightened corporations many parents are devising solutions which allow them to work and rear children responsibly. Creating a new framework of support for modern families will be vital and is not beyond our reach.

Meanwhile, the spread of communications technologies continues to transform our culture, creating new opportunities for people to share, trade, argue, talk and socialize. The Internet is not creating a generation of inward-looking solipsists, but a generation that is far more individualistic and more collaborative at the same time. This technology allows people to both personalize and socialize. Combined with the rise of educational standards around the world, the spread of communications will help underpin democratic culture. The spread of democracy may not take the classic liberal democratic form of multi-party elections. However, rulers will find it increasingly difficult to abuse their power without challenge or check. The powerful will be more easily held to account and challenged.

Globalization is promoting some truly global brands, products and standards. But equally it is creating the conditions for new mixes, dialects, hybrids. People are finding new ways to engage with and accommodate the global economy, without that threatening their sense of locality and identity. Globalism often spreads local products and cultures to international markets, rather than imposing global products on local cultures. Globalization is a complex, heterogenous process, which could take many different paths. It is not a one-way ticket to disaster as the pessimists would have us believe. The cause of reducing global poverty, inequality, poor health and hunger will be best advanced by creating a global economy which is more integrated and more equitable. The answer is not less globalization, but more globalization to integrate poorer economies and to give them a decent chance to make their livings within a more stable and equitable global economy. The agenda of globalization has to move on from markets and finance, to global governance and social programmes. If we can make that shift then globalization could turn out to be the biggest poverty reduction programme ever seen.

Above all the pessimists argue that the die has been cast, the future is already sealed. They are wrong. On virtually every issue on which they argue for gloom, there are many possible outcomes and many reasons for being optimistic. On many of these issues, from education to poverty and the environment, we have choices that can affect the future. It is not beyond our control: we are not helpless as the pessimists suggest.

The contest between optimism and pessimism is fought out over several key issues addressed in the remainder of this book: globalization, individualism, work and the environment. The costs and benefits of technology are central to these other arguments. That is why the next three chapters focus on the utopian appeal of new technologies, the dystopian fears they produce and some rules of thumb we should follow to make the most of them.

5. The Dream of Digitopia

Fantasies animate our private and public lives to an extent that we are often unwilling to admit. Modern consumer society in many ways is living out a medieval myth. Virtually everyone living at the end of the Middle Ages had probably heard of the land of Cockaigne, a magical country tucked away in a remote corner of the globe where ideal living conditions prevailed.[1] Columbus and other explorers found the New World in part because they were fascinated by the myth of Cockaigne. A detailed account of the pleasures of life in Cockaigne was set out in the *Sterfboek* (*The Book of Death*) written in 1491. It reflected the themes of many vernacular texts that were passed by word of mouth. In Cockaigne work was forbidden. Ready-cooked food appeared spontaneously. Fine food was so plentiful that houses were built from fish, game and sausages. As one Dutch account of Cockaigne put it: 'No one suffers shortages, the walls are made of sausages . . . another fact I must utter: the beams of houses are made of butter.' Beautiful women were everywhere and consented to tender offers of sex. Well-made clothes appeared on people's doorsteps. Night and day, wind and rain, hail and snow were all abolished, as people basked in permanent spring warmth. There was neither animosity nor envy. In some accounts, everyone in Cockaigne was perpetually thirty-three years old, the age Christ attained on earth. There was neither death, sickness nor frailty. No one was deaf, deformed or dumb. There were neither hunchbacks nor cripples. The waters of magical springs and lakes protected people against sickness and made them younger than they were. Everything blossomed forever and fruit was always ripe in a world where there were no weeds, worms or toads. Angels made beautiful music the whole time leaving everyone in a state of constant elation.

The myth of Cockaigne, recounted in thousands of texts with these themes, was a relief and escape from daily life in which threats from hunger, disease and bad weather were a constant source of fear and uncertainty. Much of our modern consumer culture unwittingly seeks to realize the medieval Cockaigne idyll. In modern Europe fast food is available in an instant at all hours of day and night. Restaurants that allow us to gorge on as much food as we like, for a set price, are mini versions of Cockaigne. Supermarkets groan with cook-chilled foods that are replenished every night through sophisticated supply systems. Welfare systems and pensions allow people to be paid without working. Our climate is partially controlled by central heating and air conditioning. Florida and Southern California are popular retirement centres because they deliver an external climate not unlike that of Cockaigne. Some versions located Cockaigne in Spain, a judgement endorsed by thousands of tourists and North European pensioners who retire there for the winter. Music accompanies us wherever we go thanks to mini discs and Walkmen. Alcohol and other drugs can be taken easily to induce a state of elation. Instead of magical springs and lakes to protect us against sickness we have health services and high street pharmacies. Special creams, plastic surgery, artificial limbs and organs, and genetics seem to offer the prospect of vastly extended, if not immortal life. Modern society is living out a medieval myth.

Cockaigne pre-dated Thomas More's *Utopia* published in 1516. While the two mythic places can share common ingredients – such as the ready availability of food and the good nature of the people – they differ markedly in other respects. Cockaigne was not an elite and uplifting intellectual vision of a morally better society. It was a popular myth, propagated in response to the harsh and uncertain material conditions of relatively short lives subject to food shortages, plagues and cold. The Cockaigne myth offered a cathartic release from the conditions of everyday life. It was not a high-minded attempt to redesign society along moral lines. More's *Utopia*, and many of the utopian visions that followed it, were founded on moderation, austerity and rationality. Cockaigne is devoted to gluttony, appetite and pleasure.

When the Internet arrived in most of our lives in the mid 1990s it fitted neatly into our template for collective fantasies derived from Cockaigne and *Utopia*. It was not an accident that the utopian promise of the new economy arrived hot on the heels of the collapse of communism. The new economy's entrepreneurs were heirs to what was left of the diminished revolutionary rhetoric of socialism. The Internet allowed a generation to live out a 'have-your-cake-and-eat-it' dream of getting rich very quickly, without doing much real work, while also being counter-cultural renegades who flouted con-vention and attacked established centres of corporate power. Yet the utopian appeal of the Internet and modern digital technology in general, including genetics, goes far deeper than that. Despite all the manifest failings of the first wave of the steam age, narrow band, clunky and dull Internet, we wanted to fall in love with it. We wanted it to amount to more than a mere tool. Digital technologies tap into long established utopian themes about the nature of work, community, government and freedom. This is why despite their short-comings they excite us and continue to have the capacity to make us feel optimistic about the future. Everything to do with computers and communications can be reduced to measurement: memory, processing power, speed, bandwidth, unique users, page impressions. But digital technologies also appeal to our feelings, emotions and imaginations. The dream of digitopia that took hold between 1995 and 2000 was at root a romantic story of sweeping change in which we could make the future afresh. To understand the enduring appeal of the Internet we should look not just at the power of the hardware and software but at the utopian hopes we invest in it.

A Map of Digitopia

Digital technologies inspired such inflated hopes in the 1990s because we were encouraged to see technology through utopian lenses. Digital technology lent itself to utopian interpretations because it seemed to echo so many classical utopian themes.[2]

The Journey

Invariably utopia is reached by a journey, through time or across the globe to a foreign land. The traveller leaves behind not just an old land but their old self as well. By journeying to utopia, we not only discover a new world but also reveal our better, inner selves. Examples of the utopian journey abound from More's lone explorer to the utopian islands and H. G. Wells's traveller through time. Utopia involves travel.

In our own limited and commercialized way, we still play out this utopian dream each year when we set off on long-distance plane journeys for holidays. The pages of magazines such as *Condé Nast Traveller* sell a commercialized and individualized utopia of sandy beaches, palm trees, endless white towels and baskets of fresh fruit brought to you by willing and happy helpers. The cult of finding the untouched, unspoilt, perfectly regulated community of chilled out people was the impulse behind Alex Garland's dystopic novel *The Beach*. World tourism, the leading experience industry of the new economy, accounts for about 11 per cent of world gross domestic product and is projected to rise above 20 per cent by the year 2008, when the industry worldwide will be worth more than $7.5 trillion, according to the World Travel and Tourism Council. Twenty years ago about 287 million people took international trips. In 1996 more than 595 million people travelled abroad. According to the World Trade Organization by the year 2020 more than 1.6 billion of the expected world population of 7.8 billion will take a foreign trip. Many of these people will be travelling in the hope of a brief experience of utopian living conditions.

Cyberspace, however, has provided us with a new utopian destination we can travel to while sitting at our desks. In classical versions, utopia meant travelling to a virgin land that was inhabited by a race that had different codes, customs and language. In cyberspace this new race, mouthing a strange tongue, were the anoraks and geeks. Cyberspace is a topsy-turvy world in which the power relations of normal society have been overturned. Children are more knowledgeable and adept than their parents because they have a special insight into the world they were born into. In the real world adults guide children; in the digital world it is the other way around.

The new world comes complete with a bewildering language, the hip techno-vocab of *Wired* magazine. This new vocabulary underlines just how different the new world is: it does not conform to the normal dimensions and boundaries of the physical world. Thus we must learn to live in a world of netizens, bitniks, cyclomedia, middleware, electrospheres, microserfs, cranial jacks and geodiscs. At the mundane level of business a whole range of activities has been reduced to acronyms: B2B, B2C, C2C, P2P. These serve not so much to describe a new world but to confuse and exclude the unin-itiated. The border to cyberspace is not drawn by customs controls but by this bizarre language. People who live in cyberspace bond around this techno-babble. Their claim is that a new language is needed to describe and gain access to a world that lies beyond normal reality. To its utopian enthusiasts, cyberspace is not something that we observe from afar, nor is it even a tool: it is a separate universe. As one of the early enthusiasts for virtual reality, Michael Benedickt, put it in *Cyberspace: The First Steps*, published in 1991: 'Cyberspace fulfils the dream of making it possible to transcend the physical world fully alive, at will and to dwell in some world beyond, to be empowered and enlightened there, alone or with others and then to return to earth.' It is as if cyberspace allows us all to take an excursion into the weightless world of outer space by travelling through our personal computers rather than perched precariously on the top of a Saturn rocket.

The Laws of Abundance

There was a time when technology was furniture. In the 1960s when I was a boy, my elderly relatives in Yorkshire all had enormous, wooden radiograms in pride of place in their front rooms. My auntie Mabel in Scarborough had the largest radiogram I had ever seen. The radiogram had a turntable for a stack of Bakelite 78rpm records that were stored in a compartment at one end of the cabinet. In the middle was a vast screen showing all the radio stations from far and near that could be reached by twiddling the knobs. To my knowledge, none of these stations was ever listened to; but they gave one a sense that you could connect to a much larger world, should you ever want to take that chance.

The radiogram was not just a device for playing music. It had a built-in drinks cabinet. Displayed along the top were a variety of photographs and vases, each with a doily underneath. By the time I discovered Auntie Mabel's radiogram in the mid sixties it had fallen into disuse for audio purposes. However, the culture of technology as furniture lived on, until quite recently. When my father bought our first 'stereo system' in the 1970s it too came in brown wood and it sat on top of a wooden cabinet that stored his very large LP collection. In those days technology was precious and so were the experiences it made possible. Music was not portable and personal: we listened to music in a particular room in the house at set times in the evening. Daytime music playing was indulgent and likely to infringe on other people. Albums were precious because a single slip of the stylus spelled ruin. They required a collector's care: my dad had a set of tools for LP maintenance, including a series of specialized brushes to remove dust. Technology was not reliable. When I was a child the television in particular was always going 'funny' for no good reason: the picture went fuzzy; the screen lost its horizontal hold; occasionally it would expire altogether, the picture reduced to a small white dot. In my childhood technology had to warm up before it would work; it could not be flipped on with a switch. It had to be coaxed into action. Even when I started work in 1983 at *Weekend World*, at the time the Sunday lunchtime flagship current affairs programme of the ITV network, the scripts were written in pencil and the only computer on the entire floor was kept in a room resembling a cupboard. When I joined the *Financial Times* in 1986, then already Europe's leading business paper, the print floor thronged with men running around with hot metal, while others worked at beautiful mechanical Victorian linotype machines. It is only relatively recently that technology has started to get so small and powerful that it has begun to pervade our lives. We are at the start of what will be a long process.

Technology is not brown any longer but black and silver. It does not stand on legs and is never polished. We do not show it off in the centre of the room: we want it to be small and discreet, hidden away. We expect it to come on instantly and when a modern machine goes wrong, we invariably replace it rather than going to the trouble of repairing it. Technology is not scarce and precious. In the past decade it has become overflowing and abundant.

Abundance is perhaps the key feature in virtually all utopias, from which many of their other qualities flow. Abundance – or at the very least the absence of significant unmet want – relieves the inhabitants of utopia of the need to be selfish, greedy, acquisitive or competitive. The material conditions of abundance make possible utopia's social qualities. In digitopia, information, communication and media are overflowing. Into a world of constraints and limited expectations, digital technologies have inserted the possibility of abundance. While our access to almost every other good and service might be limited – trains that run on time, routine operations, maths teachers – the supply of digital services seems almost infinite.

The founding laws of digitopia are the laws of technological abundance. Moore's law states that the power of microprocessors doubles every eighteen months. Metcalfe's law is that networks self-propagate exponentially once they get over a certain size. Hard disks are able to store more and more data, so that by 2007 the average hard disk will be able to store all the songs ever recorded and by the end of the decade every film ever released. George Gilder, the US techno-futurologist is just the most enthusiastic exponent of the idea that bandwidth is exploding so fast that communications will become free. The bandwidth at the backbone of the Internet is doubling every twelve months, as is the number of Internet hosts in the world. The costs of computer memory are halving every eighteen months or faster, while the global storage capacity of the world's computers – now perhaps eighteen billion gigabytes or more according to experts – is doubling every year. The number of human genes that can be mapped in a year is doubling thanks to advances in bio-informatics. These underlying technological trends enable narratives about the impact of digital technologies to be so optimistic. This is a world in which everything gets cheaper, faster, smaller and more available, without our even having to ask for it. Abundance allows people to behave in odd ways. Software companies can afford to give away products for free. The zero cost of creating new copies of software and music creates new communities and cooperation, from Napster's file-sharing community of seventy million users created within two years, to the cooperative developments of the Linux operating system. Resources are no longer scarce; there is no reason to compete ferociously.

Our sense of power is enhanced because so much of this technology comes in miniaturized form. Most modern technology is packed into products that you could slip into a pocket: a bottle of pills, a mobile telephone, a microprocessor, a CD containing software, an MP3 player. Technological progress packs more power and intelligence into ever smaller products. Nano-technology (machines made from atoms that could, for example, swim in your blood system) and genetics will take this several steps further. Pervasive miniaturization helps us feel like giants: we are like Gulliver surrounded by scores of minute technological helpers. It is probably no accident that many of the most popular computer games of the past decade – Populous, Sim City, Black and White – allow us to adopt the vantage point of God designing idealized communities.

Within the space of little more than a decade western consumers have learned to take it for granted that we should be the beneficiaries of an extraordinary crop of technological abundance. There is no sign that the supply will dry up soon. Digital abundance allows us to imagine new ways in which society, corporations and governments might be organized. It does not guarantee a better future, but it has opened up the possibility of innovation and invention in other walks of life it touches.

Community

In theory at least, abundance makes it possible for societies to overcome selfishness. Utopias usually offer some new levels of communal social organization that renders private property redundant. Abundance means it makes no sense to own goods privately. Conflicts over scarce resources need not occur. In utopia there is no tension between our private desires and the public interest. That clash, which is at the heart of political conflict in most societies, simply disappears in most utopias. Abundance relieves us of nasty, grubby and greedy motives that make us grasping, jealous and competitive. Instead, in utopia, ordinary mortals become rational, enlightened and far-sighted. They choose to be part of a community rather than being born into it. A society of abundance can absorb all the claims made upon it. But the price of abundance is that the individual has to submerge him or herself into the life of the society that makes it possible. This feature of most visions of utopia has deeply dystopian implications.

One of the earliest examples of the utopian linkage between abundance and community comes from Diodorus, writing between 80 and 30 BC, who tells the story of the ideal Island of Icarus, in which day and night are of equal length; cities are of geometric proportions; the people are free from disease and so live to the age of 150; and food is so abundant that rivalry of resources makes no sense. The community devotes itself to learning and reason. Cyberspace is simply the latest instance of this utopian dream of community built on abundance. The Internet has allowed us to create very large, global, complex communities based on our interests and identities, rather than class, race or gender. People can start to share rather than compete in cyberspace.

Governance

Utopian communities usually require more than mere abundance. They need a new form of government. Although some older versions of utopia rested on a benign ruler meeting the needs of an acquiescent populace, most visions of utopias after Thomas More have been founded on the idea of self-rule. Utopia is perfect because it is designed by and for people. That is only possible with a high degree of self-governance. This was perhaps More's most innovative insight: his utopia was a mature, responsible self-governing society, an expression of the power of human design to create a perfectly ordered world. Cyberspace has, its advocates claim, created a virtual assembly, a new community built from scratch, in which codes, laws, rules and customs are created, and recreated at will. There was no history with cyberspace, no indigenous people to eliminate, no forests and animals to clear. Electronics gave us a new frontier on which we could design a perfect community that was free, mobile, diverse and yet equal and above all self-governing.

The Internet's utopianism in large part stems from its use as a tool for direct democracy and self-rule, local and global. As long ago as the thirteenth century Ramon Llull foreshadowed a society in which the Pope would convene a world Parliament of all faiths to ensure peace. Llull argued that Latin should become the world's language to eliminate the risks of cultural conflict. Llull's dream will be realized by the Internet, according to its more rosy-eyed enthusiasts. It will allow comprehensive and intense global communications, mainly in English, and probably in time through automatic language translation, that will in turn pave the way for a genuinely global politics. H. G. Wells, writing at the end of the nineteenth century, envisaged a world governed by an all-seeing global consciousness; cyberspace is as close as we have come to realizing Wells's vision.

The Internet seems to be creating the possibility of a new global politics in which anti-globalization and environmentalism are just the first strands. But it could also radically alter how national and local governments could work. In *News from Nowhere*, his nineteenth-century Arcadian utopia, William Morris looked forward to a society in which the state has withered away to be replaced by productive and self-governing communities. The Internet in its way seems to offer a modern version of this hope. Citizens should be better informed and it should become harder for rulers to hoard information and keep people in ignorance. Everyone who wants one can have a voice in this world and make their views known. Political parties will still matter but increasingly interest groups and activists will be able to create networks and launch single-issue and time-limited campaigns without large institutions. The Internet promises to create a more open, informed, direct and anarchic form of democracy.

Work

In utopia the spirit of self-governance extends into work. The reorganization of work is as vital to utopia as the reorganization of governance. The tyranny of unsatisfying work is as evil and crushing as the tyranny of unaccountable leaders. In More's *Utopia* everyone works, no matter what their background, because it is a duty. As a result work is not exploitative. Work does not enrich someone else, it enriches the community at large. As people identify their personal interests with the aims of this perfect, self-regulating community, no one minds working. However, twentieth-century versions of work and utopia have taken a different tack. In Morris's *News from Nowhere* work is no longer alienating because everyone is engaged in creative craft production, in which work is an expression of their creative persona. For Morris work is no longer a burden because it is highly personalized, not because it belongs to the community. In some classical utopias people were relieved of the need to work by the blessing of abundance. As a result they were able to devote themselves to leisure, learning and reason. This has been a repeated theme of techno-romanticism in the twentieth century. The French leftist André Gorz argued in *After Work* that as technology was eliminating jobs we should prepare for a society without work. The key to his utopia was to find a way to redistribute work and its rewards so that we could all work less.

The Internet co-opts these ideas about work. In visions of the future enabled by the Internet work is both far more communal and collaborative, and yet also highly personalized and creative. People can work on the move, from home, in rapidly assembled virtual teams or in networks that span the globe. Work can become far more cooperative because tools such as Lotus Notes and other software allow people to share information across departments and organizations. Yet at the same time the content of work should become more creative and imaginative. The future belongs to knowledge workers: people who add value through their ideas and know-how rather than acting as adjuncts to machinery. Increasingly people want to work for themselves, as free agents and independents. And thanks to the power of the Internet these free agents and independents can connect to customers, clients and collaborators to share ideas, memos, reports and schedules. The Internet, at its most optimistic, seems to combine the communal impulse of More as work becomes more collaborative; the personal impulse of Morris as work becomes more creative; the anti-work vision of Gorz as the line between work, leisure and play becomes increasingly blurred.

One of the most vivid proponents of the Internet's power to transform work for the better is David Weinberger, one of the co-authors of the *Cluetrain Manifesto*. Weinberger asserts that we desperately want the Internet to be important because we long for what it seems to offer: a chance to use our distinctive individual voice in our work. Business is about managing resources, people, finances and plant by quantifying, aligning, processing and mobilizing them. The unmanaged – riots, weeds, cancer – are synonymous with something bad. But increasingly people do not want to be managed. For good reason, people are increasingly attracted to the new deal the Internet seems to offer: self-managed work.

The Power of Ideas

Almost without exception, utopians are hazy on how a utopian society might be created in practice. A few envisaged utopia emerging through the cleansing process of violent struggle. The Futurists of the early twentieth century glorified speed, machines, aggression and the convulsive power of war to sweep away all that was old, corrupt and decadent. Yet most utopians seem to believe utopia will emerge from the pervasive power of education, reason and rationality to overcome prejudice, conservatism and self-interest. Edward Bellamy, for example, in the popular nineteenth-century romantic socialist utopia *Looking Backwards*, wrote of a people who 'enjoy the blessings of a social order at once so simple and so logical that it seems the triumph of common sense'.

The Internet seems to be the perfect medium for spreading change through analysis, education, argument and rationality. Ubiquitous information technology and communications systems amplify human brainpower and rationality, just as industrial machinery amplified human muscle power, making it go further and last longer. The Internet is a utopia in which effortlessly, from the comfort of our own homes, we can enter a world of pure information and open debate, in which freedom and cooperation spread painlessly, without anything more than the occasional struggle with some recalcitrant hardware.

Technology opens up for us utopian possibilities. Of course that does not mean these utopian hopes will be realized, just because the technology makes them possible. As we shall see, faith in technology often exposes us to some steep downsides. Work can become more creative and collaborative. But new technology also opens us up to more surveillance by our employers. Working in a call centre, being prompted by the software to answer another call, is not creative knowledge work. The Internet is promoting new forms of community but not all of them are benign or morally uplifting. Digital technology may encourage a deeper democratic culture but it could also be a tool for push-button Pop Idol democracy. Technology is often at its most useful when its advocates are modest about its potential: to act as a tool to fulfil some clear needs.

However, the power of the Internet and the wave of digital and genetic technologies we are in the midst of is that they are far more than better tools for achieving what we already do. They open up imaginative new possibilities for how we might reorganize fundamental features of our lives: how we work, govern, share, relate to one another. As this technology becomes even more pervasive, so the opportunities for imagining different futures expand. We have embarked on the latest stage of a long, complicated and fraught process of social, cultural and organizational innovation to exploit a wave of rapid and profound technical innovation. Which is where Karl Marx comes in. According to Marx's much disputed account of historical development, advances in human knowledge and technology create new 'forces of production' which can be fully exploited only when new social arrangements – companies, markets, banks – come into being. Marx called these new social arrangements 'the social relations of production'. Digital technologies offer us the possibility to transform our social relations in at least five fundamental and sometimes conflicting ways. Starting with the same basic ingredients of technotopia – the laws of abundance, new forms of collaboration, new approaches to work and governance – we can end up in wildly different utopian visions of the future. Technology could change fundamentally: our economic relationships, the way we work, buy, sell, trade and invest; our social relations by allowing a wide range of self-organizing communities, local, global, bizarre, alternative, kinky and banal; our political relationships by transforming our citizens' relationships with government; our relationship with our environment by markedly reducing our claim upon natural resources; and our relationship with our own bodies as they become ever more dependent upon technology to extend their lives.

The Economic Revolution: Marketopia

At its height the New Economy seemed to be an insurrection launched from within the capitalist system. It provided people with a way to be revolutionary within a world in which alternatives to the market have been extinguished. This was borne out for me in the autumn of 2000 when I found myself addressing a gathering of venture capitalists and high-tech entrepreneurs at a resort in California's Napa Valley. It was like addressing a religious cult: a revivalist meeting in which the key texts were business plans. This small group had gathered to plot how they were going to pursue a crusade to overthrow the established centres of power with business models that would revolutionize their industry, make the world in their own image, bring benefits to workers, consumers and investors and in the process, of course, make them filthy rich, very quickly.

The Internet has spawned a library of business writing with barely concealed utopian undercurrents: Bill Gates's *Business at the Speed of Thought* and Grady Means's *MetaCapitalism*, Kevin Kelly's *New Rules for the New Economy* and Esther Dyson's *Release 2.0*, Stan Davis's *Blur* and Don Tapscott's *Digital Capital*. In the late 1990s, each month magazines such as *Wired*, *Upside*, *Business 2.0* and *Fast Company* delivered utopian tracts on the transformative power of technology and the risks of being left out of the creation of utopia.

There is no doubt that over time markets, companies, consumers and workers will operate in different ways thanks to new technology. The Internet promises to globalize the economy, linking suppliers, producers and consumers in global networks of exchange, through online retailing or vast business-to-business exchanges. Companies will increasingly be able to source standard products from anywhere in the world and determine the price through competitive online auctions. Markets should become more competitive, better informed and so more transparent: it should be increasingly difficult for companies to overcharge informed consumers who have a wealth of choices of alternative sources for products they want. Production should be far more streamlined. Links between consumers, retailers, manufacturers and suppliers should be far more direct and effective. Middlemen and middle managers, who channel and distribute information but add little value, should be gradually removed: instead consumers should communicate far more directly with retailers, who should then communicate their demands far more swiftly and accurately to suppliers. Supply chains should become more responsive, leaner and quicker. The organizations of this new economy could look quite different: less hierarchical, more networked and flatter. The organizations of the future will increasingly depend on networks of collaboration, partnerships and alliances to get their jobs done. We should be living in a far better informed and so a far more efficient, frictionless economy, in which supply and demand are far more tightly aligned. As a result the risks of misallocating resources will be reduced markedly. Competitive pressures mean that inflation should be a thing of the past. The very meaning of consumption is changing. Increasingly consumers are really the last stage of the production process, completing the product or service by tailoring it to their needs. Our houses are stocked with modern capital equipment that allows us to produce music, entertainment, documents and presentations. Consumption involves work, self-service and replication.

Some of the rules of economic life are being rewritten. The intangible assets which account for the lion's share of most of the value of most large companies – brands, know-how, research and development – behave quite differently from traditional assets – land, labour and machinery. Knowledge does not get run down when it is used, in the way that coal reserves do. It is difficult for two people to eat the same piece of cake; but very easy for many thousands of people to use the same cake recipe. We are moving into a world in which we make our livings from making recipes, not just for cakes but to make computers run better, supply chains be more efficient or to unravel genes that cause disease. New ideas are developed more rapidly, spread more quickly and travel further than ever before. For most of the twentieth century the job of management was optimization – to make the most efficient use of scarce physical resources. In the twenty-first century the job of management will be, increasingly, adaptation and innovation – to create and develop new intangible resources.

Marketopia is a capitalist cornucopia of larger, more competitive, efficient and transparent markets in which consumers are better informed and so more powerful; leaner, more efficient networked organizations, which depend upon global supply chains that are less wasteful and more responsive to demand; faster innovation to create and spread new products which create new opportunities for entrepreneurship and productivity improvements; an intangible economy in which weightless assets which come out of our heads are often worth more than those that stand on or come out of the ground.

The promise of the Internet's business revolution has been overshadowed for some by the catastrophic collapse of the dot.coms. Some hard lessons stand out from the failures of the dot.com wave. First movers do not always have the advantage. The dot.com experiment was a massive exercise in first mover *dis*advantage. Pathfinder entrepreneurs often prove a concept can work only to see large companies come into the market after them to pick up the profits. E-commerce is a middle-distance race in which stamina and patience count; it is not a sprint in which being first to market is everything. Many entrepreneurs thought brands would spread at the speed of the technology. Brands are complex and consumer habits change more slowly than technology. Entrepreneurship is not simply about speed: getting first to a market that everyone else can see, in a 'land grab'. The most impressive entrepreneurs see the world in a different way: they spot opportunities that others cannot see. Most of the first wave of Internet businesses were nowhere near as revolutionary as they thought. E-commerce companies, for example, largely delivered traditional, 'offline' business models – publishing, retailing, market making – online. Lastminute.com is mainly an online version of a traditional, cheap fares bucket shop. Nor was the content of the Internet revolutionary: it was mainly old media text and still photographs. The page-based Internet is boring. The next Internet will need less information and more imagination.

Revolutions respond to deep-felt problems. Too many e-commerce companies offered to solve non-existent problems.

Urban Fetch, the failed rapid delivery service, arrived in Britain with massive warehouses, a state of the art distribution system, a fleet of liveried vehicles and a stock market capitalization of about $300 million. Urban Fetch offered to deliver virtually any product to a central London address within an hour. But how many people really need a DVD delivered to their door within an hour? This state of the art system was mainly used to ship popcorn, videos and beer. The first wave of the Internet business revolution was all about powerful technology in search of a problem to solve. Success will go to those retailers who provide online and offline ways to buy products as complements to one another. Just as air travel and international telephone calls have grown together so will online and offline shopping. People want an 'offline' experience to give them a sense that what they are doing is 'real'. That is why many online consumers research a product on the Internet but buy it face to face or over the telephone. The future lies not in virtual shopping channels but hybrids that mix the Internet, television, print advertising, telephone sales and in person purchases.

Over the next two decades, what we currently call the Internet will transform how we conduct our economic lives. But that will not happen until this technology is faster, more reliable, easier to use and more fun. It will have to penetrate our lives far more deeply. We are still at the black and white movie era of the Internet. The business revolution, it turns out, will require first a slow social revolution in our viewing, shopping, learning and savings habits. The Internet is already allowing networked forms of organization to emerge, displacing old models of the corporation. A new generation of self-employed free agents is populating niches in the new economy. The last few years were the first skirmishes in what will be a long revolution.

The Social Revolution: Communitopia

In many ways the distinctive feature of the Internet, its capacity to promote collaboration and sharing among a large number of independent actors, makes it difficult for business to make money from it. The Internet is primarily a tool for social rather than business innovation. It allows us to converse, communicate, collaborate and cooperate with people in new ways, by sharing files, jokes, tips, information and ideas. That is why some people see in the Internet not a marketopia of more efficient capitalism, but a social revolution that will realize the counter-cultural ideals of the 1960s: an open and self-governing community of unconstrained self-expression.

The slogans of Paris students in 1968 – 'All power to the imagination' and 'It's the dream that's real' – seem to be made true by digital technology. The Internet helps build self-regulating communities of the kind that 1960s hippies could only create with the help of drugs, tents and loud music. Now you can go online to share, collaborate, jam, have sex and join in. The Internet's most successful products are generally peer-to-peer technologies that allow people to interact and share with other people, without having to go through a central organization: e-mail, SMS messaging, instant messaging, chat rooms, file-sharing technologies such as Napster and Groove Networks. In the UK in 2002, the most successful Internet site was Friends Reunited, a service that allows school friends to track one another down. It is a largely self-regulating and self-service site. To enter the site you have to register the date at which you left your school. Other people entering the site can then see that you have visited. Long-lost friends can track one another down, send e-mails and even meet up. To send an e-mail costs £5. Within months of starting up Friends Reunited had four million regular users. When the Internet is deployed to help people build self-regulating communities it explodes. It is first and foremost a tool for social innovation.

The Internet allows more and more diverse communities to form around interests, desires, obsessions and fetishes. These are not closed communities. They are fluid and open, formed around the anarchic and self-organizing ethic of the hacker, the independent, self-reliant, ungovernable frontiersman of the digital economy. One of the best expressions of this yearning for a new communitopia is the alternately uplifting and infuriating *Cluetrain Manifesto*. It begins:

Millions have flocked to the Net in an incredibly short time not because it was user-friendly – it wasn't – but because it seemed to offer some intangible quality long missing in action from modern life. In sharp contrast to the alienation wrought by homogenised broadcast media, sterilised mass culture and the enforced anonymity of bureaucratic organizations, the Internet connected people to each other and provided a space in which the human voice would be rapidly rediscovered.

The *Manifesto* goes on:

Unlike the lockstep conformity imposed by television, advertising and corporate propaganda, the Net has given a new legitimacy – and free rein – to play. Many of those drawn into this world find themselves exploring a freedom never before imagined: to indulge their curiosity, to debate, to disagree, to laugh at themselves, to compare visions, to learn, to create new art and new knowledge . . . Hypertext is inherently non-hierarchical and anti-bureaucratic. It does not reinforce loyalty and obedience; it encourages idle speculation and loose talk.

The *Cluetrain*'s insight is that the Internet is a tool for people to create self-organizing communities that can cooperate without elaborate laws and rules, without managers and rulers. People in their millions are learning how to negotiate, cooperate and collaborate, learn, create and share without being told how to do so. The Internet is spawning an insurrection against life in the command and control economy of mass marketing and global brands. Now, thanks to the explosion of media and communications, not only can you switch channels to listen to something else but you can also shout back.

Well, up to a point at least. The communities of interest formed around the Internet are fluid and democratic, but they can also seem morally and ethically thin. They are attractive in part because joining up to them carries so few obligations and commitments. We can keep them at arm's length. You might get an e-mail from a long-lost school friend but you do not have to meet them. The strongest traditional communities are more than exchanges of information and ideas; they are criss-crossed by moral bonds and obligations. Community itself is a problematic virtue. In an age that is both individualistic and increasingly dominated by big business, self-organizing communities of most kinds should be welcomed. But the Internet has also been used for self-organizing communities of paedophiles, extreme pornographers, racists, child traders, terrorists and militants. Communities are not morally equivalent. We do not just value community for its own sake but for the values it promotes: communities can be good and bad.

The Political Revolution: Politopia

A related theme is the way new technologies could enable a political revolution to transform modern government and the powers of citizens. The grounds for such a transformation – as well as the doubts about it – are set out in books such as Andrew Shapiro's *The Control Revolution* and Lawrence Lessig's *Code and Other Laws of Cyberspace*.

The Internet could transform the way we interact with government and the state – as taxpayers, voters, citizens and consumers – and in the process lay the grounds not just for better government but for more self-governance. At the outset digital technologies may simply make the old state machine more efficient and responsive. In the long run they could break it up and allow more self-governing solutions to emerge.

The initial agenda for most governments is to implement e-government programmes which should offer huge benefits in the way that government raises finance (e-tax systems); procures services and recruits staff (B2B exchanges for the public sector); delivers services to consumers – for example, through e-learning, e-health programmes; giving citizens more scope to self-service their needs by allowing them to fill in forms, make applications, get licences over the Internet rather than on paper and by going in person to a government office. That should be just the start.

The Internet should also change our relations with government as voters and citizens. It should become more difficult for government to keep us in the dark and deny us information. A more informed citizenry should have more opportunities to voice their views and take part in democratic decision-making continually, should they wish to. When citizens can voice their own views directly, what need is there for parties and representatives to play their old role of acting as political middlemen to articulate and represent people's views? The combination of growing direct democracy, citizens' self-service and the localized communities the Internet helps to build, could in turn pave the way for more self-government: people finding their own shared solutions to problems rather than turning to the state to deliver them.

Digital technologies could play a critical role in promoting more effective, personalized, responsive government as well as sowing the seeds for more self-government and direct political action. But democracy requires informed debate and reflection. The Internet might give us constant push-button, instant polling but that would give us government by rolling electronic plebiscite, with opinion swung by the tabloid press. Democracy rests on citizens having competing views that must be aired and reconciled: you have to confront people whose views you do not know and whom you might not normally meet. The Internet all too easily could provide us with a sealed and personalized world in which we get only the news we want, from the sources we want and engage with communities that share our views and express our interests. Democracy is about people having to adjust their views to competing inter-ests and demands. The Internet's appeal is that it allows us to submerge ourselves in the world that suits us.

The Environmental Revolution: Ecotopia

Technology has long played an ambivalent but potentially powerful role in dreams of an environmentally sustainable future. Most dreams of ecotopia – Marge Piercy's *Woman on the Edge of Time*, for example – use old pre-industrial technol-ogy such as windmills to deliver a low consumption and more human economy. But other visions of ecotopia, influenced in part by science fiction, give new technology a far more prominent role. In the book that gave Ecotopia its name Ernest Callenbach describes a society that has learned to harness new technology to promote a better quality of life and with it environmental benefits. The train that Callenbach's protagonist boards to travel to Ecotopia, for example:

looked more like a wingless airplane than a train. At first I thought I had gotten into an unfinished car – there were no seats: The floor was covered with thick spongy carpet, and divided into compartments by knee-high partitions; a few passengers were sprawled on large bags like leather cushions that lay scattered about. One elderly man had taken a blanket from a pile at one end of the car and laid down for a nap. Some of the others; realising from my confusions that I was a foreigner, showed me where to stow my bag and told me how to obtain refreshments from the steward in the next car. I sat down on one of the pillows, realising that there would be a good view from the huge windows that came down to about six inches from the floor . . . By the time you notice you are underway in an Ecotopian train, you feel virtually no movement at all. Since it operates by magnetic suspension and propulsion, there is no rumble of wheels or whine of vibration. People talk, there is the clink of glasses and teacups, some passengers wave to friends on the platform. In a moment the train seems to be flying along the ground, though it is actually a few inches above a trough shaped guideway.

The spread of digital technologies has provided further powerful fuel for ecotopian dreams. Shawn Fanning, the twenty-something renegade founder of Napster, is an unlikely environmental hero. Napster, the online music community, uses a simple yet powerful software programme that allows a computer user, armed with a modem, to download music files from someone else's computer. At first sight this technology appears to have little to do with protecting the environment from climate change or pollution. The entire music industry is embracing Napster-style technology. In the long run that innovation could phase out the production of compact discs, tapes and all the materials, packaging and transport associated with these physical products.

The innovation-driven, information-rich economy holds out a tantalizing promise for environmentalists: economic growth with far fewer environmental side-effects. In an economy in which competitiveness turns on innovation, the opportunities to design entirely new production systems that use fewer materials and energy have never been greater. The Dyson vacuum cleaner, to take one example of a radical innovation, has been designed to be recycled. A product innovation designed to make a product easier to use for consumers has created the opportunity to improve the product's environmental performance. At the same time the production process for making the Dyson is designed to be more environmentally friendly. In contrast traditional vacuum cleaners, where change has been incremental, offer fewer opportunities for big strides to improve environmental performance. The more radical innovation there is in the economy the more there will be opportunities to shift production to make it more environmentally friendly.

Technology is the best tool we have for making far better use of scarce resources and thus protecting the environment. Modern technology is not uniquely harmful: some of the most dramatic species extinctions were carried out in Australia and America many thousands of years ago by men armed with spears and stones, bows and arrows. On the contrary the more sophisticated technology has become so its environmental benefits have increased. Throughout the 1970s there were repeated resource panics about what would happen when oil, land and food would run out for the world's rapidly growing population. Those panics have proved misplaced largely because modern science has allowed us not only to discover new resources but also to use resources far more efficiently. These physical resources are mainly fixed in our minds by what we think it is possible to do with them. Scientific and technological ingenuity helps to expand them. It is technological advance that has allowed us to move from whale oil (an ill-managed natural and renewable resource) to oil (a managed finite resource) and from wood, coal and oil to hydrogen.

The most dramatic examples of how innovation and new technology have expanded the capacity of the physical world come from agriculture. If agricultural productivity were the same as it was in 1961, then we would need 82 per cent of the world's landmass to feed the world's population. Between 1961 and 1998 India's population doubled, but the amount of land under cultivation increased by only 5 per cent because it was used so much more productively.[3] The worst recipe for food production and the environment would be to return to high land use, low productivity agriculture. The future of the environment ultimately will not be determined by how much we care about it, nor how strictly we regulate industry but how ingenious we are in developing technologies that allow us to satisfy our needs while reducing the harm we inflict on the environment. The best way to save the planet is to promote innovation to improve resource productivity and recycling. It is perfectly possible that by 2050 we could be using silent cars running on hydrogen fuel cells or solar power; fossil fuels would be used only rarely; genetically modified crops might be growing in fields full of butterflies; a world population of nine billion could have rising living standards and ample food delivered from a declining amount of cultivated land and new generation of managed wildernesses that have been returned to nature. New technology will redefine our relationship with the physical world, allowing us to use it in less harmful ways.

Of course it will not be simple. Amazon.com may appear ethereal when you log on to buy your books. But it is very much in the real world of pollution and congestion when the van draws up to deliver them. The new economy means increased efficiency, which means reduced prices, which means more consumption. The accelerating rate of product innovation and ceaseless advertising mean constant demand for the newer version of computers, hi-fis and MP3 players. Technology has enabled a dramatic increase in resource productivity, our appetite to consume is quickly filling the extra environmental 'space' that technology opens up. Still, innovation will be the environment's ultimate saviour. The question for public policy is how we harness the power of innovation to the cause of the environment rather than simply to making better MP3 players. Technology at least opens the possibility of an environmentally and socially sustainable future. Nothing else does.

Post Humanism: Genetopia

Utopians have never been satisfied with producing a utopian society. They want to produce utopian people by replacing the flawed, real people who inhabit the real world, with individuals who are capable of living up to the demands of a perfect society. In Plato's idealized society, children would escape the accidents of their birth and upbringing by being brought up by the collective. Utopia was a society of orphans, in which the society took responsibility for its future generations and dared not leave the task in the hands of individual parents with all their failings and frailties. Now genetic technologies may be on the verge of realizing Plato's ambition: allowing children to escape from the vagaries of their parenthood.

Parents have long tried to mould their children. Genetic technology will give them additional tools to achieve their goals.[4] The Platonic urge for perfection through design is perhaps on the verge of being fulfilled, not by mass social engineering but by the mass availability of genetic technologies that may allow parents to redesign their offspring. In Lee M. Silver's genetic dystopia *Remaking Eden* parents who can afford to do so, buy genetic upgrades and improvements for their children. The human race will divide, Silver predicts, into a gene-enriched race and the sub-standard naturals, who have to stumble on without the improvements that genetics can bring. Just as computers, cars and houses can be upgraded with new software, accessories and extensions, so humans, in theory at least, will become open to constant improvement through implants, chips and add-ons.

It is not too difficult to imagine a future, perhaps no more than a few generations off, when parents will consider it irresponsible to leave reproduction to passion and chance. There may be some organic parents – Silver's naturals – who choose to stick with the old ways. But with 4,000 potential genetic defects many parents will opt for technologies that allow them to choose at least some aspects of their child's genetic make-up. Such a leap may be a smaller step than we think. Over a long period we have become used to plastic surgery, flattering glasses, IVF treatments and genetic therapies, which all in different ways use technology to extend our choice over our bodies. It is not inconceivable that private firms will start offering a service in which our genes will be inserted into pigs to grow replacement organs for us. Under this scenario our bodies will increasingly become modular: much of it will be what we were born with, but in old age especially, we will acquire body-enhancing technologies – pace-makers, nano-machines to clear clogged arteries, hearing aids, artificial joints, replacement organs grown in host animals. Surgeons will plug these new components in for us, much as we insert a new hard drive into a computer. Some people may think we are not prepared to move that far that fast, yet even as recently as the 1950s the idea of a cornea transplant to save someone's sight was regarded as morally repugnant. Who is to say that we will not travel as far in the next fifty years?[5]

This desire to produce the utopian body, to turn the drive for utopia away from society and into ourselves, will involve not just choosing from the available stock of human genes but from technological plug-ins as well. According to some prophets we are moving into a post-human era, in which people will increasingly become robo sapiens, part machine, part human. One such prophet of the post-human future is Hans Moravec, the head of the Carnegie Mellon Mobile Robot Laboratory. In *Mind Children: The Future of Robot and Human Intelligence*, Moravec argues that what he calls carbon-based life forms such as humans, will be overtaken by 'silicon based life forms': intelligent machines. Bill Joy, the chief scientist at Sun Microsystems, has issued a similar warning that human inventiveness is about to create a catastrophe for the species. Moravec's version of the post-human future is one in which human consciousness, the core of identity, can be excavated from the brain and decanted on to silicon. We can live on, he says, at least as a disembodied consciousness. Never mind that it would be a pretty miserable existence. The appeal of this and other visions is that we might, one way or another, cheat death and claim a form of immortality.

As Peter Menzel puts it: 'There may be general resistance to implanting chips in people's brains, but when a bio-chip is developed to easily enhance memory or linguistic skills or mathematical abilities, how long will people just say "no"? . . . It could be true the next stage in evolution could be from man to machine.'[6] In the coming century then the way we think about what it is to be human may undergo profound transformation as technology and organisms converge to the point where they become indistinguishable. The reason this technology of post-humanism will keep coming at us is that it claims to satisfy a deep urge to cheat death and control the future. Steven Spielberg's film *AI* is an exploration of the appeal this rescue from death has for us, as well as how complicated and prone to failure it will be. The central cyborg character David is a digitized archive of human possibilities: love is just another software programme.

Other advocates of the post-human future include a US group called the Extropians, who have issued a manifesto on the Internet. It says:

Posthumans will be persons of unprecedented physical, intellectual and psychological ability, self-programming and self-defining, potentially immortal, unlimited individuals. Posthumans have over-come the biological, neurological and psychological constraints [to] evolve into humans. Extropians believe that the best strategy for attaining posthumanity is to be a combination of technology and determination, rather than looking for it through psychic contracts or divine gift.

Posthumans may be partly or mostly biological in form but will likely be partly or wholly postbiological – our personalities having been transferred into more durable, modifiable, faster and more powerful bodies and thinking hardware. Some of the technologies we currently expect to play a role in allowing us to become post-human include genetic engineering, neural computer integration, molecular nanotechnology and cognitive science.[7]

It goes without saying that this exploration of the possibilities of genetopia could lead us into all kinds of trouble. Kris Pister, an electrical engineer at the University of Berkeley, California is leading a team working on the creation of 'Smart Dust' autonomous robots no larger than the average gnat. Each tiny machine will be able to sense and move but will be relatively simple. However, when they combine into a small cloud these machines will be capable of undertaking more complex tasks, such as controlling the environment in offices, cleaning windows and monitoring people's health. Beyond Pister's Smart Dust machines is nano-technology, machines made on a molecular scale, that could, for example, strengthen the human immune system.

The pessimistic case has already been made by Neal Stephenson in his nano-centric novel *The Diamond Age* in which clouds of Smart Dust wage aerial guerrilla warfare; people are covered with the stuff to allow government, corporations and their enemies to monitor their movements; criminals are put to death by having killer nano-machines injected into their bloodstream. Bill Joy, Sun Microsystems co-founder and chief scientist, warns that sophisticated technology distributed throughout society could pose an unmanageable threat. 'The threat to humanity in the last millennium – nuclear, biological and chemical weapons of mass destruction – was largely confined to the military arena.' Now we are putting hugely powerful technologies in the hands of everyone. As a result: 'We are on a course for human destruction.' The desire to find genetopia will unleash a death wish. But that is only one, extreme version of the future. Consciousness is not a detachable component of the human body. Modern robots have the intelligence of only the average insect. Instead of machines wiping us out we should be capable of designing them to help us, as adjuncts to our bodies and minds rather than competitors. As Shigeo Hirose, one of Japan's most respected roboticists, puts it: 'If we can engineer robots to be intelligent we can also engineer them to be moral. We can build them to be saints because they do not have to fight, as we did, for our biological existence.'

The Digital Sublime

The last decade has witnessed the globalization of what was until recently, and with the exception of Japan, a largely American love affair with technology. The technotopia of the Internet and the genome did not emerge in a cultural vacuum. It took distinctively American forms. Utopian, democratic and national hopes for the transforming and uplifting power of technology have played a central role in American life for at least the last 150 years, providing the nation with much of its sense of purpose and confidence.[8] This is a tradition that stretches from the first railways, and the bridges that carried them, through to skyscrapers, neon-lit cityscapes, aeroplanes and space rockets. In their time all have been the focus for a collective awe and celebration at the public display of techno-logical achievement. The rise of the Internet, combined with Nasdaq's take off into orbit, fits squarely into that tradition of technology invoking a sublime sense of public awe. Indeed in some respects the rise of the Internet filled the void left behind by the domestication of the space programme. When I was a child the launch of an Apollo moon shot was cause for wonder and fascination. Our family gathered around the television to watch James Burke explain what was happening. In the US millions flocked to Cape Canaveral to watch blast off in a state of reverence. In the 1990s we flocked instead to the Internet to wonder at the scale of what was being undertaken. Yet in two important respects our experience with the Internet was different. First, we were not mere spectators, we were players in the technological spectacle. Second, this was a global experi-ence from the outset, not something that was confined to America. In this case the entire world was wrapped into the US experience of technology as religion. The roots of this respect for technology lie deep in American culture. The *San*

Francisco Examiner, for example, commenting on the celebrations of the fiftieth anniversary of the opening of the Golden Gate bridge in 1987 described the bridge as 'a gateway to the imagination' which was as much a 'state of the spirit' as it was a mere road. Technological progress and achievement are a way for America to make visible its productive and inventive genius.

That sense of awe comes from being in the presence of something much more powerful and larger than yourself: something so large that its dimensions are difficult to comprehend. Edmund Burke, writing in the eighteenth century on the nature of the sublime, listed a series of qualities objects had to possess to produce a sense of the sublime: obscurity, power, vastness, magnitude and infinity among them.[9] That is why the Grand Canyon, 28 miles long, 18 miles wide, 15,000 feet deep and the product of two billion years of geological change, produces such a sense of awe. In the nineteenth century American technology started to take over from objects of nature as the objects of awe. The orator Edward Everett, in 1852, for example, greeted the railway locomotive as a 'miracle of science, art and capital, a magic power . . . by which the forest is thrown open, the lakes and rivers are bridged and all Nature yields to man'. Little more than a century later it was space travel that provoked this sense of awe. Witnesses to the launch of the space shuttle Columbia in 1981, part of a crowd of more than half a million, spoke of having an exalted, quasi-religious experience. Those people were making a pilgrimage. In the 1990s America made a collective technological pilgrimage into cyberspace to experience a similar state of transcendence.

This sense of awe at technology was not largely a European phenomenon. Europeans have not, by and large, embraced the vertical city centre, although many Asian cities have done so. Europeans banned or restricted the neon signs that so excited New Yorkers in the 1920s. Europeans seldom flocked to watch rockets being launched and did not treat nuclear bomb test sites as tourist attractions. Technological progress is part of America's manifest destiny, to discover endless new frontiers. Europeans have held this technological rapture at bay. But in the 1990s the global communications revolution drew us all into the technological rhapsody, at least to some degree. Yet awe at technology commits one to constant innovation, to deliver new objects to be awed by. Familiar technology can no longer fill that role. Railways that provoked wonder in 1830 were commonplace in 1870. New Yorkers flocked into the streets to see the first planes fly overhead. Twenty years later only extreme daredevil stunts would have the same impact. Space travel is now conducted in 'shuttles', the language of commuter travel. The Internet was fascinating in 1995 and boring five years later.

As Don DeLillo put it:

Technology is our fate, our truth. It is what we mean when we call ourselves the only superpower on the planet. The materials and methods we devise make it possible for us to claim the future. We don't have to depend on God or the prophets or other astonishments. We are the astonishment. The miracle is what we ourselves produce, the systems and networks that change the way we live and think.[10]

Technology is an affirmation of our power and inventiveness. But it also can make us feel powerless and insignificant. Technology can make us feel triumphant and terrified in quick succession. To provide us with a tangible sense of progress, technology must learn to overcome the disquiets it produces, to which we now turn.

6. The Terror of Technotopia

Despite my continued excitement at the utopian promise of technology, I have grown to loathe almost all advertisements for high-tech products. Sometimes I feel myself wanting to shout at billboards that are simply minding their own business. This feeling came over me in the autumn of 2000 when I was in America on business and the hype about the Internet was still in full swing. As I went from airport to airport, I saw many of the same advertisements again and again, selling simple utopian messages about the lives we could lead with the technology they were selling. Let me give you a couple of examples.

In Washington DC, on the side of a bus stop I came across an advertisement for a Handspring personal digital assistant. A personal digital assistant, such as a Palm Pilot or a Psion, is a small computer that includes an address book, a diary and other features that help you to organize your life. The Handspring advertisement followed the format that all these advertisements take. It showed an example of the 'model' day you could follow if you bought one of these devices.

These days always, without exception, start with:

7.00 a.m.: Visit gym

Only maniacs go to the gym at that time of the morning and so committed are they to exercise that they do not need a reminder. This entry is invariably followed by a reminder of emotional significance:

Buy Louise anniversary present

This means: although I am obsessed with my body, I have a long and loving relationship with Louise. In mid-morning there is some event that involves building your skills.

10.00 a.m.–12.00 p.m.: Sales training seminar

This means: I am a person going somewhere, building up my skills, advancing my career, taking my work seriously. But then at lunchtime, to show that your life is in balance, there is time for:

Lunch with Louise

when you give her the present.

But you don't of course drink any wine at lunch because in the afternoon the schedule usually includes something like:

3.00 p.m.–5.00 p.m.: Make key customer presentation

This is the event at which single-handed you save the company you work for and secure your future as an executive, so you can pay for the house you and Louise will move into and which will serve as home for the five beautiful children you will soon have. However, the complete day, brought to you by Handspring, is not finished:

7.00 p.m.: Soccer with guys

This means: even though I have a loving relationship with Louise and a demanding career which is full of promise, I still have time for my buddies and some male bonding.

So this is what it looks like.

The Perfect Day Brought to You By Handspring

7.00 a.m.: Visit gym

Reminder: Buy Louise anniversary present

10.00 a.m.–12.00 p.m.: Sales training seminar

Lunch with Louise

3.00 p.m.–5.00 p.m.: Make key customer presentation

7.00 p.m.: Soccer with guys

When you buy a Handspring you don't just get a diary and a calendar you can buy into an entire lifestyle. Designed to fit your life neatly into a Powerpoint presentation, no event requires more than a bullet point to describe it. The trouble with ads like this is that they bear so little relation to the messy, chaotic and often boring lives we lead in which pages of the diary are left blank for weeks on end, apart from dross like 'pick up the dry cleaning' and 'pay bills'.

I would like to do an advertisement for a personal digital assistant based on a 'model day' which entirely consisted of:

Call in sick/Sleep in late (with Louise)

That surely would be closer to how most people would like to live their lives rather than donning the American corporate straitjacket supplied by the Handspring. The Handspring ad falls into a trap waiting for all high-tech gadgets: the designers of the product think they know how consumers will want to use the technology they have invented. The truth is that consumers often ignore the features designers create or find uses for gadgets that the creators never dreamed of. A classic example is the growth of text messaging on mobile phones. In April 1999 there were just one million text messages a month sent by mobile phones. By October 2000, according to Nokia, that had reached twelve billion and by 2002 the figure was expected to be 100 billion. Mobile telephone operators and manufacturers did not expect 'texting' to become a major activity. It developed as a result of consumers deciding to innovate and teaching one another to use the phone for their own ends. Just because the technology makes it possible does not mean the consumers will want to use it.

The Handspring is not the only advertisement to have annoyed me. Another that I saw many times on my tour of the US was a poster for Lucent, the communications technology company, extolling the virtues of the mobile Internet. The poster in question shows a young professional woman, smartly dressed in a grey business suit with a short skirt. She is crouching on her haunches in the marble walled lobby of what looks like a large office building. People in business suits are walking past her. As she crouches, she is moving the cursor on her laptop computer that is balanced on her knees. With her other hand she holds a mobile telephone to her ear. She is smiling as if she is engaged in a wonderful, fulfilling and intimate experience. The catchline for the advertisement is something like: 'The Freedom of Mobility'.

But anyone who has used a laptop knows that it takes three to five minutes to boot up a laptop from scratch. This woman has been crouching on her haunches like that for a good three minutes. The smile cannot be real because her legs must hurt. She is controlling the computer with one hand while using her mobile phone with another. She can be balancing only because she spent her early years at a circus school. If you or I tried to do this we would end up in an unseemly pile on the floor. Would she have called her office from this position, perched precariously on her heels in an office entrance hall, in full view of hundreds of other people? I think not. This woman has been tracked down by her office because she forgot to leave behind some information her boss needs urgently. She has been taken by surprise. She would not be smiling; she would be flustered, anxious, apologetic and possibly late for her next meeting. After seeing this poster time and again I wanted to shout at the Model Woman Mobile Worker of the future: '*Go to a desk. Sit down. Get yourself a cup of coffee. Plug your computer into a mains socket and hook it up to a landline and do it properly.*'

I could go on – and on – about the way new technology companies misunderstand what consumers might want to use technology for. There was the chief executive of BT's Open World broadband service, who told a conference I was attending that his service, when hooked up to web cams installed in your home, would allow you to 'see your daughter's birthday party from the office'. I wanted ask: 'Why don't you just go home and be there in person?' All these advertisements about how technology helps us 'stay connected' only make sense because in some deeper, more fundamental sense we fear we have grown more disconnected.

These advertisements should not be taken too seriously. But they are texts in our creed of hope in technology. Technology is becoming so pervasive that it should no longer be understood as a tool but as the medium in which we live out our lives. Within a decade the phrase 'The Internet', if it is still used, will be less a description of a discrete infrastructure and more a metaphor for a constant state of connectedness. That connectedness will be the product of a messy, chaotic, incremental and unplanned process, in which new hardware is being introduced as old equipment is being adapted, new generations of standards and software are constantly overtaking the old, public and private investment duplicate and complement one another. The outcome of this process, encompassing computers and mobile telephones, broadband landlines and satellites will be, within the next decade, a communications infrastructure with comprehensive global coverage that will allow sophisticated person-to-person communication, using voice and text, alongside graphics that look like computer games.

Much of this traffic will be carried along wide, high-speed pipes to a myriad of devices which will have inbuilt capacity to store large quantities of content. People will go online through a wide array of everyday objects – wristwatches, telephones, screens on the fridge door, in-car communication consoles, the television – not just their computer. Some of this technology will be woven into the clothing we wear. We may put on our personal communicator much as we might put on our socks. The content that these devices convey should be increasingly tailored and personalized to our needs. We will all carry around with us little parts of the telecommunications infrastructure. By the turn of the decade the web should be ubiquitous, instant, interactive and intimate. People will still meet face-to-face to trade, vote, argue, protest, learn, flirt and fall in love but increasingly we will take it for granted that our lives will be orchestrated around screens both large and small. Meanwhile, over the next decade and beyond genetic engineering and nano-technology will seep like a rising tide into our bodies through the food we eat, the medicines we take and the way we reproduce. Technology will no longer be like a set of tools that make our arms or legs more powerful. Technology will become part of the ether, the environment and medium for our lives.

When technology migrates into the hands of consumers and allows them more freedom and choice, by saving them time or allowing them to extend and improve their lives, then it is virtually unstoppable. Regulators, conservatives and doom-mongers might put their fingers in the dyke but they will fail to stem the flood. However, technology's power can also lead to myopia and hubris. Advocates of new technology often mistakenly assume that they know in advance how consumers will want to use a technology, when in truth most of us, most of the time, are operating in the dark. Advocates of new technology are so busy telling us what technology can add to our lives, that they do not stop to think about what it could take away. Risks and dangers are often overlooked or minimized. Technology can often increase the range of options available to us, to listen to music, send a message or take a journey, but often only at the expense of eliminating other options – writing a letter, taking a walk. If technology advances without serving human needs, then it can be imaginative, dynamic and clever without being particularly useful, valuable or significant. In those circumstances new technology can simply add a new layer of complexity, cost, confusion and cacophony to our lives.

The problem is not just that technology has unforeseen and unintended downsides. It goes beyond that. The power that technology now has means that for all of us, at least some of the time, technology can be a source of terror as much as hope. We are increasingly dependent on electronic life-support machines that blink and bleep into life in the morning. Yet this life-support machine entraps us as it sustains us. This dependency was foreseen by the American poet W. S. Merwin who wrote a futuristic parable about a people who tire of remembering. To rid themselves of this burden they persuade inventors to build small, precise machines, easily worn on the body, that will remember for them. These machines simplify and categorize experience so that remembering becomes easy and the owners become more efficient. But then a horror strikes. The first man loses his machine and becomes a 'ghost'. Incomprehensible to others and himself, he loses the capacity for memory. To cope with the gravity of the crisis people become even more dependent upon their machines, backing them up and adding to them. But one by one people who have lost the ability to remember start to forget where the machines are that store their memories. These days most of us carry remembering machines around with us. Our dependence might not have become as extreme as that of the people in Merwin's fable but it is growing all the time. In Merwin's imaginary land the stages of a person's growth and development are no longer measured in physical terms but by the kind of machine they are attached to. We already account for development in this way: young children are wedded to their games consoles; adolescents to their mobile phones and pagers; working age people to laptops and Palm Pilots; the old to their pacemakers and hearing aids. Each stage of life is defined by a new way that technology infiltrates our lives.

These fears are graver than the worry that technology may have unintended downsides. The fear is that technotopia contains the seeds of its own dystopia. In the course of the twentieth century, the city passed from being a symbol of utopia – the rational, radiant, planned, shining white city imagined by the architect Le Corbusier – to Ridley Scott's 1982 *Blade Runner*, in which the city is dispersed, chaotic, ungovernable, dark and delirious. It is all too possible that the hope we now invest in technology, to extend life, clean up pollution, make the streets safe, improve education, overcome barriers of culture and eliminate constraints of time and space, will turn sour, just as the promise of the modern city soured for many in the twentieth century. In an effort to save the utopian vision of technology from itself, we have to address the dystopian tendencies already at work within technotopia. We have to find solutions – organizational, political and social – that take account of people's fears about the future, without retreating from the promise implicit in innovation to create new ways for us to organize ourselves.

Digital Dystopia

According to those who see digitopia turning sour, new communications technologies do not amplify and enhance human
brainpower and creativity. They displace and disempower it.
The world is not unified by communications but fragmented
into millions of parallel channels. Our horizons are not
expanded but increasingly shrunk to the screen in front of us.
Modern, abundant media do not represent the world to us in
new ways but eclipse it altogether in an electronic fog. Paul
Virilio, the modern French critic, for example, in his recent
book *The Information Bomb*, describes a world dreadfully out of
control, in which scientific extremism leads to a series of awful
accidents and genetic plagues that spread viruses of all kinds.
Our societies are in the grip of a technological arms race,
Virilio argues, in which science drives an incessant search for
limitless improvements in performance in computers, robots
and genetics. He is far from the first to worry that advances in
communications will cause havoc. Plato attacked the written
word as a degeneration of memory and poetry as a distraction
from hard questions of philosophy. Samuel Taylor Coleridge
denounced the novel as an inferior and psychologically harmful form of writing. In the 1920s the House of Commons held
heated debates about the need to regulate the spread of the
telephone because unfettered access would impose an impossible burden on MPs as constituents would be able to contact
them at any time. Campaigners against the cinema and the
comic predicted they would lead to falls in literacy, sanity and
civility, long before the same arguments were made against
television and computer games. The contemporary reaction
against the always-on media world sits squarely within this
tradition. Terrifying scare stories about technology are as likely
to prove false as extravagant utopian promises. Yet that does

not mean modern worries should be dismissed out of hand. For technology to deliver a tangible sense of progress it needs to address not just people's hopes but their worries as well.

Cacophony

Abundance is the foundation for the digital economy's utopian appeal. But what do we get abundance of? Digital abundance is invariably measured in technical terms – bits and bytes, processing power and storage capacity – not the quality of the experience it provides us with. Our abundance of media and information comes with the mixed blessing of increased confusion. As channels on our televisions proliferate so do the number of boxes beneath them for cable, video on demand, video recording, DVD and the new breed of Tivo personal video recorder. At worst this seems to give us only an abundance of mediocrity and sameness: scores of digital television channels showing remarkably similar content that is recycled endlessly in slightly different formats. We live in an electronic entertainment culture that is constantly going round in circles, finding ways to repeat itself in slightly different ways. Once a format, for example for a television comedy such as *Friends* or *Frasier*, is successful it gets repeated and copied endlessly. We seem to get more opportunities to see the same content rather than more opportunities to see a greater diversity of content.

This may be a reflection of a fundamental mismatch. Digital technologies have dramatically increased our ability to store, distribute and consume electronic content. But that is not yet matched by an increased ability to create content. The costs of creating new content in video, television and cartoons, for example, have gone down. Tools for content creation – computers of one kind or another – are increasingly used. On websites such as Friends Reunited the users are the content.

However, our ability to write better stories, dramas and jokes has hardly been enhanced by new technology. These creative skills are human, tacit and social.

Worse, the digital era seems to be characterized by growing cacophony. We are besieged by a bombardment of the loud, trivial, meaningless and insubstantial. As information and media become more ubiquitous, so they seem to become more insubstantial. For someone seeking solitude, silence or a moment's quiet reflection, the constantly connected world constitutes an ever-present threat of interruption. The scope for self-reflection is being reduced. The more active, open and questioning our imaginary life the less in thrall we are to the status quo. It is imagination that drives change not just information. But in the web of new technology with its endless stimulus to watch and perform we seem to use our imaginations increasingly to play games and perform roles, rather than imagine entirely different futures. We are awash with a flood of verbal and visual signals that never leave us, which mean we are never alone. As Mark Slouka put it in his essay 'In Praise of Silence and Slow Time': 'Silence and solitude are being eroded and encroached upon as surely as the wild. Silent, unmediated reflection, the domain of the spirit, is under siege.'[1]

It should be no surprise that one of the most powerful reactions against digitopia is a desire for retreat and withdrawal into a private, domestic, low-tech life. We spend far more of our time waiting and hoping to be prompted, stimulated and guided than our parents or grandparents. They may have lived in smaller, more enclosed worlds. They may not have travelled as far, nor heard news as fast from far and wide. And yet possibly they retained a greater inner space for their thoughts than we do in our constantly stimulated world. The always-on, available-everywhere media does not just shrink the physical world we live in: it can threaten to shrink our inner world as well.

The train to Heathrow airport carries designated Quiet Zones in which the television does not play. Not only are these Quiet Zones hard to find they only highlight that the rest of the train should be renamed the Noisy Zone. When our family first started travelling by car in the early 1960s – a dark green Morris 1100 – there was no radio, CD player or telephone, just the sound of a very noisy engine. The modern car is an entertainment complex on wheels. When we bought our last car the salesman spent forty minutes explaining how it worked: most of that time was devoted to the radio and none of it to the engine. The toilet is rapidly becoming the last place where one can escape modern media: it can be only a matter of time before that succumbs.[2]

The cacophony that surrounds us means that we are constantly in danger of being distracted, turned away from what we were doing. A person who is constantly distracted becomes bewildered, perplexed, agitated and confused, as their attention is scattered across many shifting and temporary attractions. For events, stories and programmes to claim our attention amidst this babble, they have to be hyped beyond all recognition to make what is often little more than celebrity gossip seem significant. It is odd to think that our parents and grandparents made it through major wars, depressions, disease, political turmoil, decolonization and disasters without the help of CNN, but they did.

I am not recommending a return to a rose-tinted, pre-technology past. Listening to a radio commentary of a football game huddled around a single set in a living room is not the same as watching that game live. Nor do I think information technology always closes down the scope for imagination. Far from it: the Internet is often a tool for the imagination, whether that be kids playing with Paintshop or people making their own movies. As I argued earlier the space for artists to reflect on the suffering and horror of war has been opened up by our information about how awful it is. Information and imagination often work together. But it is worth remembering that as technology advances it can quietly take experiences away from us while at the same time providing us with new ones. We need to address how we make the digital era less cacophonous and more imaginative. We need to invest more to create spaces – physical, cultural and personal – which are free from cacophony, which encourage reflection, thought and imagination. Private investment is seeing to it that technology is not in short supply. Public investment should increasingly equip us with spaces – museums, galleries, parks – which free us from cacophony. These spaces do not need to be low-tech; on the contrary they could be very high-tech. But instead of encouraging speed, distraction and noise they should encourage calm, reflection and relaxation. Our education systems need to equip the young not just with the skills to use computers but to use them creatively and imaginatively: to find their own sense of purpose and creativity. They need to be digitally literate. Living with the babble of the information age feels like being engaged in a long driving lesson in which we are bombarded with signals, lights and instructions, directing our attention this way and that as we fumble with the controls, our reflexes constantly on the alert and on edge. To learn to drive one must master these conflicting signals, filtering the important from the trivial.

From Choice to Coercion

Utopian vision expresses people's desire to escape fate, tradition and history and so to make society in their own image. The Internet and genetics base their appeal on this utopian desire to design life from a blank sheet. Yet all sorts of dangers lurk in this apparent opportunity, among them narcissism, intolerance and ludicrously over-inflated ambition. Advocates of new technologies have a dangerous tendency towards self-exaltation: the belief that we are gaining complete control to create, stimulate, redefine and manipulate notions as fundamental as space, time, community and even our bodies. New technology is an expression of human creativity but all too easily that can turn to hubris.

Take the extraordinary explosion of telecommunications bandwidth as an example. Fibre optic cabling allows information to be transmitted in particles of light rather than in electrons. Light particles will soon carry everything we can conceivably say, write, compose, play, record, film, draw, paint or design, in vast quantities. The entire content of the Library of Congress could be passed through a top-of-the-range high-tech optical switch in less than three seconds. The capacity of fibre to transmit information has been increased by a factor of 16,000 in less than five years. Waiting will become a thing of the past: any film, song, television programme, web page will be at your fingertips, they say.

But what will we do with all this additional communications power? George Gilder, the high-tech guru and author of *Telecosm*, argues that we will use it to eliminate what he calls 'latency': waste, waiting, middlemen and all those in-efficiencies which clog up the way organizations work and slow them down. We will live in a world of instant gratification, trade and communication. This desire to eliminate imperfections reflects a long-standing utopian revulsion with the wasteful and deviant. There is a hygienic tendency in utopianism, a desire to cleanse society and systems of imperfections. But then a perfectly honed system with all the latency taken out of it has little room for idle speculation, invention, daydreams or surprise. It is often in the unforeseen gaps that life is lived out at its most intense and creative. I have my best ideas when I am daydreaming, walking or driving the car. If we eliminated those gaps to make sure we were constantly connected, always interacting and doing something useful, then we would lose something vital.

The new-tech advocates invariably fail to recognize when their vision of expanding choice shades into intolerance. Vince Khosla, one of the most successful venture capitalists in Silicon Valley, argues that as technology moves faster, so people will have to learn to get a move on as well. Slower moving people will feel rushed off their feet: they will become casualties sacrificed in the name of progress. Technology will set the pace of life for us, like a digital treadmill. We will have to adjust to the rhythm it sets for us. Khosla predicts that within two decades there will be more than fifty billion computers in the world, in tiny chips embedded in almost every household appliance and piece of equipment. They will constantly talk to one another and to us. People will have no choice but to swim in this electronic medium. It will be a basic currency of life. As an example, Khosla told *The New Yorker* magazine: 'We will be connected all the time, monitored by internal chips. Doctors will call us when something is wrong.'[3] Our bodies will be part of a vast communications network. Other people – perhaps the insurance companies that may insist we wear the medical monitoring chips they give us – will tell us when we should go in for a planned service so we waste as little of our, and our doctors', time as possible. It sounds as if technology will be running, prompting, directing, stopping and starting us as much as the other way around.

Your Personal Straitjacket

For an individual the utopian desire to design the world in your own image surfaces under the mantra of 'personalization'. One of the most attractive claims of digitopia is that we will move away from mass, commodified products and services to those tailored to our needs and wants. Everyone will become a 'market of one'. We can already set up our own bank accounts, when we want, devise our own television schedules and mix our own music compilations. No longer will we have to compromise and accept services designed for a mass market; in future we can have what we want, when we want it.

A world constructed entirely around our interests and needs sounds perfect. The life of a king will be made available to everyone. But just imagine if this promise was made good and taken to an extreme: life would quickly become awful. We would live in straitjackets of our own creation. We could choose to hear only the news that we wanted and choose not to hear news that offended, upset or shocked us. Nothing in this world designed around us could surprise us. It would reflect our taste: it would be a giant electronic mirror, reflecting our prejudices. We could each day retreat back into a sealed world of our own liking and making, in which the surprising and unusual, reflecting the tastes of other people, might never have to intrude. We would not have to confront anything we did not know in advance that we liked. The pleasure of personalization and the sense of control it brings could quickly lead to isolation and solipsism. Carried to an extreme it would be a recipe for mass self-centredness, which could find its most powerful expression in genetics.

The more powerful our technologies become the more we will face the dilemma of how far we want to create the world in our own image. One feature that makes a society exciting, democratic and innovative is that it is full of surprises because it is not completely planned, at an individual or social level. Our sense of our individuality does not just come from our inner interests and desires. It also stems from a recognition that we differ from other people whom we interact with. Living in a purely personalized world, cut off from that social interaction, we would collapse in on ourselves. We need to work out how we should live in a world that is both more personalized and more social.

Indecent Exposure

In most visions of utopia virtually every aspect of life is conducted in public because in a perfect society there is no conflict between the community and the individual. Some critics argue we are in the process of realizing this utopian dream, turned nightmare, through constant communal surveillance through our networks of closed circuit television cameras, web cams that broadcast from bedrooms and devices linked to global satellite positioning systems. It is not simply that new technology is extending the range of surveillance to track our movements and activities. We are ensnared in much more complex and subtle ways in this electronic web. The web that is always on is helping to create a culture in which voyeurism becomes a mass pastime; surveillance is a commonplace feature of life; exhibitionism, confession and exposure of private aspects of people's lives become the currency of the media. Television used to be a periodic entertainment that people turned on at the end of the day to watch fairly passively. Now screens are all around us, all the time. We watch them, perform for them and are tracked by them.

There is no better example of the potentially double-edged nature of this technology than the Global Positioning System, the largest constellation of military satellites ever to have orbited the earth. The system was originally developed by the US military to locate soldiers lost in dense jungle in Vietnam. The twenty-four satellites, with four spares, circle the planet twice a day moving in six orbital planes. The satellites function as reference points, like man-made electronic stars. Within a few years every mobile telephone, laptop, watch and camera could have a tiny GPS receiver embedded within it. It should be possible to locate it down to the nearest three metres. This global electronic positioning grid has been made possible only through massive US government spending and amazing scientific advances. The GPS receivers of 1985 were five feet tall and had large cables running from them. They cost $300,000 a piece. Now that functionality has been put on a tiny chip that costs about $150 a time. The benefits of this system are enormous. When someone makes an emergency call from a mobile telephone the emergency services should be able to pinpoint the telephone's position automatically. A device in your clothing, briefcase or bag should be able to tell you not only where you are but how to get to where you want to go. By 2020 every place in the world could have an electronic geographic tag attached to it. As James Spohrer, a GPS specialist at IBM, told *The New Yorker*: 'Devices that know where they are will soon be everywhere. We will map every metre of this planet. And not just this planet.'[4] You need never be lost again. You will never have to ask directions and waste time on wrong turns.

Yet if the system never allows you to get lost, it always knows where you are, just as the mobile telephone companies already know all the telephone numbers you make calls to. The mobile Internet and global positioning may allow us to work wherever we want to, but will also allow our employers, our partners and the police to track us down, whether we like it or not. In offices of old it was commonplace for someone to leave their jacket hanging over the back of their chair to make it look as though they were at work while in reality they were in the pub. In future we will need electronic versions of that trick.

In Transit

Digitopia offers a seemingly never-ending supply of promises that not only will the future be better but it will arrive soon. Innovation-driven societies constantly supply greener grass for the other side of the valley. And yet, this constant orientation towards the future, what is coming next, can be unsettling. The fact that the future always promises to be better means the present must be less than satisfactory. We live in a disposable, interim, upgrade society: we are always in transit, always on the move to somewhere else, a new standard, a better version, and so never fully satisfied with what we have got. The business models of new economy companies are built on constant upgrades to drive consumer demand for products that embody real or imaginary improvements. An innovation-driven society is shadowed by the prospect that the present will soon be outmoded, left behind, second-rate. We love novelty but it makes us dissatisfied with what we have got.

As we are constantly in transit, never still, the faster we can get to the future, indeed the faster we can do anything – consume food, download the news, read a book – the better. Speed only became a major component of utopian visions in the twentieth century, with the Italian Futurists and the technotopians who have followed in their wake. Marinetti's Futurist Manifesto published in 1913 celebrated speed and scorned obstacles, caution, slowness and nostalgia. The Futurists associated everything slow with nostalgia for history and pessimism about exploring the unknown. They imagined a world filled exclusively with man-made products that were superior to those of nature, in which legacies, traditions and ties to the past had been eliminated. Unwittingly the new economy clothed itself in Futurist rhetoric. Vince Khosla, the Silicon Valley venture capitalist who warns that the future may be too fast for slow people, is a latter-day Futurist. In the new economy everything is judged by how quickly it can be accomplished: how fast information can be processed, connections made, data downloaded, plants grown, ideas turned into products, animals fattened. The new economy was a giant celebration of speed. It bred a deep intolerance of delay and waiting: a culture of mass impatience. There are all sorts of downsides to a world that cannot wait. We spent most of the twentieth century investing heavily in going faster. Now perhaps we need to start investing consciously in making sure we can slow down. We measure our dissatisfaction with computers in milliseconds but find it very hard to address issues that require much longer timescales: tackling environmental degradation or child poverty, for example. The desire for quick results makes citizens intolerant of governments that find it hard to address complex problems that will take a long time to resolve. At times it seems all too easy to agree with Franz Kafka's observation: 'The masses are rushing, running and charging through the age. They think they are advancing but they are simply running on the spot and falling into the void.'

Ignorance

We live in an ignorance economy. As a society we are made better off by our acquisition of knowledge. But as individuals we grow relatively more ignorant. Take the mobile phone as an example. Tens of millions of people around the world use mobile phones. They greedily buy up the latest versions, with lighter batteries, more efficient semiconductors and more powerful software and services. Yet only a tiny fraction of the population could explain how a mobile telephone works. The millions who use mobile telephones do so by relying on the knowledge of a tiny minority in the whole population. Each time we pick up an Ericsson, Motorola or Nokia, we pick up the intelligence of the engineers, scientists, designers and software programmers who made it possible. Our lives are made richer by our ability to rely on the knowledge of other people: our willingness to remain ignorant.

As the economy becomes more knowledge-intensive and our lives more interdependent, our ability to trust the knowledge of other people will become more vital. All of us are made richer by our ability to remain ignorant. By remaining ignorant we avoid having to go through the time-consuming business of acquiring knowledge. We allow other people to do the learning and inventing for us. In science, it is not just recorded facts that are expanding at an overwhelming rate, but also the theories that explain them. As these theories have proliferated so have the disciplines and specialisms that surround them. Physics, for example, has split into astrophysics, thermodynamics, particle physics and quantum field theory, to name but four. Within each of these branches nestle many sub-specialisms. Each of these fields is based on a theoretical framework at least as rich as the whole of physics was a century ago. The more we discover and invent the more specialisms we create. The more specialists there are, the harder it becomes for the non-specialists – the rest of us – to understand their knowledge. Stephen Hawking, at the end of *A Brief History of Time*, concludes that we are close to a complete theory of the world and that when that theory is available we shall be 'close to the mind of God'. Yet in other respects knowledge seems to fracture as it grows. In our knowledge-rich yet relativistic age we find ourselves in a world increasingly lacking certain, shared and fixed frameworks of belief, in which claims to scientific truth are disputed as soon as they are made. We do not have a single history but a multitude from every point of view. We do not have shared moral codes but different cultural traditions which explain and justify how people behave. As knowledge has grown so we have had to abandon the idea that we can view the world as neutral, objective observers because all our perspectives on the world are necessarily contaminated by our culture and language.[5] Learning how to cope with our growing ignorance amidst this bounty of knowledge will be vital to our sense of stability.

Saving Digitopia from Itself

Digital abundance can quickly turn into a cacophony of constant trivia and distraction. Utopian faith in the power of human design and creativity is meant to allow us to overcome the constraints of nature, fate and tradition. Yet our own power prompts fears that we are becoming self-centred, intolerant of imperfection and hygienic in our pursuit of the perfect design for life. The dream of an open and accountable community, with unconstrained communication, becomes the always-on, ever-tele-present society of mass voyeurism, surveillance and exhibitionism, in which the line between the public and the private has all but disappeared. The promise of innovation means we live in an interim world that is always in transit to somewhere else. We live in a high-tech accelerator. As a result what we crave is slow, human, personal experiences as well as excitement. People are inventing new versions of the 1970s trade union tactic of the 'go slow'. As our society becomes increasingly knowledge-rich so we, its ordinary citizens, increasingly become ignorant and dependent upon specialist knowledge we cannot hope to understand. As knowledge grows it fragments. The economy of ideas and imagination is a world of opportunity without constraint and yet as a result it is more unstable and less reliable.

Innovation through science and technology, but also in other fields, is the most potent force for improvement in our lives. Technology will open up ways to transform our world far more than politics in the century to come. At the start of the twentieth century mass utopian dreams were focused on projects for rational, large-scale planning, top down experiments in social mobilization: fascism, communism, nationalism, city planning, mass-production industries. Given the largely disastrous track record of these grand political utopias in the twentieth century, we may be better off investing our hopes not in a vision but in a fundamental social process of innovation and creativity as sources of hope. Innovation and creativity, unlike utopian visions, have to be open to change, improvement, criticism and new ideas. Innovation is a constant process: it is never closed and finished. Its appeal, on the contrary, is the way it constantly throws the world open, to new possibilities and interpretations. That is why innovation, expressed through culture, science and technology, can provide us with a powerful non-utopian source of hope for the future. The twenty-first century is likely to be dominated by the story of whether innovation can deliver on its promise of transformation or whether it is defeated by its own myopia and hubris. How we might achieve that is the subject of the next chapter.

7. Innovation Rules

We are getting older and younger at the same time. The developed countries of the world are at the vanguard of a revolution in life expectancy that is spreading to poorer developing nations. That revolution will not only continue the twentieth-century extension of life expectancy, it should also in time allow more of us to lead better quality lives for longer in what was once called old age. We are creating a new phase of life and a new social group – the young old – people who well into their seventies expect to live life much as they did in their forties. In a sense, this is yet another example of how new technologies, in this case the technologies of genetics, are being used to allow us to extend the range of familiar, almost nostalgic experiences: we will give up our sense of youth only when we absolutely have to. Genetic technology will allow us to hang on to it for as long as we possibly can, just as digital technologies will allow us to carry around the music and films of our youth.

In the past century science, medicine, technology and public services, providing clean water and sewerage, helped us to extend our ability to control the most basic aspect of our lives: when we die. In the nineteenth century, life expectancy in the UK was about forty years. In France in 1800 it was thirty and in Denmark in 1845 it was forty-four. In the UK now life expectancy is seventy-five for men and more than eighty for women. In the last fifty years life expectancy in the UK has risen by two years every decade. As Professor Tom Kirkwood said in his 2001 Reith Lectures, it is as if every decade we have got 20 per cent extra for free. As a result a growing share of the world's population is becoming older. In the nineteenth century just 1 per cent of the world's population was aged over sixty-five. That percentage has already risen sevenfold and by 2050 it is expected to reach 20 per cent of the world's population, according to US government figures. In previous generations it was quite common, even in developed countries, for children to have no knowledge of their grandparents, because they tended to die so young. I knew only one of my grandparents; the other three died before I was born. Now it is far more likely that families, though perhaps dispersed, will embrace three if not four generations. While conservatives might bemoan what they regard as young people's lack of respect for their elders, the truth is that more and more young people will know their grandparents and great-grandparents, and so make up their own minds about them.

This extension of the average lifespan in the developed world has already spread to much of the developing world. World average life expectancy was thirty years in 1900. Now it is about sixty-seven, according to the World Bank. In China, life expectancy in 1930 was just twenty-four years. Now it is close to seventy. More than 85 per cent of the world's inhabitants can expect, with reasonable confidence, to live for more than sixty years. This trend should continue with the greater availability of the basic ingredients of longer life: affordable food, antibiotics, vaccines, clean water, electricity and basic education. In the twentieth century the extension of life expectancy was mainly due to fewer people dying young. Infant mortality has declined by more than 50 per cent even in developing countries. But this century life expectancy will continue to rise because of the application of science to the other end of the age range: old age.

In the decades to come science, in the form of genetics, chemistry and biology, will start to tell us more about why bodies wear out, get old and die. Death rates are already declining fastest among the oldest groups in the population. If you make it to seventy these days, you have a reasonably good chance of making it to ninety. In future that will become increasingly common for more people. In addition, older people will live much richer quality lives. The seventy-year-olds of today are more like the sixty-year-olds of two generations ago: they are fitter and healthier, they will have eaten better food and lived and worked in better conditions than their grandparents. As a result we have the tantalizing prospect that more and more people could live better, longer lives, with perhaps thirty or forty years in which they are fit, out of the corporate rat race and free from child-rearing responsibilities. If the late twentieth century was set alight by youth culture, the first decades of the twenty-first in developed countries will in many ways be made in the self-image, and self-delusions, of the young old. The droves of eighteen-year-old students travelling around the world in their gap year will be outnumbered by their grandparents doing much the same thing. (Put it another way, many parents and grandparents will do things that will embarrass and alarm their offspring.) Of course this extension of life expectancy does not come without significant challenges and downsides for pensions policy, retirement ages, long-term care of the elderly, and in the developing world the need to feed and clothe populations that are rising in large part because of the decline in death rates. The blessing is mixed. But that should not obscure the fact that longer better lives are a blessing.

This expansion of lifespan is one of the most tangible and exciting examples of how science and technology can improve life chances when they are applied to solving significant human problems. When technology is not tackling important human needs, it can be dynamic, creative and exciting while making life more confusing and complicated. Innovation too often entails complication.

For the foreseeable future our capacity for innovation, to generate and apply new ideas, to communicate, educate, treat disease, improve health, heal the environment, will be the most likely source of major improvements in our well-being. We will achieve more by creating new resources and solutions, which can be fairly distributed, rather than simply redistributing a stock of existing resources. In the next few years more technology will come at us, whether we like it or not. It will get smaller, more powerful and more pervasive. Yet, as we have seen, the overblown utopian promise of new technology can all too quickly deflate. For many people science is not a source of progress but a source of new risks, dangers and uncertainties. How can we maximize the rewards from innovation while minimizing the risks? The first task is to understand the general trends and features of the technology-rich world we are moving into. The second is to set some very general rules to guide innovation.

Five Features

The technology that will become available to us over the next few years will have five main features.

First, it will become increasingly pervasive. We have been used to seeing technology as a set of tools that we pick up to carry out discrete tasks. The industrial technology of machines was really an extension of human muscle power: it made muscle power go further with gears, levers, engines, brakes that were operated by human action. The first wave of mass computing and the Internet amplified and spread brain power, to allow us to share information and ideas more readily. But increasingly technology will not be simple discrete tools that we pick up, as we might do a spanner. Technology will become a pervasive part of our environment, part of the media through which we live our lives. We will communicate using ubiquitous and common platforms that will allow us to stay connected, and be traced, wherever we are. Technology will be embedded in windows, furniture, clothing and environments. Hotels, airports, offices and schools, for example, could soon start operating on wireless local area networks that will allow people to connect to the outside world, wherever they are, using a variety of devices. The line between a fixed infrastructure of pipes and cables, and devices that plug into them, will become increasingly blurred. We may well call down software from the web around us and store more of our information in spaces on it, so that we can access it easily on the move. Equally, we will find ourselves perhaps carrying around with us small parts of the telecommunications infrastructure.

Second, at the same time as becoming increasingly pervasive, technology is becoming increasingly personalized and individualized. Technology will increasingly be tailored to our needs and preferences. At a more fundamental level it will become part of our person. Mobile devices such as personal communicators will become smaller and more powerful. Computing power will be increasingly woven into our clothes. It may also be at work in our bodies, as pacemakers, nano-machines, patches to regulate our metabolism and genetic recipes to forestall the onset of diseases of ageing. Technology will be both a seamless part of our environment and part and parcel of our clothing and bodies. It will be shared and personalized.

Third, all this technology will become increasingly intelligent, in the sense that it will need less instruction from us to do our bidding. Technology such as the software that will be embedded in set top boxes on digital televisions will increasingly be able to observe and learn about our habits and preferences and serve material to us. We might want to reject its suggestions, or turn off that feature from time to time. But computer and communications technology will increasingly have the capacity to learn and adapt to its users, rather than being passive tools. At the moment we interact with most new technology through incredibly narrow channels: by tapping on a computer or fiddling with a handheld control. In the near future, the range of interactions will increase as technologies become more interactive, more aware of mood and touch and controlled by speech as well as typed in commands. That means we may increasingly be in conversation with technology rather than simply controlling it.

Fourth, the process of change and innovation will be complex and evolutionary, at times rapid and at others faltering. Technological progress will rarely mean new technologies sweeping away older forms altogether. It is increasingly likely, rather, that we will use layers of old and new technologies, adopted at different speeds by different parts of society. It will be an increasingly uneven, chaotic process, in which old technologies will be improved and upgraded to extend their useful life, as new ones are introduced. Some of these new technologies will fail (as various forms of mobile communications did in the 1980s), others will complement existing technologies (the video seems to have increased the appetite for film viewing and so cinema attendance), while others will displace established technologies (digital television will in time replace analogue television). Yet when old technologies are displaced by new ones, the habits associated with older technologies will linger on. It is quite likely, for example, that most of the UK will move over to digital television within the next decade. But it is extremely unlikely that all television viewers will exploit the full range of services digital television has to offer. My children and my parents both have access to digital television and mobile telephones, but they tend to use them in quite different ways. We are accustomed to thinking of technology moving in great waves, sweeping all before it. In future we will have to think of technology in more evolutionary terms, developing new varieties that colonize different parts of a habitat, while older varieties still hang on to areas where they are established. We will have to come to think of innovation as laying down new layers of technology on top of existing ones, which themselves may be partially recuperated by technical change. The future of transport will include more efficient public trains and trams, a nineteenth-century technology, as well as new generations of high-tech, electronic cars. We will generate energy from wind and solar farms, but also from much improved gas- and coal-fired power stations. Technology might once have swept across technology-poor societies, moving into relatively open habitats. But in societies that are already technology-rich it will be a more complex story.

Fifth, technological change will increasingly breed new hybrids. We will not all switch, suddenly and completely, from the old to the all new. Instead we will become increasingly adept at mixing and matching old and new, high and low tech, to meet our needs. As the range of devices and networks people can use for communications widens, so does the range of different combinations people can come up with to meet their needs. Increased international telephone traffic has not reduced or substituted for international air travel: the two have grown in tandem. We will buy some goods, such as books and groceries, over the Internet. But other goods and services we will want to buy face-to-face. People will increasingly find new ways to combine old and new, high and low technologies to achieve their ends. We are moving into a world in which people will increasingly want high-tech genetic treatments for disease but also organic and herbal remedies and massages. The more amenable technologies are to this mixing and matching, to allow users to create their own hybrids, the more likely they are to succeed.

Technological innovation in the next few years may well follow these five themes. It will be more pervasive, personalized, intelligent, evolutionary and hybrid. Technology will be less a set of discrete, stand alone, relatively passive tools, which operate only with human instruction. Worriers and pessimists see several interconnected risks with unfolding technological innovation. The capacity to learn about and engage in innovation is now highly distributed, largely thanks to the spread of education, communications and computers. As a result it is far easier for people outside respected bodies, professions, governments and universities to learn about innovations with far-reaching potential. Armed with the right tools people can start doing things for themselves. Imagine a hacker of the year 2030 who does not spread computer viruses but real, biological ones. The risks of this widely distributed know-how go up because the technologies themselves are so pervasive and can spread so easily. Technological risks are harder to spot and stop. It was difficult for anyone other than a government to build a nuclear missile and it was difficult to move such missiles without being detected. It is much more difficult to identify and stop a terrorist group using a biological weapon. We are moving into an era when innovation is increasingly uncertain. We are pushing at barriers and boundaries that we should transgress only after careful thought: boundaries between brains and computers, humans and robots, cells and nano-machines, natural crops and genetically modified ones. As a result it is far more difficult to calculate and control bigger risks, which might take many years to become apparent and be harder to eradicate. When technology was just a set of tools, the risks associated with it might be confined. When technology is part of our environment, risks and viruses might spread within it very rapidly. One response to these apparent risks is that we might adopt stricter controls and precautionary principles and even renounce some aspects of technological innovation as too risky. We should learn to say 'no'.

In the twentieth century, utopians – communists, futurists and science fiction writers – worked on the same subject matter: how technology and science would bring revolutions in work and political power. The utopian tradition expressed a faith in the liberating potential for science and technology to give us richer, longer lives, in which work was less of a burden and more a source of fulfilment, in a society ruled by open democracy, cooperation and rational debate, among educated and well informed citizens. The dystopian account – from greens, leftists, conservatives and communitarians – is of a society overrun by rampant technology, that is beyond public control or comprehension: a society in which work has become drudgery, every nook and cranny of private life is infiltrated by surveillance and politicians and the media lord it over the citizenry thanks to the technology they control.

It is perhaps impossible to devise hard and fast rules to steer us away from technological catastrophe, especially when innovations bring completely unintended benefits as well as drawbacks. Innovation stems from an open, distributed process, in which there is constant experimentation. Innovation proceeds often by breaking rules rather than following them. Instead I want to suggest two general approaches to innovation which are likely to improve the chances of it delivering benefit, rather than harm. The first is that innovation is more likely to be legitimate the more it addresses significant needs – for education, health, democracy, a better environment – rather than adding more functionality to devices that already do quite a good job entertaining us. When innovations improve the quality of life for very large numbers of people in tangible ways and extend their sense of control and choice, they are very difficult to stop. The second is that innovation is more likely to be successful and legitimate, the more it is understood as an open social process, rather than a purely commercial or professional one. The knowledge economy rests on social foundations: societies that are better able to attend to these social foundations will be better placed to create, absorb and intelligently reject innovation. The common theme is that innovation is becoming an increasingly dispersed, democratic and social process in which there are many players, public and private, large and small. Rather than attempt to put the genie back in the bottle by tightly regulating innovation or disallowing certain avenues, it would be far better in the long run to build on the increasingly democratic and open nature of the process by improving the quality of public debate and involvement. Innovation is neither a purely commercial nor a purely scientific process; it has to be seen as a social activity.

Innovate or Die

One of the defining features of the dot.com bubble was that so much technology was deployed to service such trivial and esoteric needs: the faster delivery of non-essential, non-emergency goods; electronic guides to cities for which there were already many good guide books; online fashion stores and advice that took ages to download. The Internet bubble was not just a financial phenomenon. There was something deeper at play. We longed for the Internet to change our lives for the better, to open our way into a brave new world. It has not, at least not yet. As we saw earlier, digital technologies will have a profound impact on our lives, creating new possibilities for us to socialize, work, debate, vote, produce and trade, as well as create, show, publish and display creative work. If technology and innovation are to maintain and deepen public support, then they have to serve widespread and basic needs, which improve the life chances of many people, rich and poor, by allowing all of us more choice and control. The more basic and widespread the sense of improvement, the more likely that innovation will command continuing support. That is why in the long run democratic innovations, which put technology in the hands of people, to collaborate with one another without having to go through established channels, will succeed. The Internet and modern telecommunications are increasing peer-to-peer networking and communications. Genetically modified food will be a success if it can be shown to be safe while also enhancing food productivity in developing countries such as India. Medical genetics will progress depending on whether it treats common diseases that afflict many people, such as cancer.

A prime example of the role innovation can play in meeting basic and widespread needs is the environment. Innovation and technology are often accused of damaging the environment. Pesticides, chemicals, industrial processes and the internal combustion engine are the creators of pollution, the hole in the ozone layer and global warming. Often environmentalists rail against industrialization and technology as the sources of most of our ills in a world badly out of touch with a sense of natural balance. Yet new technology is not uniquely destructive. Some of the largest species extinctions in history were achieved by men wielding stones and spears. While new technologies such as CFCs have had a deleterious impact, new technology and science have also played a vital role in reducing the impact of human industry on the environment. Modern domestic heating systems are far more environmentally friendly than domestic coal fires. Water quality has improved in the rivers of many developed countries through more effective anti-pollution technologies. Many of these technological improvements, moreover, have been introduced because they make good economic sense as well as protecting the environment. The modern aluminium drinks can weighs an eighth of its counterpart of twenty years ago. As it uses less material the modern drinks can is cheaper, less environmentally damaging to make and to dispose of. Nevertheless technology is often seen as the source of our environmental problems rather than a solution. Former US vice-president Al Gore captured some of this spirit in *Earth in Balance*, published in 1992, in which he warned that we had constructed a false world of 'plastic flowers and Astroturf, air conditioning and fluorescent lights, windows that do not open and music that never stops, sleepy hearts jumpstarted by caffeine, alcohol, drugs and illusions'. Gore suggested that the rescue of the environment from modern industry was a continuation of the struggle against the totalitarianism in the shape of Stalinism and Nazism. Gore, as many other environmentalists, gets very close to blaming technical ingenuity for creating a world dangerously out of control, in the grip of a death wish.

Nothing could be further from the truth. The key to our chances of dramatically reducing the environmental impacts of modern society lies in our ability to innovate new environmentally friendly products and services. Our future society will be more environmentally sustainable only by rapidly developing and judiciously adopting new technologies. It will be environmentally sustainable only by being technologically rich and intelligent.

I have no wish to enter into the detailed debate over Bjorn Lomborg's provocative and stimulating book *The Skeptical Environmentalist*, in which the Danish statistician and polemicist tackles the evidence for many widely held beliefs about the savagely deteriorating state of the planet. Lomborg is surely right that on many counts – life expectancy, education, poverty, hunger – the world is in better shape than many of the extreme doomsayers would have us believe. It is also clear, as Lomborg acknowledges, that while on many counts things have got a lot better in the last few decades, in global terms they are nowhere near good enough. In response to Lomborg's argument, Tom Burke, the environmentalist and former adviser to the British government, countered that there are limits to the extent that we can degrade biological systems, the sea, air and land, and still go on benefiting from the goods and services they offer to absorb waste, provide raw materials and produce energy. Our ability to extend the limits of these biological systems or to evade those limits altogether, however, largely depends on our ability to innovate new products and services. That means applying new technologies to existing products and processes to make them cleaner or inventing entirely new ones that leave no environmental mark.

The environment should be at the heart of innovative activity, both public and private, to develop less environmentally damaging products, services and methods of production. Traditional innovation policies have placed little emphasis on the environment, while environmental policies have traditionally focused on incentives and regulation to encourage consumers and producers to take up already available technologies. The key in future will be to use regulation to promote environmental innovation that gives us many more options to satisfy people's desire for greater well-being, to travel, keep themselves warm, eat good food, while damaging the environment far less. Innovations such as the introduction of lead-free petrol and gas-fired power generation have had a huge impact on carbon dioxide emissions. Environmental innovation is not just about applying new technologies to clean up existing old processes. It can create entirely new products and processes as well.

One outstanding example is the Californian initiative to mandate that 10 per cent of cars offered for sale in the state would be 'zero emission vehicles' by the year 2003. A similar regulation was adopted recently for transit buses: 15 per cent of buses acquired for Californian fleets should be zero emission in 2008. As a result of the initiative, in what is the world's eighth largest economy, key components of electric vehicle technology have improved dramatically in terms of performance, cost, size and weight. Advances have also been made with new materials to create lightweight car bodies. The major automakers have already put more than 2000 ZEV on to California's roads. More 50:50 vehicles are emerging: battery cars that have a fifty-mile range and a 50mph top speed. Ford bought a Norwegian company that makes small cars with aluminium and plastic bodies to create the 'Think' car. Honda and Chevrolet both have new small cars with hybrid, battery and petrol engines, which have ranges of about 700 miles. To compete, traditional cars in California are now increasingly super-ultra-low emission vehicles, generally fuelled by natural gas. As the debate has progressed the California Air Resources Board has adapted the mandate to encourage innovation along a variety of paths, rather than focusing on a single technology: battery-powered vehicles. What is now underway, with California acting as the world's laboratory, is an exploration of several different ways to migrate road users and car producers to far less environmentally damaging forms of transport. We will solve our environmental problems when industry has innovated solutions which consumers have an incentive to buy. In the end, as the California experiment shows, a mixture of innovation and consumer demand will drive environmental improvement. Regulation matters in so far as it helps this process along. To be green we do not all have to go back to bicycles. Clean cars should soon be a mass product.

Another example of an environmental innovation that could have far-reaching implications, as Martyn Turner and Brian O'Connell explain in *The Whole World's Watching*, is the fuel cell, which generates electricity using hydrogen and oxygen, leaving water as a byproduct. Hydrogen is difficult to isolate and store, so most fuel cells work on hydrogen-rich substances – methane, methanol and ethanol. Innovation in this field has been rapid. One of the main fuel cell producers, Ballard Power Systems in Vancouver, decided to go into commercial production only in 1989 but by 1996 prototypes were under development for buses and cars. The company plans to make fuel cells that are 90 per cent efficient, in terms of power and zero carbon emissions, by 2010. Ford has a 15 per cent stake in Ballard and has teamed up with Daimler Chrysler in the development of fuel cell-powered cars. Joseph Romm, executive director of the US lobby group the Centre for Energy and Climate Solutions, argues that fuel cells could provide the basis for distributed home-based power generation systems. Romm is also a believer in renewable energy, such as wind and solar power. According to one scenario of the future compiled by the energy company Shell, a third of the world's new electricity generation capacity could come from renewables by the year 2060, with solar energy as the fastest-growing source. With innovation along the right lines we could be heading for a future in which by 2020 the internal combustion engine could be considered as old-fashioned as valve-operated radios are today. Innovation is moving us inexorably from high to low to zero carbon fuels.

Some of this environmentally beneficial innovation will come from companies seeking more efficient products and processes and as a result creating environmentally sustainable products. A growing number of companies is finding these win–win solutions, which are good for the environment and the financial bottom line, as Amory and Hunter Lovins and Paul Hawken set out so convincingly in *Natural Capitalism: the Next Industrial Revolution*. That is one reason why a faster rate of innovation should be better for the environment. As more companies have to fundamentally rethink products and processes for competitive reasons, the more they should have the opportunity to redesign processes along environmental lines. The global market for environmental products and services is projected to be very large indeed. The OECD estimates it could be worth $570 billion in the year 2010, up from $210 billion in 1992. However, the problem is that innovation is undertaken without the speed and scale required. Often it takes twenty-five years to introduce a new technology, in part because technologies take a long time to develop but also because the speed of introduction is often constrained by how fast existing products and plant are retired from use. Ambitious target setting, of the kind used in California, will be vital to create markets for environmentally sustainable products that can be satisfied only with innovation. The British government's mandate that 10 per cent of electricity generation should come from renewable sources by 2010 is a big step in the right direction. EU measures to make producers responsible for the disposal of their products should be the start of a long-running debate over how best to promote and reward design innovations that make products recyclable. Investing more strategically in basic and applied research into new energy technologies and materials, as well as encouraging venture capital funding for spin-offs from universities, will also be vital.

Through innovation, both technical and social, it is possible we could see major cities teeming with cars that are not powered by internal combustion engines by the year 2050. Given the populations that will by then live in cities, especially in the developing world, this will be a major improvement in living conditions, health and the environment. The phrase, innovate or die, never had greater resonance.

If technological innovation helps to improve the state of the environment, extend access to education, improve the conditions for democracy, extend life expectancy, improve health and reduce hunger, then it will be seen as a vital force for good. If on the other hand it does not, or if corporations alone dictate how innovation proceeds, then it will be constantly fraught with tension and doubt. Commercial and scientific innovation thus needs to be part of a much larger social and democratic process, through which societies can set parameters and priorities for innovation. Companies should welcome that debate, not retreat from it.

Social Foundations

It has long been recognized that innovation is a social process, in which ideas are developed collaboratively through networks and face-to-face interaction. The more uncertain and fuzzy the innovation, the more likely it is that it will develop only through intensive collaboration in networks and clusters of the kind that Silicon Valley exemplifies. People invariably need to meet, face-to-face, to explore and resolve complex problems, especially when innovation is at its earliest, fuzziest stages when its outcome and direction are most uncertain. Creativity is possible only if people are willing to expose themselves by revealing untried and untested ideas. Encouraging people to take that risk is difficult unless they feel trusted. Trust is a vital lubricant of innovation because it encourages risk taking and trust thrives amid networks of collaboration. Yet the significance of social capital extends well beyond its role as a lubricant for innovation.

The vital resources of the knowledge economy – imagination, creativity, a capacity and appetite for learning – are socially created through families, friendships, hobbies, private passions and education. These assets are not created commercially, through the market, for profit, but socially and culturally. They are created only when people interact with one another in lessons, debate and performances. These social processes that create knowledge and a capacity for learning start with the family and early education but they extend well beyond that. It is very difficult to promote a widespread capacity for learning, in which people are encouraged to think for themselves, pursue their own interests and develop their own curiosity, without a wider democratic culture which promotes diversity and dissent. Access to and participation in an open culture which values artistic expression is another vital component. Cultural creativity is essential in encouraging a wider capacity for people to think laterally, to look left and right for ideas, as well as straight ahead. A society in which learning is an everyday, mass activity will not just be better able to generate and create ideas, it will also be better able to scrutinize and absorb them. That is why many of the Nordic countries, with well educated populations, are highly technologically advanced and yet engage in informed and active debates about environmental and other risks posed by technology. Innovation is no longer the preserve of men in white coats and experts. The capacity for innovation is widely distributed across society and consumers expect to have their say in the process. It is not a linear process in which knowledgeable experts deliver the fruits of their insights to a passive audience. These days innovation is far more open and disputatious. A successful knowledge-driven economy, then, rests on social, cultural and democratic foundations. In the long run societies that attend to these social foundations will be better able to innovate and match innovation to social need, than those that neglect their social foundations and rely on a knowledge elite to drive innovation.

As knowledge and innovation come to play a larger role in economic life, so the social dimensions of economic activity take on greater significance. In what follows, I want to focus on one particular connection between the social and economic aspects of life in an innovation-driven economy: the role of the family.

The social foundations for growth matter more because the economy is increasingly driven by learning and innovation. Yet the instability and flux of the modern economy make it all the more difficult to maintain its social foundations. At the centre of this tension is the modern family. The family is at the heart of the creation of human and social capital. It is where we first learn and trust, cooperate and compete. In a knowledge economy, the family should be at the heart of supply side economic policy. Yet the family is beset by all the pressures, fissures and fractures of the modern labour market. According to *Social Foundations of Postindustrial Economies*, the Swedish sociologist Gosta Esping-Andersen's sweeping survey of the welfare state, the labour market and the condition of the modern family: 'The household economy is alpha and omega to any resolution of the main postindustrial dilemmas, perhaps the most important social foundation of postindustrial economies.'

The relationship between the family and the modern economy has developed through at least four stages. Until the early nineteenth century, in virtually every western society, households were economic enterprises. The labour of fathers, mothers, children, relatives and hired hands was essential for the household to make its living. Work was conducted from home, by merchants and bankers, as much as by artisans and farmers. In the sixteenth and seventeenth centuries the term family covered not just immediate family members but also servants and other relatives who might be long-term guests. A father was not only the head of the household but invariably also the owner-manager of the family business. Economics, welfare, education and authority all flowed through the authority of the father. Authority and obedience, not affection, were the guiding principles of family relations. Nor were the boundaries between the family and the community well defined. The community, in the shape of the church or aristocracy, could intervene in family affairs. The family and the household were a quasi-public institution.

With the growth of industry and the cities, paid work moved out of the home. Fathers went out to work. Mothers were increasingly left in charge of the family and household. The household became a place in which children were reared and workers recovered after a day's work. Young people gained more independence. Male authority was less omnipresent. By the middle of the nineteenth century men and women, who had worked together in family enterprises for centuries, were regarded as belonging to separate spheres, work and home. Men had to work in a harsh and demanding public world. Women were defined as virtuous domestic beings who tended the children within the distinctly private household. Children, long regarded as dutiful workers in the family enterprise, became tender innocents in need of maternal love and nurture. The apparently timeless notion that a woman's place is in a home that is a haven of comfort, affection and intimacy was largely a creation of this period.

As the twentieth century progressed the dominant 'separate spheres' approach to family life – based on clear boundaries between home and work, men and women, child and adult, public and private, production and consumption – developed, not least during the era of mass consumerism in the 1950s. Yet it also came under growing strain. More women were educated and started entering the workforce, particularly with the growth in part-time service and retail jobs. Advances in medicine – the pill and abortion – gave women far more control over when they had children. The growth of educational provision meant that children spent less time at home.

The distorted ideal of the nuclear family, based on the male

breadwinner in stable, full-time employment and a housewife
rearing children in a well provided for home, reached its peak
in the Golden Age of the 1950s when it was just about to start
coming apart. That kind of family no longer fits with women's
expectations, nor those of many men, nor with the reality of
work in the modern labour market.

Work has not only become more knowledge intensive but
also more flexible. Companies increasingly do not provide
people with jobs, but a shifting portfolio of tasks to be com-
pleted. An efficient factory production line required that each
worker do exactly and only what was required of him, over
and over again, as quickly as possible. Today the average
employee has to do many different things, often at different
times. Usually this means workers moving from task to task,
project to project, varying the intensity of work and working
hours accordingly. From the point of view of companies that
have twenty-four-hour operations, often dealing with global
supply chains and demanding retail customers most of whom
are also working long hours, the best solution is to have
very flexible employees who are prepared to work whenever
needed, often with changing schedules and without looking
at the clock to figure out their overtime. Companies reward
workers who are regularly prepared to sacrifice other activities,
namely their relationships with lovers, spouses, relatives and
children, for the sake of work. Arlie Hochschild says in *Time
Blind*, her study of modern work in large US corporations:
'While the mass media so often point to global competition
as the major business story of the age, it is easy to miss the fact
that corporate America's fiercest struggle has been with its
local rival – the family.'

At the same time, the demand for those with few skills
and little education has fallen, along with their wages, compared to those who have the skills to work in high-tech,
high-productivity jobs or to compete in global markets for

professional services. The wages and employment prospects of the relatively poorly educated used to be reasonably good when there were still plenty of unionized manufacturing jobs. But these days the main source of work for this group is the service sector, where low productivity often means low salaries. Sustaining a family on the paypacket of a single bread-winner in a low-productivity, relatively low-wage service job is increasingly difficult.

Different societies are seeking different solutions to the problem of how to provide for family stability in the midst of a changing labour market. In countries such as Spain and Italy, where the traditional family, albeit in modified form, is still the bedrock of welfare, the main thrust of policy has been to protect the employment and earnings of male heads of household. While unemployment in Spain is high compared to the rest of the EU, its rate of unemployment among heads of households is very low. Male breadwinners can still provide for their families, which then soak up youth unemployment. The average Spanish unmarried young man leaves the familial home only at the age of twenty-eight. However, there are serious limits to how far this approach can go. Female partici-pation in employment in these countries is generally low: it limits women's opportunities to gain satisfaction at work and so underutilizes the talents of creative and well-educated women. Job protection rules for those already employed make it more difficult to create jobs for those without work, espe-cially in the service sector. As a result long-term unemploy-ment is higher than in countries with more flexible labour markets. In addition, as young people leave home later and marry later, families are having fewer children. The traditional family is becoming less fertile, which in turn helps to under-mine the future financing of the welfare state. There will be fewer future workers to pay pensions.

These drawbacks are one reason why in the US and the

UK especially there has been a different approach. In both countries two-earner families increasingly predominate among those in work – with both adults in a family working for a living, out of choice or necessity. Families with single breadwinners are becoming rarer. Women's demands for satisfaction through work and desire for financial independence are a big driver. But in addition economics plays an increasingly critical role, especially for those with fewer skills and less education. Work in the modern service economy is often less well paid than comparable jobs in manufacturing and more risky than it used to be. The best way for a family to protect itself against the instability of a single breadwinner losing their job is for both adults to work. This spreads the risk and allows both adults to operate in social networks that link them to employment prospects: you are far more likely to find a new job if you are already in work or know someone who is. Two-earner households are far better equipped to cope with the insecurity the modern, flexible labour market creates for families. That is why in the UK one of the main thrusts of policy has been to open up opportunities for job creation and employment, especially in the service sector and among small firms.

But even well-paid two-earner couples find their working lives under strain. Adults frequently seem to have too little time for one another. Demands of work pull them in many different directions. Many women and men at work in the service sector stitch together a living from several part-time jobs. The burdens on the family, and expectations of it as a source of comfort, nurture and care, are growing just as its capacity to deliver is being reduced. Esping-Andersen again: 'Families, always a vital source of social support when markets fail are themselves now failing.' Children suffer when families live in poverty. That is why increasingly both parents go out to work. But the nature of modern work for two-earner families only creates other tensions, which often leave children poorly provided for. Family life is often tense because families are at the heart of a fierce contradiction. Marriages are less stable and children therefore experience higher risks of poverty that usually follow divorce. Costs of purchasing childcare are prohibitively high for poorer families. In *Sustaining the New Economy* Martin Cornoy sums it up:

The new workplace requires even more investment in knowledge than in the past, and families are crucial to such knowledge formation, especially for children but also for adults. The new workplace however contributes to greater instability in the child centred family, degrading the very institution that is vital for future economic development.

The most important social, and arguably the most important economic, policy for the knowledge economy is to put families on a more stable footing. Given the centrality of the family to social and economic well-being and given the strain traditional family models are under, there is an overwhelming case for public support for innovation that helps new kinds of family units, more suited to modern conditions. The old model of the traditional family and its relationship to work is no longer tenable. Families have changed enormously and so has the nature of employment. We need a new relationship between work and family life, that works for companies, parents and children. Some of the outlines of what the family might become in the knowledge economy are becoming clearer. There will be considerable and growing diversity of family types and lifestyles. More people will be single in future, either through choice or divorce and separation. There will be more step-parent families and more one-parent families. Genetics and reproductive technologies will change the options for birth and child-rearing. More single people are likely to become parents by choice. Same-sex couples will bring up their own children, at least in the US. Global companies and welfare systems will be dealing with a widening array of possible family forms and so with a widening range of demands to reconcile work and relationships. There is no 'one-size-fits-all' solution.

The family of the future will be based on couples as its 'core'. Most of these couples will be men and women. They will play more symmetrical roles, both working and taking care of children, than they have in the past. Families are becoming more networked. Two-earner couples will rely increasingly for childcare on paid help – nannies, child minders, cleaners – as well as relatives, especially grandparents, and nearby friends. Promoting this service economy to sustain the modern family is a vital policy. Home will be partially reintegrated into the system of production. For many it will become a place of work, as well as leisure, as people use computers from home to work. Services to make it easier for parents to work from home will be vital. People will experience more changes in family circumstances through their lifetimes: from being single to being married, having children, getting divorced, remarrying, leaving a career, etc. Helping people through these upheavals will also be vital.

The family will be one of the most controversial objects of public policy because it touches so many aspects of life. Families produce the basic raw material of the knowledge economy. Home is where the human capital is. The issue of how societies can develop a new family form to suit the needs and opportunities of the new knowledge economy will be with us for years. That is why serious companies need to engage with the issue of family support in an innovative and strategic fashion. Policies to promote and extend rights to parental leave are vital, as is a national network of childcare provision and more widespread availability of nursery places.

Stressed out parents need a better network of public and private support to be good parents and committed to their careers.

The role of the welfare state, at least in the eyes of its architects, was never to be the prime, still less the sole, provider of welfare. They believed the best recipe for promoting welfare was for families to have the resources to do so for themselves. That required policies of full employment and family stability. The welfare state was designed for a different world and needs far-reaching reform. But in a sense the aim should remain the same: to help parents provide for family stability and invest in their children's future, in a flexible labour market, where most jobs are in low-wage, low-productivity services. The welfare state's modern job is to help parents and families cope with the pressures and insecurity of the modern economy so that they can make good on their commitments to children, to invest in their minds and imaginations. The welfare state should operate at the point where the needs of the modern labour market and the needs of families collide to the detriment of children and so to the future human and social capital on which the knowledge economy depends. The welfare state needs to be bent, adapted and redirected to that goal. A step might be to dispense with the vocabulary of welfare and social security and instead focus on policies for learning and the family. Or to put it more bluntly: the best social policy for the knowledge economy is – women and children first.

8. The Age of Self-rule

When I was young our family had a single grey telephone, with a dial that clicked and whirred as you wound it round to make a call. It sat on a special table in our draughty hallway. Having the telephone in the hallway meant that telephone conversations did not penetrate into the heart of the house; the outside world was kept at bay. To use it, you had to sit on an uncomfortable, wooden straight-backed chair and stop whatever else you were doing – listening to music, watching television – to engage in a separate activity: making a telephone call. It was impossible to talk on the telephone while flicking through channels on the television. Its usage was strictly rationed until after 6 p.m. when off-peak rates came into force. I was in my twenties when I first made a telephone call of any length during the hours of daylight. Most remarkable, our family did not have its own telephone line. Ours was a 'party' line that we shared with a family two doors away. They could make a call only when we were not on the line. It was an arrangement neither family thought to question. The telephone was a scarce resource. We were lucky to have one.

Our household now, with two adults and four kids, ranging in age from two to eighteen, has multiple phone lines from cable television and ISDN, as well as a number of mobile telephones and several landlines. The telephone is not a narrow entry point through which the outside world can enter the house in strictly controlled bursts. The outside world constantly seeps into our house through multiple points of entry, and at all times of day and night. By the end of the average day, many of our handsets have migrated into the bedroom of our eighteen-year-old, Henrietta. By then she has access to more telephone processing power than the average BT exchange had a couple of decades ago. Abundant technology allows her to conduct her relationships with friends and develop a sense of herself in a quite different way from teen-agers of my generation.

The modern phone allows Henrietta far more privacy than I had when I was young. She can text or speak to her boyfriend several times an evening, from rooms of her choosing. Her voice mail allows her to screen out people she does not want to speak to. Arrangements, dates, deadlines, telephone numbers can be checked at will. But as well as allowing Henrietta more choice and discretion, abundant technology has allowed her and her friends to be far more sociable and collaborative. When I was her age, I used to have occasional, sometimes lengthy, conversations with particular friends. Henrietta is in constant communication with a host of people in a collective, criss-crossing conversation that might include gossip, discussions about television, sharing homework notes and making social arrangements. Henrietta and her friends are a telephonic tribe. They work, plan, judge and organize collaboratively. On a Friday night they graze across North London like an electronically orchestrated herd, coordinating their movements until they converge on the same place. At times it seems as if Henrietta cannot survive without being connected: she is anchored by her constant conversations. She and her friends are collaborative individualists.

The twentieth-century information and technology revol-ution will become a cultural and social revolution in the twenty-first century. As technology pervades our lives, pro-viding the medium in which we work and socialize, so it will change our sense of ourselves: what individuality means. The cause for optimism, it seems to me, is that in the decades to come the collaborative individualism which Henrietta has grown up with could become a much larger, if not dominant, part of our culture. In the closing decades of the twentieth century we were encouraged to celebrate a deformed and diminished version of atomistic individualism, associated almost entirely with the freedom to consume. Do not get me wrong: Henrietta's generation are great consumers. They like shopping. But they also want and expect something more than that. It is constitutive of their way of life that they are connected to and cooperate with others, and that these connections might stretch over long distances and even cultures. This younger generation, which grew up with new technology, expect to use it not just to shop but to express themselves. They aspire to a sense of individuality with creative self-expression at its core as much as consumerism. They want to be the authors of their lives, at work as much as in pleasure. The twenty-first century networked economy will provide fertile ground for the expansion of the scope of individualism, beyond consumerism. That is why we should feel optimistic.

The primacy of narrow, atomistic individualism is being challenged by a wide variety of currents even in cultures where it is dominant, let alone the many societies in Europe and Asia where individualism is not and likely will not be dominant. One of the chief contests of the twenty-first century will be over the possible varieties of individualism, narrow and broad, instrumental and creative, within different kinds of market-based societies. Free market policies have left us with the impression that the only possible form of individualism is the distorted ideal of individualism as consumerism. If that were true, it would be good grounds for pessimism. But that narrow individualism is far from the end of the story. Our aim should be to promote a far richer notion of individuality, in which collaboration, creativity and citizenship play a much larger role.

Utopian Individualism

The ideal of the autonomous, self-regulating individual is one of the most powerful cultural currents of our times. It is not only central to consumerism and markets but also to our moral standards. As the outstanding Canadian philosopher Charles Taylor explains in *Sources of the Self: The Making of Modern Identity*, a history of the rise of individualism, the development of this notion of the autonomous individual, who is due respect because they are capable of deciding their own aims in life, grounds our ideas about how society should be organized:

We as inheritors of this development feel peculiarly strongly the demand for universal justice and beneficence, are peculiarly sensitive to the claims of equality, feel the demands to freedom and self-rule as axiomatically justified, and put a very high priority on the avoidance of death and suffering.

The universal moral concerns and standards espoused by anti-globalization protesters arise from this Enlightenment ideal of the individual. Their criticism of globalization is that it leaves too many people so far short of the respect these moral standards imply. If we dispense with this ideal of individual autonomy, in favour of vaguer notions of community and faith, then we dispense with some of our most important moral intuitions, which should help provide some moral yardsticks for globalization.

This ideal of the autonomous individual is spreading around the world through markets, travel, communications and the practice of democracy. This idealized modern self does not take its role and purpose from an external authority, such as the Church or the army. It is a 'lone ranger' figure, who finds him or herself only when they are outside, or even at odds with, pre-ordained roles and codes. Our image of ourselves in western, liberal democratic societies, is largely that we are self-actualizing, rational, choosing agents. The more we can understand and realize our individual desires and aspirations, the truer we are to ourselves. The more we can cut ourselves off from extraneous influences the better, because that enhances our chances to understand our own inner drives and desires. For the philosopher Adam B. Seligman in *Modernity's Wager: Authority, the Self and Transcendence* the modern self is sacred: the ultimate source for moral authority comes from within, rather than from external religious or communal authority.

Modern technology will undoubtedly amplify the appeal of this notion of individualism and self-realization. Deregulation, the spread of markets and above all the power of technology have created unparalleled opportunities for us to explore and make choices. Medical technology allows us growing choice over when and how we have children and what qualities they have. Digital technology enables us to access services, news, music and entertainment of the kind we like, when we like. We can use the Internet to scour for the best deals. Political parties do not have a monopoly on political organization: increasingly people can organize themselves into campaigns and movements to pursue their interests. This culture of self-rule is spreading around the world with the power of communications. The Philippine government was recently brought down by a campaign orchestrated by text messaging on mobile telephones. A lively debate about the future of Iran is conducted on Yahoo sites on the Internet instead of in cafés in Tehran. China's attempts to control access to the Internet have themselves become the focus of democratic protest. As US Internet commentator Andrew Shapiro puts it in *The Control Revolution*: 'Technology does not just change how we process information, compute and communicate. It also changes who is in control of news, information, experiences and resources.' The Internet allows us to challenge the rights of powerful institutions to make choices on our behalf: increasingly we can do things for ourselves, from booking a holiday, to researching a drug, to questioning a politician. The Internet may be the technology that realizes the dream of the sovereign, self-sufficient individual. Shapiro says: 'To an unprecedented degree, we can decide what news and entertainment we're exposed to, whom we socialize with, how we earn, and even how goods are distributed and political outcomes reached. The potential for personal growth and social progress seems limitless.'

However, as Shapiro acknowledges, this explosion of personalized information and activities could well turn out to be a mixed blessing. An entirely personalized world, in which we never had to confront something unexpected, would be sterile. It would be like living within a self-imposed straitjacket. The spread of the Internet will extend the scope for individual choice but also intensify the doubts many already feel over the benefits of greater individualism.

The Destructive Self

Individualism is a curse for arch-pessimists, such as US strategic thinker Edward Luttwak, who argues in *Turbo Capitalism* that individualism, propelled by markets and encouraged by the moral relativism of an 'anything goes' culture, threatens to unravel society. Our bonds to one another, Luttwak claims, are becoming no more than contracts to be renegotiated at the drop of a hat. Excessive choice corrodes our character. It leaves us feeling uprooted and anchorless: we constantly have to rebuild the foundations for our sense of identity and self-worth. In a mainly service economy, all professions become a shallow performance to win consumer approval and get rich. Spin and style take over from substance.

These doubts about individualism focus on two main issues. First, how can a society of committed individualists sustain the levels of cooperation needed to tackle the increasingly intractable collective problems we face, such as the degradation of the environment? Second, how can people sustain a sense of meaning and purpose in their lives, if their identities are entirely defined by the shifting and shallow forces of consumerism? Take cooperation first.

The utopian, sovereign individual finds himself only by being at odds with communal authority, by standing out and being different. That is why 'being cool' has become so essential in popular culture. Yet under what conditions does this autonomous individual cooperate with others, or even recognize the need to address the collective consequences of a myriad of individual decisions: traffic congestion, environmental degradation, the social consequences of family breakdown, underfunded public services? A purely instrumental, atomistic individual engages in cooperation only when they absolutely have to, in a crisis or emergency, such as war, or in response to the threat of disease; when they are forced to do so by the coercive power of the state, for example, to pay taxes; when they choose to do so because cooperation furthers their own self-interest. The trouble is that none of these motives – crisis, coercion and contract – seems to provide a durable basis for the kind of sustained cooperation needed to fund shared public goods such as a first-class public transport system, good state education and a vibrant, open democracy. Strong communities probably need their citizens to make deeper and lasting commitments to one another based on belonging, duty, loyalty and passion as well as constantly recalculated, mutual self-interest. According to Taylor:

In a world of changing affiliations and relationships, the loss of substance, the increasing thinness of ties increases apace. A society of self-fulfillers, whose affiliations are more and more seen as revocable, cannot sustain the strong identification with the political community which public freedom needs . . . the extreme mobility and provisional nature of relationships can lead to a feeling of inhabiting a narrow band of time, with an unknown past and a foreshortened future.

To create a stronger sense of community without turning to coercion, or relying on a sense of crisis, we need to encourage a more rounded and socially engaged sense of individuality, one that recognizes social commitments without having them forced down our throat. We will create a more durable sense of community only if we build it on a spirit of individuality that recognizes the importance of wider social obligations and attachments. We cannot impose a sense of viable community on a society of narrow, selfish individualists. We need a different recipe.

The second problem created by narrow individualism is the shallowness of identities built largely on consumerism. I am not against consumption. Far from it: I cannot do without occasional bouts of shopping, especially for clothes. Shopping brings me great pleasure, and in the modern economy consumption is increasingly taking on new forms: when we share recipes, or swap music files, or watch videos, we are taking part in a process that is more like replication than straightforward consumption. Learning is increasingly becoming a leisure activity. Increasingly products are valued not just for their utility but for their brand: what they stand for. Each year, especially during the key religious festivals of modern life – school holidays – millions of people make a pilgrimage across Europe's well-worn routes to pay homage at the holy site of the brand: Disneyland. It is not just that Disney itself is a master brand but that everything associated with the experience is branded. People wear branded clothes and shoes. They eat at branded restaurants that sell food as part of an experience. Brands provide children's rites of passage: their first Nikes, an Adidas track suit, being photographed eating at Planet Hollywood, to freeze the magical moment when you became part of a brand experience. Brands now perform some of the functions of religious rituals. If we were to see ourselves entirely through the products and brands we consume, others – the brand masters – would be defining what we stand for. The ideal of individual self-rule is that we, and not corporate marketing departments, are in charge of making our identities. In truth, this overinvestment in brands probably afflicts only a narrow group of 'fashion victims', the ultras of the consumer economy, who cannot be satisfied without the latest thing. My sense is that most people have a self-knowing and critical attitude towards brands they enjoy.

However, slavish dependence upon brands is just one issue thrown up by identities built on consumption. The main shortcoming is that consumption is only one avenue down which we might find a sense of self-worth and achievement. Another major avenue is to explore our capacity for learning and creativity as the basis for our sense of self. Our parents and grandparents mostly worked in a largely industrial economy, dominated by hierarchical, large organizations, which offer little scope for self-management, initiative and creativity. In the old industrial economy work was necessity and consumption provided a realm of freedom. In the emerging knowledge economy, however, things could be quite different, at least for a significant share of the workforce, for a part of the time. Opportunities for self-expression through creative work and learning will expand. It is becoming more possible than it was in the industrial era for more people to imagine how they might express themselves through work and creativity. This could change, fundamentally, how we think of our identities. Work based on creativity and learning will become ever more important to our sense of self, alongside consumerism.

The Hybrid Individual

Two predictions seem relatively safe. First, thanks to the spreading power of communications and markets, individualism will continue to be a hugely powerful force in the decades to come. Second, the spread of individualism will provoke a series of reactions as people seek to address its shortcomings and downsides. It is far from clear what the products of this contest might be. One is certainly conflict. It is a distinct possibility that our culture will be shaped by its extremes, the clash of different fundamentalisms: the individualist fundamentalism of free market liberals and the appeal of anti-market, religious or nationalistic fundamentalism.[1] The September 11th attacks suggest that in the years to come a cultural stalemate between different value systems will sometimes flare into violence. Pessimists see only conflict, a clash of civilizations, ahead of us. Yet an optimistic account of the future is equally plausible, it seems to me. That optimism should be based on our ability to adapt our identities to these different pressures. The centrepiece of that adaptation could be a much more rounded notion of individuality, that embraces collaboration, creativity and citizenship. That would mean moving from an idea of individuality based purely on the exercise of choice and rights, to a broader notion of collaborative individualism in which people recognize that they bear responsibilities to one another. Rather than promote a diminished individualism based on consumerism we should encourage children to explore a sense of individuality that will find expression through creative work, learning and political engagement.

Creativity and collaboration, not consumerism, should be at the core of individualism in the knowledge economy of the twenty-first century.

So while there may be outright conflict between individualistic and communal cultures, there will also be a great deal of evolutionary adaptation that will spawn hybrid senses of identity. Modern identity, within western liberal democracies and in developing societies that are open to the market, will be a product of how different cultures mix, mingle and cross-fertilize: market individualism and citizenship will cross-fertilize with religious and ethnic attachments. This process of cross-fertilization will create new hybrid identities. There could be at least four different strands to these new varieties of individualism.

First, modern culture is creating a generation of highly collaborative individualists, such as Henrietta. Far from being atomistic, the new varieties of individualism are likely to be relational and cooperative. Much of what provides us with meaning in our lives comes from our non-contractual relationships with lovers, family, friends, neighbours. In these relationships obligations are not bartered or bargained. Technology will play a big role in developing these social connections in our lives. Far from becoming more isolated we may well engage in more relationships, with a wider range of people and with a much wider range of intensity. Thanks to technology, we can constantly connect to friends and family through phone, fax and e-mail. The modern, multi-media, networked society seems to be a riot of social interaction, rather than a place of isolated individualists. So much so that one fear is that we might become 'over-related': too rich in relationships. As US cultural commentator Kenneth Gergen puts it in *The Saturated Self: Dilemmas of Identity in Contemporary Life*: 'These relationships pull us in myriad directions, inviting us to play such a variety of roles that the very concept of an authentic self with knowable characteristics recedes from view. The fully saturated self becomes no self at all.'

To pessimists the connected self is no more than a node in many communication networks. Yet this fear that we might pass, within a generation, from breeding avid individualists to a generation that has no strong sense of their individual identity, seems overdone. Henrietta's generation of collaborative individualists want to be themselves and to work in teams; they like having their own style but they socialize in large groups and clubs. They are far more able, it seems to me, to understand and tolerate cultural and ethnic difference and to empathize with one another. In *The Protean Self: Human Resilience in the Age of Fragmentation* US academic Robert J. Lifton argues that the connected, collaborative self, with many overlapping relationships, multiple roles and even multiple personas, may well be a sensible adaptation to life in the constantly connected world. We should not mourn the passing of the utopian model of the self-sufficient, atomistic individual but instead welcome the fact that a sizeable chunk of young people seem to be finding ways to be more collaborative and more individualistic at the same time.

Second, people increasingly want to find a source of meaning in their lives that comes from outside themselves: a religion, membership of a community, taking part in a campaign, an attachment to a sense of history. That search will be part of modern identity, not a throwback to an older era. Creating our identities afresh, over again, from our own materials is very hard work. Instead of this entirely do-it-yourself individualism, we may well see more people choosing to invest part of their identity in causes which are larger than them. Just as people increasingly want hybrid solutions in technology, so that for example we use digital technology to deliver better versions of old music, so people will also look for hybrid solutions to find a sense of identity. While the modern idea of the choosing, sceptical, self-controlled self will spread, so it will mix and mingle, for example in large parts of Asia or in North Europe, with other sources of identity that provide people with a sense of community, belonging, meaning and moral purpose. The archetypal modern self developed by being at odds with the authority of religion. In future modern identity may increasingly adopt, adapt and accommodate religious and spiritual beliefs, within a modern setting. If people make a return to notions of faith, community and tradition in the next few years, as well they might, it may promote rigid fundamentalism in Islam and Christianity. Yet that is just one possibility. Another is that many people will find a particularly modern kind of religious identity: one that is chosen, open, questioning, plural and tolerant. This will be religion as an individual commitment and journey. Religion, faith and spiritualism may play a larger role in the lives of people who will also happily use mobile phones, drive flash cars, watch digital television and enjoy holidays in the sun.

One lesson for public policy is the importance of investing in civic spaces that provide the opportunity for spirituality and reflection. That means investing in art and culture, libraries and galleries. In a more technological world, art should play an ever more important role to help people express their deepest feelings. If we confront a complex, shifting, dynamic world with a language limited to webspeak and pop videos, we will always be in danger of disappearing down a cul de sac. We need a range of artistic expression that matches the complexity of the society we live in. Art has vital qualities that we can turn to in moments of confusion and crisis. Just as people turned to the television to help guide them through events after September 11th, so also they turned to art for qualities the media cannot provide. W. H. Auden's 'September 1 1939', an evocation of New York on the day

Germany invaded Poland, was among the first poems to be aired in the wake of the attacks.

The evolution of public memorials, for example, tells us something important about what we look for in modern expressions of spirituality. Memorials used to be religious symbols, or lifelike representations of heroes in action. Yet most modern memorials seem to be minimalist in tone and design: plain walls, blank boxes, empty chairs, on to which people can project their feelings. Almost without realizing it, minimalism, one of the most difficult forms of high art modernism, has become one of the main modern languages of popular memorial. Maya Lin's Vietnam memorial in Washington is an outstanding example. Peter Eisenmann's proposed holocaust memorial in Berlin, originally conceived with the sculptor Richard Serra, is a field of plain concrete pillars.

The open space for art to explore issues like love, war, work, science and terror cannot be managed in detail by anyone, including public policy makers. Artistic expression is being constantly reinvented, reinterpreted, refashioned, re-channelled and repackaged. While we should not seek to manage the open space for artistic expression, we can choose to fertilize it. In an increasingly secular western world, public, civic art will have a vital role to play to connect us to that sense of a deeper meaning. That is perhaps why we are in the midst of a worldwide museum building boom. Tate Modern, the Lowry and Walsall Art Gallery are our cathedrals.

Third, the new varieties of individualism will build on the desire for self-rule. People do not just want to be consumers; they also want to be governors, at least part of the time. Being a governor implies taking responsibility for the way you make choices; being prepared to be held to account for decisions which have a bearing on other people. We do not make choices in a moral or social vacuum. Increasingly people do not just want consumer choice; they want to be participants in the exercise of political power, they want to be part-time co-governors of society. Taking a role in governance implies taking responsibility for decisions that affect other people. Sorting out traffic congestion or global warming is not just an issue for politicians, it is something each of us has to address in the daily decisions we make. We cannot hope to have safer, cleaner streets, unless we as citizens are prepared to take some responsibility for making them safe and clean. We cannot expect the police to do it all on our behalf. Self-rule is about knowing when to make choices yourself and when to delegate that power to other people. It requires us to be open to the views of other people, with whom we may disagree, rather than lock ourselves away in our own personalized world. Thanks in large part to the spread of digital technology, we citizens and consumers have much greater power to make choices. The challenge will be how we educate ourselves to use this power creatively and responsibly.

If it suits us to consume information more directly, rather than through trusted intermediaries such as broadcasters, then we have more of a responsibility to check whether the information is true or not, before we pass it on. If we want to invest in stocks and shares directly, rather than going through a broker, we have to bear the risk. In the 1980s and 1990s the agenda of politics and culture was all about expanding choice. In the coming two decades, we will need equal emphasis on our capacity for self-rule: our capacity to make choices responsibly.

The fourth ingredient will be a much stronger emphasis on creativity, learning and productive work, voluntary and paid, as sources of satisfaction and achievement. Trends in the way we work will make creative individualism ever more important. As material consumption and production come to occupy less of a role in economic activity, so intangible personal assets, such as knowledge and creativity, will become more critical. For individuals, companies, regions and societies the critical determinants of wealth and well-being will increasingly be the way knowledge is produced, shared and used. The prime sources of poverty, both material and spiritual, are the lack of these immaterial assets that crucially affect people's quality of life. People without these personal assets have increasing difficulty in finding work that is well paid. Rich people can be wealthy but time-poor, stressed out and unhappy, materially well off but feeling spiritually impoverished. We should focus on promoting a work ethic based on our capacity for creativity.

The ethic of creative, productive individualism is being fed from both ends of society. Young people, especially those working in cultural and creative industries, regard work as an expression of themselves: they are working creatively, as well as earning a living. They want to negotiate an accommodation between creativity and commerce. Working for commercial clients is a price they are prepared to pay for a measure of independence and as an outlet for creativity. These young entrepreneurs in cultural industries are creative and collaborative individualists *par excellence*.[2] At the other end of the age range, new technologies, improved public health and medicines have helped to extend dramatically the average lifespan. People can now expect to live long and productive lives well beyond their retirement from formal employment. Increasingly people are turning to voluntary work and learning to find a sense of purpose beyond their first working life. The young, active, productive old will become a new social force in the next few years.

These immaterial and personal assets do not just include knowledge and skills. They also include: a capacity for self-expression; self-esteem and confidence; an appetite to learn, formally and informally; the ability to sense opportunity; the ability to get on with people from diverse backgrounds; a sense of self-respect and pride in where you come from. One of the most critical issues for public policy is how we make sure access to these personal assets is fair and equitable. A century ago the most important issues in terms of distribution of resources were about the physical and material conditions of life: 80 per cent of household consumption in countries that went on to become members of the Organization for Economic Cooperation and Development was accounted for by food, clothing and shelter. These ingredients now account for less than 30 per cent of OECD household consumption. Nobel prize-winning economist Robert William Fogel writes:

The *modernist* egalitarian agenda was based on material redistribution. The critical aspect of a *postmodern* egalitarian agenda is not the distribution of money income, or food, or shelter, or consumer durables. Although there are still glaring inadequacies in the distribution of material commodities that must be addressed, the most intractable maldistributions in rich countries such as the United States are in the realm of spiritual and immaterial assets.[3]

Self-esteem cannot be redistributed in the way income can. Attempts to do so deliberately in some parts of the US school system appear to have backfired. Governments cannot take knowledge and a sense of purpose from one group and give it to another. Addressing the maldistribution of these personal, intangible assets will require a massive investment in education and learning. Welfare programmes will increasingly have to focus on building up human and community capital, rather than simply transferring money to alleviate poverty. These 'assets of the spirit', as Fogel calls them, cannot be parcelled up and handed out; to a large extent they have to come from within. They have to be personally produced; they cannot be delivered by the state. This agenda also requires changes to the way we work and the way companies manage. Entrepreneurship and learning need to become mass, everyday activities.

The Evolution of Individualism

We like to think that modern societies are relatively free from the rituals that organize tribal societies. But our society is replete with rituals through which people go to find their sense of self. Henrietta, the heroine of this chapter, had at the time of writing, just embarked on one such ritual – the Gap Year – in which thousands of eighteen-year-olds leave home between school and university for an extended period of travelling and work abroad to start to find themselves. For those suffering from mid-life crises, bookshops groan with self-help manuals designed to help us unlock and master our inner selves. As Charles Taylor remarks modern people are always concerned with the question 'what is the meaning of life?' because in our age that meaning has to be individually created, with much hard work. Although ideas of community have become fashionable and appealing in the last ten years, it would be a complete mistake to think we should dispense with the ideal of individual self-rule.

This ideal of individual autonomy is deeply rooted in western culture. It is not the creation of modern consumerism and neo-liberal politics. Central to our ideas of justice, democracy, freedom, equality and empathy is the idea that individuals are due respect as sovereign and autonomous agents who are capable of making up their own minds rather than accepting instruction from higher authorities, whether those be religious, managerial or political. Our sense of our dignity and self-worth comes from considered self-control, not mere expression of hedonistic desire. Modern western liberal democratic society, for all its shortcomings, aspires to high standards of equality, justice and the relief of suffering because it seeks to uphold this ideal. Individual self-rule is not the reason why society is unravelling. Far from it: it is part of our moral bedrock.

However, in the last decades of the twentieth century individualism came to be defined in terms of the market and consumer choice, and against collectivism and state planning. Individualism was co-opted for political and commercial purposes. As a result the core story of individual self-rule has been debased at great cost. A society of atomistic, narrow, instrumental individualists would quickly undermine itself. People might well not invest enough in the public spaces, civic institutions and democratic processes that secure the public platforms on which people can play out their choices. Atomistic individualism, far from amounting to freedom, would create a vast fog in which we would find it increasingly difficult to discern how collective consequences, for good or ill, could be avoided or for that matter created by individual actions. We need to rescue the ideal of individual self-rule from this fate.

Just as the tide of narrow individualism remains powerful, so are the counter currents that will help us to create new varieties of individualism that promise to be richer and more rounded. These new varieties of individualism will be made up from several different strands. Atomistic individualism might rule the roost in America and to a lesser extent in England. But in Scotland and in North European and Asian societies it has not dug such deep roots. In societies such as Sweden, Denmark and Finland, where the state is more respected and community organization is stronger, individual-ism will take quite different forms from say in Essex or Cali-fornia. In Asia, corporate and consumer cultures from the US will mingle with older religious and communal traditions. The consumer individualism of the industrial economy was about promoting a sense of identity based around the possession of consumer durables to be enjoyed in a private space at home. The individualism of the networked economy will be far more relational, collaborative and sociable. Henrietta and her friends are both more individualistic and more naturally collaborative than their parents' generation. They have grown up with technology that allows them far more choice but also more sociability. They can lock themselves away in their rooms with their computers but they can also network, locally and globally, with many more people. They will do both.

Some people foresee an irreconcilable clash between individualism on the one hand and religion and community on the other. Many people, however, will try to reconcile the pull of these different forces and in the process create new hybrid forms of identity. People will turn to art, architecture, nature and wilderness to find a sense of the sacred within secular culture. Many people, to varying degrees of intensity, will look to wild nature as a moral standard. A century that may well be characterized by our growing power to manipulate genetic material, to extend choice, may also be marked by a growing reverence to the idea of 'nature' as a store of moral meanings. The prospect of these new varieties of individualism should make us feel at least mildly optimistic. A monoculture based on atomistic, instrumental individualism will not smother the world. Instead we are far more likely to witness individualisms that express themselves through religion, citizenship, creativity, community, crusades and campaigns. Individualism will evolve and adapt: from individualism as choice, to individualism as responsible self-rule; from consumerism to individualism as creativity; from atomistic individualism to collaborative individualism. The networked economy will allow us to create new forms of organization that are more decentralized and yet more coordinated. At the same time it will create huge opportunities for a more engaged, creative and collaborative individualism. With so much private investment going into creating the technologies of consumerism, public policy and investment should focus on creating the space for that creative and collaborative individualism to emerge.

9. The End of Capitalism

The end of capitalism is nigh. Well, perhaps not nigh, but the end is coming, slowly and almost certainly not through revolution. At the very peak of its powers, when capitalism had vanquished socialist planning, changes already set in train within modern capitalism were laying the seeds for its successors, variants of market-based societies that will emerge in the decades to come but which may not be capitalism. Indeed the very qualities that allowed capitalism to triumph over socialism – its greater capacity for innovation, learning, adaptation and invention – are the source of the new forms of market economy that could be post-capitalist. We should rejoice: by the mid point of the coming century a substantial proportion of the workforce of advanced market economies could be working in the market but outside capitalism. Let me explain why and how.

In capitalism markets are pervasive and workers are paid a wage to produce commodities which their employers own and sell. The distinctive feature of capitalism, as opposed to other forms of market exchange, is that work and labour itself become commodities, to be bought and sold. Karl Marx saw this as the source of the aggravated class antagonisms that would define capitalism. Either you own the means of production or you do not; either you are an employer or a worker. In the modern economy the embodiment of this relationship is the employment contract: the employee is hired by the employer and so has to accept the employer's authority to issue instructions, at least within certain limits. However, if firms and other organizations are not based on the employment contract, they do not count as capitalist firms. In volume 3 of *Capital* Marx said: 'Let us suppose the workers are themselves in possession of their respective means of production and exchange their commodities with one another. These commodities would not be products of capital.' If workers own their respective tools and machinery, on an individual or collective basis, and trade with one another, the system is not capitalism, according to Marx.

My argument is that the modern market economy is moving towards a future in which this will be true for more and more people, at least in the advanced economies and at least for part of their working lives. According to the economist Geoffrey Hodgson in *Economics and Utopia*: 'By definition, firms largely using genuinely self-employed workers are no longer capitalist firms. If such a practice became widespread then the socio-economic system would no longer be capitalist.' It would not be socialist either, because there would still be private property and markets. It would be a weird, hybrid evolution from capitalism.

Why should the modern economy be moving in this post-capitalist direction, at least for a substantial number of people? It is really very simple. As production processes become more complex and sophisticated, they require more knowledge and skill in the workforce. The driving force of economic growth is the capacity to learn, innovate and adapt. Thomas E. Cliffe Leslie observed more than a century ago that 'the movement of the economic world has been one from simplicity to complexity, from uniformity to diversity, from unbroken custom to change, and, therefore, from the known to the unknown'.[1] This puts a growing emphasis on the capacity to explore, learn, innovate and create. As the management academics Michael Porter and Claas van der Linde put it in 'Towards a New Conception of the Environment–Competitiveness Relationship': 'Detailed case studies of hundreds of industries, based in dozens of countries, reveal that internationally competitive companies are not those with the cheapest inputs or the largest scale, but those with the capacity to improve and innovate.' Success goes to those who are quick to learn and adapt. In a complex, open and dynamic system such as a knowledge-intensive modern market economy people have to learn and learn again how to adapt. The American specialist on work and technology Shoshona Zuboff said in *In the Age of the Smart Machine*: 'Learning is at the heart of productive activity . . . learning is the new labour.'

Marx foresaw capitalism as a continual process of deskilling. That is certainly part of the story, and remains so today in fast food outlets and service factories such as call centres. But work in the knowledge economy increasingly involves people applying their judgement, skills and creativity, personal assets that are beyond the complete control of employers. It is impossible to observe, monitor and instruct this kind of knowledge work in the way managers could when work was the completion of repetitive manual tasks. It is impossible to see, and so to manage in detail, what is going on in people's heads. The more that work involves the application of knowledge and creativity then, the more that traditional forms of managerial control are undermined, and with that the classic employment contract. It will be increasingly difficult to specify in advance what workers will be expected to contribute, when part of their role will be to innovate, create and adapt to unforeseen changes. Increasingly a significant share of the workforce will become akin to independent contractors, selling not themselves to a company but a service, outcome, capability or skill. Marx defined workers as those who did not own their means of production. But in a knowledge economy, in which technology is cheap and ideas are the source of value, more and more of the assets that matter will be owned by this new breed of independents. Firms will increasingly become alliances of these independent knowledge workers, brought together to jointly store, combine and create knowledge. The culture of work in these companies will have to be highly collaborative, to bring people together, voluntarily to share ideas. But it will also have to be based on respect for individuals, who ultimately own their own knowledge and skills, and who might choose to walk out of the door with those assets. The culture of work will have to be more social and more individualistic. The only way to make this work is if knowledge workers are increasingly able to self-manage their work. The employment contract that allows managers the right to issue instructions will become increasingly at odds with this emerging self-managing culture of knowledge work.

This does not mean that there will be no divisions between social classes, nor that inequality will disappear. But it does mean that for a growing number of people, working within a market economy, the classic employment contract will mutate into something quite different. That new relationship between workers and companies will have to recognize two key aspects of modern work: first, key knowledge assets are owned and controlled not by companies but ultimately by individual workers and second, these capabilities emerge from a social base of interaction and learning, that often goes on outside the firm. Firms will increasingly need to attend to these social and collaborative aspects of learning. This will be a hybrid economy of markets and private property, in which some aspects of work are post-capitalist and in which social aspects of life, particularly those that support learning and creativity become more important to the economy. It is not socialism, but nor is it red in tooth-and-claw capitalism. It will be a market economy with widespread individual ownership of key economic assets, mainly knowledge and skills, which in turn depend on a solid foundation of social institutions that promote education, learning and creativity. Hodgson sums it up like this:

Capitalism necessarily entails the widespread use of the employment relationship . . . yet transformative processes within capitalism are undermining this relationship. We are thus facing the possibility – no matter how long it may take – of modern capitalism being transformed into a system in which the employment relationship is no longer central. By common definition, such a system would no longer be capitalism.

The irony is that free market capitalism succeeded over the planned economy of socialism because of its superior capacity for innovation and learning. But the growing importance of knowledge and learning in time will corrode and outmode traditional capitalist forms of organization based around the employment contract. A different kind of economic system will be born, not from socialism, but from an evolution within capitalism.

This should be cause for considerable optimism. History is not over. The market capitalism of the 1980s and 1990s is not its end point, nor the exhaustion of alternatives to capitalism. It will provide the starting point for new kinds of market economy to emerge. Just as we should expect and hope for new varieties of individualism to emerge, so we should also expect different kinds of market society to evolve as well. We should not wax nostalgic at the evolutionary failure of state communism. It did not work. We should be thankful that such a mistake is unlikely to be made again. But nor should we succumb to a radical chic pessimism that the urge to create a more humane, post-capitalist economy is a spent force. In some respects we are in a better position to imagine a world in which more people spend more of their time in post-capitalist modes of work, albeit within a market economy.

Some people at least could be heading into a post-capitalist economy, of sorts. How do we expand this space beyond capitalism and ensure more people can occupy it? The answer is not revolution on the streets and workers' committees running the economy. At least two parts of the answer are about the nature of learning and work.

First, we have to promote a much wider distribution of key economic assets and capabilities, particularly the capacity to learn, so that more people have a chance to be in charge of their economic lives. Promoting a wider and lasting culture of learning, in which people become as used to learning as they are to washing, will be central to that. We need to promote learning driven by curiosity. Again this should be the cause for optimism. We have only just begun to take education seriously as a mass activity. We still do not do it terribly well. Even the UK has had a mass secondary education system for only a little more than fifty years and it is only in the last fifteen that higher education has become more than a minority pursuit. The pessimists like to bemoan the dumbing down of our high culture, without acknowledging that access to much of high culture was confined to an elite. In the next two decades we could see the flowering of a new mass culture of self-motivated learning. Culture is as likely to become more intelligent, curious and informed as it is to dumb down: another cause for optimism.

Second, knowledge and skills are not enough to allow people to exploit the opportunities for independent, post-capitalist forms of work. People also have to have confidence in themselves, the desire to claim authorship over their work and to see themselves, in small as much as large ways, as entrepreneurs, to sense opportunities and realize them. For that we need a whole range of reforms to make entrepreneurship and independent work a mass, everyday aspiration for most people, for at least part of their working lives. Work in the modern economy does not have to be relentlessly deskilled and humdrum. Increasingly people could claim greater control over their working lives, exert a sense of authorship at work and gain a feeling of achievement. Opportunities to organize work around life, rather than to organize life into the small areas left behind after work, will grow. All this should be grounds for optimism. The conditions for making independent work a possibility for most people start with learning.

Curiosity Culture

When did you last wash in a public bathhouse? I ask because public baths were part of the solution to the problems of public hygiene created by urbanization and industrialization in the nineteenth century. The way that problem was solved should help us understand what we need to do to create a society in which knowledge, information, education and learning are mass, everyday and even enjoyable activities, on a par with cooking, washing, eating and watching television.

To make that possible we need to create a mass culture of curiosity. To understand how such a culture might come about it is worth looking at how the culture of cleanliness emerged in the nineteenth century. The growth of cities and industry created a huge problem of cleanliness. The middle classes could afford to be clean. The working classes were dirty. That might have been fine when people lived in rural towns. But in large cities dirtiness posed a peril to public health. The solution was social innovation on a grand scale. Medical expertise developed to understand the importance of hygiene in preventing disease. Public works programmes, led by visionary engineers, delivered clean water and disposed of sewerage. Families that had washed only for special occasions learned to wash on a regular basis. Initially communal public baths were the solution. But thanks to plumbing, bathtubs and sinks, washing became a private and personal activity made possible by private enterprise: Lever's invention of the domestic bar of soap. In the space of a few decades Britain went from being a generally dirty to a mainly clean population thanks to this mixture of public infrastructure, social innovation and private enterprise, which created a mass culture of cleanliness. More than a century later cleanliness is not a chore but a pleasure.

Our attitude towards acquiring knowledge and learning is like the early Victorians' attitudes towards cleanliness before the advent of soap. Learning is often seen to be the preserve of a privileged elite. Until quite recently, very few people continued in education after leaving school. (Imagine a world in which 80 per cent of the population stopped washing for the rest of their lives at the age of eighteen.) Learning largely takes place in special zones outside the home. (Imagine all of us trooping off to the public bathhouse each evening before going to bed.) Education means accepting the instructions of older people. (Imagine being told by a public official which shampoo to use and when.)

The Victorians created a culture of cleanliness to cope with the demands of social and economic change. To adjust to the increasingly knowledge-driven economy, we have to do the same with curiosity and creativity. They have to become a taken for granted part of our everyday lives, which like washing, cooking and eating, are a source of pleasure as well as a necessity. The generation, acquisition and application of knowledge through learning, experimentation and innovation are critical to our economic, social and political lives. Economic growth is increasingly driven by the creation and application of new recipes: new ways to combine the ingredients of technology, software, people, buildings and equipment, to make us more productive and effective. If we want a prosperous society everyone should be able to play a role in making and enacting new recipes for the way they work, learn, shop, design, trade, save and entertain.

Knowledge also matters increasingly as a social glue. What we know and choose to inquire into helps to define who we are and what matters to us. Knowledge is vital to our sense of belonging. We identify with people who have the same passions, hobbies and interests. Knowledge is social: it is generated and validated through collaboration and debate. As local community has dwindled as a source of common identity so knowledge has become more important. Six out of ten people say they have more in common with people they share a hobby or an interest with than their neighbours. Local communities thrived not just on proximity but on shared viewpoints. These days we engage with people who share our view of the world without having to live next door to them. Sharing knowledge is the new basis for community.

How and why we acquire knowledge is also central to our sense of citizenship and so to democracy. For traditionalists, what we know is a defining badge of citizenship. Citizens should speak the home tongue, know key facts from history or be able to explain the meaning of the constitution. Radicals, on the other hand, argue that truth and knowledge emerge from open debate among intelligent, informed, compassionate people. To be a full citizen, the radicals argue, you have to be able to engage in democratic debate. These two views of the relationship between knowledge and citizenship coexist in our culture. The traditionalist agenda dominates in primary and secondary schools where education is largely a matter of being instructed in what adults decide you need to know. Even radicals who believe education should unlock the free spirit want their children to be able to write, spell, learn their times tables, get up when the bell goes and wait in line. This kind of education is about socializing us into the society around us. However, the radical view dominates in universities: after a period of enforced socialization up to the age of eighteen we are rewarded with a brief period of individuality before we have to submit ourselves to the authority of work and managers.

However, with the spread of the Internet, cheap communications and the media, the ideal of open inquiry, traditionally confined to an intellectual elite, is becoming a mass aspiration. A period in higher education is fast becoming the norm for young people. Expansion of opportunities to learn, explore, discover and inquire will help create a more open, participative and democratic culture. The problem facing public policy makers is not just to make the school system work better, the issue which has commanded most attention in the last two decades. The fundamental problem is this: the key asset on which our society rests economically and socially – knowledge – is created and shared by millions of individual investments each of us decides to make, across our working lives. How do we encourage millions of people, many of whom hated formal education, to see participation in the circulation of ideas and knowledge as exciting, rewarding and easy? Self-motivated learning is driven by curiosity. How do we excite a mass appetite for curiosity?

Consider the way the British palate has taken to Indian food over the last two decades. We are no longer frightened by exploration; we welcome it. Twenty years ago Indian food was a minority taste to be handled with great care, for fear of burning. Now curry is a central part of our lives. Somehow, we have to make curiosity as popular as curry over a similar timescale. That is why the main public policy response, policies for 'lifelong' learning, will not be enough. Valuable though these initiatives are they make learning sound like something that is done to you, but not an activity you would choose to undertake. To create a culture of curiosity we have to work with the grain of other tendencies in our culture. Adults will not accept top down models of learning. The curiosity culture is most likely to emerge out of the coming together of three trends: shopping, technology and individualism.

Shopping infiltrates every aspect of our lives. We have to mobilize consumerism in the name of curiosity. US shops outnumber primary and secondary schools by a factor of 10.3, libraries by twenty-five times and universities 252.9 times. For each UK university there are 2,174 shops. Most of us go to museums, hospitals, churches and libraries relatively rarely. In contrast all of us shop most weeks, most of our life.[2] Shopping has an essential quality the culture of curiosity desperately needs: an ability to attract people's attention. Shopping emerged as a mass activity at the end of the nineteenth century just as European societies began to take mass education seriously. Yet while many children are taught in Victorian school buildings, sometimes with recognizably Victorian methods, shopping has gone through several waves of innovation, from the Victorian arcades to department stores and supermarkets, to out of town malls, factory outlets and online retail. To keep people interested, shopping is in a constant process of reinvention. Learning will become a mass activity only when it acquires some of that capacity for innovation. But it cannot become shopping. Shopping can be episodic and fickle. Items can be bought, discarded, returned, traded in. Learning and curiosity in contrast require tenacity, patience and application. Learning starts only when people do it for themselves: it is about contributing rather than merely consuming.

The culture of curiosity has to use the abundance of technology to give free rein to imagination and curiosity. The Internet allows people to get at vastly more information than ever before. The culture of curiosity has already taken hold in health, for example. Finding out about illness has become a huge area for informal, online learning. The average patient can now question a doctor confidently about their diagnosis and treatment after spending a couple of hours on the net. Online learning programmes allow people to learn at the speed and in the style that suits them. Usage of these technologies takes off when people collaborate, to share files and swap information. The great successes of the Internet have been as much social as commercial innovations, largely self-governing, peer-to-peer file-sharing networks such as the music community Napster which had seventy million members at its peak. Of course we should not get myopically optimistic about new technologies. The familiar technology of television will play a critical role. According to a recent Henley Centre survey for the Discovery Channel 70 per cent of viewers use television to explore their special interests; 84 per cent to find out new things and 59 per cent to get ideas for things to do. Moreover, old technology in the form of teachers will still be vital. The drop-out rate on online learning courses in which there is no teacher support is well above 90 per cent. Learning is a social and emotional experience in which people feel anxious and excited. It needs to be conducted person-to-person as well as through a computer.

Finally we are exploring new links between intelligence and individuality. Thanks to educational psychologists such as Howard Gardner it is increasingly difficult to think of people as simply being 'smart' or 'stupid'. People display different kinds of intelligence that are drawn out in different settings. Traditionally intelligence has been associated almost exclusively with our rational and analytic capacities, which are promoted by an academic education. In the last decade, partly thanks to the work of writers such as Daniel Goleman, it has become clearer that we also have emotional, spatial, social and artistic intelligence.[3] For Howard Gardner, in *Intelligence Reframed: Multiple Intelligences for the 21st Century*, the unique potential of each individual rests on our ability to combine these intelligences in different ways, just as a painter combines colours. Learning needs to be organized around individual curiosity not just because we are all much more assertive consumers, but to respond to the individualized nature of intelligence. Of course there are limits to how far personalized education can and should go. Kids can be quite conformist. They often find it painful to stand out and be different. Education should not simply reflect people's prejudices and tastes. It should challenge as well as develop the way people tend to think. Respondents to the Henley Centre survey endorsed this: 78 per cent said people should learn subjects they are not interested in.

We need to shift from a public sector, top down, instructional model of learning to one that is driven by curiosity. We need to move from education as an obligation, to learning as leisure. In this world minimum standards of quality might be assured by officially appointed gatekeepers but above that minimum, as in other competitive markets, the decisions would be made by consumers, making choices and rewarding innovation. Standards would be set as much from below as from on high by unlocking individual aspirations and personal targets. Learning would not be a standardized product for a mass market but tailored to individual needs and kinds of intelligence. This cannot be a purely consumerist model. A curiosity culture would promote participatory and contributory learning, in which peers learn, often informally, from one another as well as from teachers and texts. Learning would take place anywhere that a taste for curiosity can be excited: a doctor's waiting room, airports, on trains, in football grounds, through computer games. The key is for people to learn because they want to and without thinking of it as a special activity. We have to forget 'learning' and focus on the satisfaction of curiosity. Such activity has to be exciting, emotive, personalized, participatory and carry over into the rest of your life. It cannot exist in a hermetically sealed box labelled 'education'.

In the Henley Centre survey 77 per cent of people said acquiring knowledge made them more adventurous; 80 per cent said knowledge was essential for them to lead a longer richer life; 72 per cent said what they knew was vital to their sense of individuality and self-confidence and 80 per cent said they got a feeling of excitement from expanding their horizons. The satisfaction of curiosity is part of the experience economy in which we value services for the experiences they give us, the way they quicken the pulse or provoke calm reflection. If public policy makers want to achieve their goal of promoting mass learning then they have to mobilize the power of entertainment, drama and television. Imagine a world in which we had maths taught to us by Celador, the makers of *Who Wants to Be a Millionaire?*; science explained to us by Bazal, the makers of *Ready Steady Cook*; biology explained by the team who made the *Blue Planet* series; the history curriculum explained by the *Time Team* and French taught to us through a soap opera such as *Friends*.

The need for television to play a larger educational role could not come at a more propitious time as the nature of television is changing fundamentally. We have been used to the set sitting in the corner of our living room, the faithful dumb receiver that brought us scheduled programmes at the flick of a button. By the end of this decade the television will be a complex tool. It will be connected to the outside world via high bandwidth pipes that will carry masses of content. The set top box controlling our TV will have a hard disk capable of taking perhaps 16,000 hours of content. The box will have the processing capacity and software of a powerful computer. The interactive remote control will allow us to reach out to the world, to share content with other people, as well as bringing it into our living rooms.

Children already learn a great deal, on their own, through digital means. The screen in the living room is fast becoming the delivery point for a plethora of audio-visual goods and services. One priority for education will be to equip children to participate, shape and have their own say in this world. The 'digital divide' is not simply to do with access to technology. It is also how much use people can make of this technology for their own ends. Children learn to use these media largely through trial and error – through exploration, experimentation and play – and collaboration with others both face-to-face and virtual. Computer game playing, for example, is a 'multi-literate' activity: it involves interpreting complex three-dimensional visual environments, reading both on-screen and off-screen texts (such as games magazines) and processing auditory information. In the world of computer games, success ultimately derives from the disciplined and committed acquisition of skills and knowledge. Much of this learning is carried out without explicit teaching: it involves active exploration, 'learning by doing', apprenticeship rather than direct instruction. Compared with the exciting and often demanding multimedia experiences children have at home, classroom work is bound to appear unexciting. There is a widening gulf between the styles of learning cultivated by formal schooling and those children engage in outside school experiences, for their own benefit. Children are increasingly immersed in a consumer culture that paints them as active and independent; yet in school, a great deal of their learning is passive and dependent. Our goal should not just be to enable children to learn by having fun using these technologies but to make sure they become at least as literate in digital media as they are in reading, writing and arithmetic. Children need to be able to evaluate and use information critically and creatively if they are to transform it into knowledge and embed it into their own work. Print literacy involves writing as well as reading. Digital literacy should involve using this technology for your own creative ends as well as consuming the information it delivers.

The intelligent television will sit in millions of living rooms and bedrooms. It will be far more ubiquitous and familiar than the computer. Its programming content will be far more compelling than the web. The intelligent television could be the centrepiece of a mass culture of curiosity. Is the current television industry capable of realizing the enormous social potential of the intelligent television? The answer is almost certainly not yet. The Henley Centre survey found that 50 per cent of people said there was nothing memorable about the last television programme they saw. Television needs to get its act together if it is to fulfil its potential as the centre of the culture of curiosity. In the year 2102 will people think that school buildings are as odd as we now think public bathhouses are? Perhaps, but only if we have the courage to trust and feed our appetite for curiosity as the motive for learning. We would have to look forward to a good lesson in the way that we now look forward to a good meal. In the coming century learning has to develop from being instruction and delivery of parcels of knowledge to the excitement and satisfaction of curiosity: a curiosity culture.

Authorship at Work

That approach to self-motivated, curiosity-driven learning will be all the more important because of changes to the character of work driven by the centrality of innovation. We live in an increasingly intangible economy, in which assets that cannot be weighed or shipped in railway cars – brands, ideas, software, relationships – deliver more value. The spread of information and communications networks means that new ideas and products travel faster than ever before to larger markets. Chief among those corporate assets is the combined intelligence and imagination of people who work for a company. Companies increasingly rest on their ability to excite and combine the intelligence and ideas of the people who work for them, to devise new products and services.

This innovation-driven economy spreads alarm as well as offering great promise of a better future. More rapid and discontinuous change means more upheaval and instability. For those in work that will mean more transitions between technologies, working practices, occupations and organizations. Many will find those transitions painful and unsettling. Capacities to cope with change – financial resources, inner confidence, the ability to sense new opportunities and learn new ways of earning a living – are not evenly spread. There are many places in the UK, places with skills and cultures of work that grew up around large employers in manufacturing, where people are completely cut off from the new economy. They are marooned.

This increasingly knowledge-driven economy will deliver quite different experiences of work for different people. It may spawn a liberated new generation of independent knowledge workers who are confident enough to demand decent rewards for their intellectual capital. But equally new technologies will allow more surveillance of service workers, 24/7. The boundaries between home and office are blurring for many professionals. That can both mean liberating flexibility or unwarranted intrusion. The new economy is creating a hyper-mobile, cosmopolitan workforce of highly skilled professionals. But at the same time there is evidence that more service jobs and micro-companies are working within local economies of tourism, retailing, leisure and entertainment.

The new world of work will mean quite different things for people with different skills, backgrounds and social networks. But several generic themes stand out which will shape all our working lives in future, and which our education and training system should be helping people to prepare for. One capability all people will need is creativity, to find and solve problems facing customers, for example. As innovation becomes more important, so should a capacity for creativity. Except the reality is that quite a lot of work will not be that creative, even though it may well require high skills and initiative. Creative people are often seen as slightly deviant. Globalization, competition and relentless pressures from financial markets mean that companies will not tolerate deviations from very demanding standards for performance and quality. As much as we might like to imagine that work will be more creative, it will also require meticulous attention to detail and quality. Another core capability will be the ability to work with new technology as more and more jobs will require a working knowledge of computers and communications. But most young people seem quite at home with computers. Indeed many learn so much under their own steam, often at home, that they find information technology lessons at school a bore. Many future jobs will be in human and personal services: education, healthcare, domestic services. Rather than promote yet more learning for technology in computer classes, we should perhaps invest in art and drama, music and sport, to develop human capacities for empathy, understanding and care.

In an economy driven by the generation, acquisition, application and exploitation of distinctive know-how, it would make sense to prepare people for work by making sure they study to a high level in some specialist areas, to build up a core of knowledge in maths and sciences for example. There is ample evidence that the British economy has been held back by a lack of research and technical skills in industry, for example. Yet as education improves in quality and more of the population gain degrees and professional qualifications there is a danger that we are entering a period of qualification inflation. Every vocation, profession and career is now accompanied by formal qualifications. Yet skills and capabilities that cannot be taught and standardized because they are based on tacit knowledge or lessons learned from experience, may matter more as formal knowledge becomes more important. Rather than encourage people to undergo more formal education before work, by starting school earlier and making formal education last longer, perhaps we should encourage young people to learn more outside school and beyond the classroom, to acquire the distinctive experiences and views on life which will really matter.

Perhaps most importantly we should aim to put most people in a position to claim authorship over their work. Let me explain what this capacity for 'authorship' means, before examining why it matters so much and how people can acquire it. The idea of authorship overlaps with many of the other ideas that swirl around the future of work: creativity, empowerment, self-employment and self-management. The idea of authorship at work means creating something which embodies your voice, your distinctive view of the world and the set of experiences that you bring to work. To see work as a process of authorship is to see it as a form of self-expression, not a task imposed upon you from the outside. When people are authors of their work, they feel they shape it and own it, in some sense. The craft that authors apply to their work gives them a sense of satisfaction and achievement. Work is a form of creative expression. Work involving authorship cannot be managed well through detailed attention to process and yardsticks. Authors need editors not managers. Providing people with the sense that they are authors of their own work means managing by outcome and deadline rather than by process and time keeping.

The value of authorship applies not just to a single job but to how people weave together careers in the modern labour market. Increasingly people are authors of their own careers, putting together the mix of training, assignments, projects and time off from work that best meets their aspirations. Thirty years ago more people might have seen their future working life as fitting themselves into a career template in a profession, trade or community. These days we want to be authors of our own career trajectories.

This culture of independent self-management, which allows people to see themselves reflected in their work, is increasingly central not just to so-called 'knowledge worker' jobs, for example in the professions, advertising and design, but also to front-line service jobs. In a world of automated call centres and electronic customer relationship management, customers will increasingly value human and social contact: staff who can take the time to understand and then respond to particular customer needs, rather than sticking to a crib sheet. The key capability that people must learn to acquire is how to exert a sense of authorship over their work and careers.

For many people cut off by change, left behind in communities created around manufacturing industries, access to work is still the critical issue. A humdrum job in a call centre with precious little sense of authorship is still better than no job. However, even in these jobs at the entry level of the labour market, initiative, problem solving and character will come to play a more important role. People who enter the job market in these 'service-factory' jobs will move on and into better paid forms of work only by developing a sense of authorship about their work. One of the deepest problems in areas long dependent upon large employers in manufacturing industries is that there is only a limited culture of self-employment.

People are not ready to think of working for themselves. They lack the confidence, skills, networks and finance to start a small business on their own. As well as seeking to provide more 'jobs' in these areas, we need to encourage a longer term social and cultural shift so that more people are better able to make and take opportunities for self-employment. People who are self-employed suffer from many forms of anxiety: the money might run out, key customers might fold, ideas might dry up, you might fall ill. Yet the difference when you are self-employed is that more of these anxieties are under your control. You can at least do something about them. The anxiety bred by working for a large company is that so little of your working life is under your control: the company might be taken over, reorganized, downsized. Life in large companies is made anxious by all the bureaucracy and rules: personnel reviews, strategic change programmes.

The most profound problem afflicting modern work, to use a rather unfashionable word, is a deep sense of alienation: the feeling that your work is not your own, it does not belong to you and does not reflect your values, desires and aspirations. This sense of alienation is at the heart of the central paradox that companies face in their approach to work. The global, always on, 24/7, financially driven market demands that work is highly organized and target-driven. Nothing can be left to chance. All costs have to be justified. No deviation from demanding standards for quality and productivity will be tolerated. Yet the growing need to compete through innovation and branding implies that work needs to be an open and creative process, to which people must feel personally committed. The 24/7 work culture, in which people never feel their time is quite their own, leads to a quiet withdrawal, a sense of reluctance or caution on the part of employees, which means they are less willing to engage in the kind of highly committed, creative work needed to drive innovation. The way out of this trap, for both companies and employees, is to encourage a sense of authorship at work.

For workers, the idea of authorship at work will become far more important as companies seek to appeal to successive generations brought up to value and articulate their sense of independence. This generation will also have more opportunities, through self-employment, extended study and micro-entrepreneurship, to pursue this sense of independence if employers do not provide it. The creativity and innovation demanded by the modern economy is impossible without work becoming a form of self-expression, at least some of the time. Entrepreneurship, the capacity to sense an opportunity and articulate it compellingly, often comes from having a distinctive view of the world. Entrepreneurs have a strong sense of authorship: they give voice to their ambitions through the kinds of companies they build.

In a world in which people are likely to have more than one career, more than one period of adult study or education, several different kinds of employment contract, it will be increasingly difficult for people to make sense of where their work life is headed by reference to external yardsticks. When I started work almost twenty years ago there was a template that budding journalists had to follow that provided some shape to their career. That has long gone. These days people need a much stronger inner sense of direction and purpose to shape their work amid much greater fluidity.

The most efficient organizations are those where people understand what they need to do, want to do it and, armed with the right information and incentives, get on with the job without being told to do so. Authorship and self-management are the keys not just to creativity but in the long run to reduced bureaucracy and improved efficiency. We live in a world in which companies cannot afford to have their costs and quality far out of line with global competition. Yet we also live in a world in which innovation and creativity matter so much that companies cannot afford to have a workforce that is disloyal, disengaged and alienated. In the long run, companies will square this circle only by creating a sense of authorship at work, so that people can see themselves reflected in their work, rather than simply working because it is demanded of them.

Authorship, like creativity, is a capacity that is very difficult to promote evenly. The British education system still struggles to deliver more quantifiable skills – literacy and numeracy – across all of society. So the chances of it delivering something as complex and intangible as a 'sense of authorship' are probably quite limited. While a sense of authorship might be developed and learned, it has to come from within. It cannot be taught and delivered from outside. And it takes time, trial, error and experimentation, as much in the 'real world' of work as in the classroom. Learning at school should increasingly teach children to sense opportunity and to seek and solve problems. They should learn how to borrow and abduct ideas from other disciplines and people to augment their own. As well as going to careers advisers, children need to be encouraged to become more able to understand and assess their own strengths and weaknesses. The more that work depends on a sense of inner direction, the more important it will be for people to be able to reach down inside themselves to understand what makes them tick. Systems of self-assessment will be as important in education in the future as external assessment in exams. Both the liberal arts and science will play a role in encouraging this sense of inquiry and self-expression. Learning needs to deliver a new mix of specialization and breadth. Specialization at later stages of schooling should reflect the ambitions and aspirations of children. But they should be expected to study a range of subjects organized around this special interest, because increasingly all careers will depend on being able to marshal knowledge from different disciplines. Perhaps above all education and learning need to inculcate a spirit of self-management. We assess children primarily on their ability to understand and follow instructions, to take and carry out orders, to deliver on tasks set for them. Increasingly we will need to assess them on the tasks they set for themselves, their ability to find and solve problems that motivate them and how well they manage their own work.

We will deliver that shift in the culture of learning only with very far-reaching changes in the way that schools and colleges are organized. The best schools already know how to excite a sense of personal commitment from students, within a framework for study set for them. The best schools encourage students to set demanding targets for themselves. They combine a clear sense of order and discipline with the engine of self-motivation and self-expression. Three fundamental changes stand out. First, education will have to become more personalized, to reflect the ambitions and motivations of children. We have to teach children from an early age to take responsibility for their own motivation and drive. We can do that only if they see in their education something vital to their sense of self and sense of achievement. Second, we need to promote a culture of self-management in learning, so that as children get older they self-manage their work, set their targets and are assessed by not just what they produce to order but what they come up with themselves. Third, that kind of learning needs to extend beyond the classroom. Kids learn at home, at play, in sport and drama. Learning to become the author of your own work can take place anywhere. Indeed, as schools are currently organized, the place it is least likely to happen in is the classroom.

Spreading this sense of authorship matters not just to the culture of work in companies, but because more people, at some stage of their lives, are likely to want to work for themselves or act as an entrepreneur. Entrepreneurship in the modern economy is less about heroic individuals and ever more about how people collaborate to form teams. Collaborative entrepreneurship is an activity more people can be drawn into, in large and small ways, without risking everything. The expansion of a culture of entrepreneurship, in which people can feel they make a difference, is another cause for optimism, because with it more people will get a sense of real achievement.

Entrepreneurship for All

We are used to thinking of entrepreneurs as special individuals, marketing visionaries such as Richard Branson, renegades and evangelists such as Anita Roddick, inventors such as Clive Sinclair, traders such as Alan Sugar or true consumer champions such as Stelios Haji-Ioannu of EasyEverything. This ideal of the entrepreneur, a charismatic, maverick, lone hero, is a myth we need to consign to the rubbish bin.

The basic entrepreneurial unit of the knowledge economy is not the individual but a partnership or team that brings together different skills and applies them to different stages of a venture's growth. Teams that combine different skills and know-how identify and exploit entrepreneurial opportunities to grow businesses.

Entrepreneurship has become a team-based activity because entrepreneurial ventures are built through several stages, often over several years. A single individual 'entrepreneur' may impart energy, vision and ambition to this process but he invariably lacks the complete mix of skills and know-how that a venture needs to move from one stage of its growth to another. The rise of the modern team-based entrepreneur is a prime example of the way in which modern creative work demands a culture of collaborative individualism. Modern collaborative entrepreneurship develops through six stages.[4]

First, successful knowledge-based businesses are built on distinctive knowledge that competitors will find hard to imitate. This knowledge base is most obvious in science-based businesses such as ARM, the Cambridge-based semiconductor maker, or Renovo, based at Manchester University, which is developing new treatments for scarring. But valuable knowledge is not always formal, technical or scientific. The knowledge at the core of a company's capability can be tacit or craft-based. Jez San's Argonaut Software, the computer games developer, for example, was built on the tacit, informal and untaught skills of computer games programmers.

The same is true for independents who trade on their know-how. Often the special know-how these independents have is not a skill, but particular knowledge of their customers and local markets. One accountant's skills may be no different from those of another. What distinguishes them is the intimacy of their knowledge of their customers and what they need. In a world in which self-employment becomes more common it is increasingly important for people to concentrate on what makes their service distinctive.

Second, entrepreneurs sense opportunities that others do not see. Entrepreneurship is in large part a process of experimentation, discovery and learning. The most impressive entrepreneurs do not simply move quickly to exploit a market that everyone thinks they can see. That was one of the problems with the first wave – more like a herd – of e-commerce companies. They all stampeded in the same direction. There was nothing entrepreneurial about the goldrush: it was a race. The best entrepreneurs go against the flow; the most impressive are those who can see an opportunity that most people overlook or doubt is there at all. Entrepreneurship is not just about speed: it is about doing something different.

Entrepreneurs sense opportunity by both seeking and scanning for ideas creatively and efficiently. They are hungry for new ideas, which they often acquire through their extended networks of friends, colleagues and contacts. They set out to seek new ideas; they do not expect them to land in their laps. They are not afraid to ask the dumb, naive questions that experts rarely ask but which can yield fundamental insights. Entrepreneurs scan information very efficiently. They need very little but high-quality information to make rapid decisions.

This process of seeking and scanning ideas to sense out opportunities is highly social. It is not something that can be done by trawling through public databases or working with published material. It depends on whom you know and how you can tap into their ideas. That is just one reason why entrepreneurs cannot be loners: they need to be highly social to learn about new opportunities. Most entrepreneurs do not come up with their best ideas sitting at home in a darkened room. They hungrily devour information.

Entrepreneurs thrive amid a consensus of doubt and scepticism that holds other people back. The best are able to spot emerging trends from the fog of uncertainty that often surrounds new technologies and emerging markets. In a sense they are masters of precognition: armed with a minimum of information they can work out quickly and confidently what is going on around them. Often the original inventor of an idea – a scientist, boffin or geek – cannot really see its commercial potential. That is why so many impressive companies are built on partnerships that bring together an inventor, who has valuable and distinctive know-how, and a business entrepreneur, who can see its commercial potential. The experimental process of trial and error often takes a long time. Entrepreneurship is an activity in which things rarely go according to plan. Instead business plans and models have to be tested, revised and rewritten as entrepreneurs sense, adapt and respond to changes in the environment as new competitors emerge, technology develops or markets implode. The initial concept might come from a flash of genius. But turning an entrepreneur's wishful thinking into something more realistic generally takes years of hard slog.

Third, to be successful a company has to package its know-how in a form that it can exploit. Having a good generic technology or skill is not good enough. Knowledge has to be turned into something that can be used over and again, very easily, by consumers and without allowing competitors the chance to imitate your core capability. A good example is Cambridge Display Technologies, which make a new kind of screen for computers, televisions and mobile telephones, based on a plastic that emits light. The original discovery was made by a chemist and a physicist working together to explore the potential for plastic in semi-conductors. Despite the promise of its technology CDT has, until recently, struggled to make commercial progress because it had a generic technology but not a specific product. The company made commercial progress only once it realized it needed to work in partnership with other companies, such as Epson the printer manufacturer, that could help to turn the generic technology into a saleable product. Often an idea can be packaged into commercial form only if it is taken out of the hands of the original inventors and put into the hands of people with skills in marketing, manufacturing and distribution. Invariably at this stage the original founding partnership of inventor and entrepreneur has to be expanded to accommodate more people. It is a tricky transition.

Fourth, a company can turn a concept into a business only by mobilizing additional resources behind it. Entrepreneurs excel at rallying money, people and resources to their cause. Knowledge entrepreneurs are ideas and purpose in search of assets and resources. Large companies are generally assets and resources in search of ideas and purpose. To mobilize resources entrepreneurial teams need to be multi-lingual: they have to be good storytellers, to communicate the excitement of the project; they need to be able to communicate to investors in financial numbers; they need to be good networkers and negotiators to form the right partnerships. A lone professional can achieve a lot these days working on their own, using the Internet and with e-mail. But increasingly independents are being recruited to play a role in larger corporate teams and projects. And one asset that independents can bring to these teams is a network of other people with different skills who might play a role. Self-employed networks work on favours and referrals. To succeed it helps to be part of one. Socialize to survive.

Fifth, entrepreneurs act confidently in the face of uncertainties and doubts that put off other people. This requires a blend of confidence and flexibility, vision and opportunism. Entrepreneurs have to show great confidence in the idea behind their business, especially when a company is only small. That confidence rarely comes from having a detailed strategy. It comes from a sense of commitment and self-belief in the project. Yet entrepreneurs also have to be flexible as market conditions change, new competitors emerge and investor sentiment shifts. As an entrepreneurial team expands to focus more on delivery, the founder entrepreneur's job becomes one of inspiration: to give the team a sense of confidence, mission and purpose. Entrepreneurs must thrive amid the uncertainty and doubt that would alarm or exhaust more risk-averse people. They have to believe in what they are doing far more than the average corporate manager.

That sense of inner confidence can come from extreme youth: entrepreneurs who have never seen trouble before do not know when they should feel frightened. The likes of Jez

San, founder of Argonaut Software, who authored his first hit computer game while he was still at school, fit this bill. Yet confidence can also come from wide experience: having seen it all before. The likes of Robin Saxby, the seasoned chief executive of ARM, the semi-conductor company, fit this bill.

Sixth, entrepreneurs need to know when to start to pull back from a business they have created. The entrepreneur who can spot an opportunity is not necessarily the best person to lead a company into a more mature phase of growth. An entrepreneur can only succeed by being deeply committed to their company. No wonder then that persuading that person that their contribution is no longer needed is one of the most difficult jobs in business.

'Meet my boss, he's two'

Modern capitalism is not the end point but a stage in evolution. It has laid the seeds for its own successors, which will mutate and evolve into different kinds of market economies in future. Many varieties of market economies should be possible. It should be a cause for optimism for us that these changes could be at work from within the market economy. As knowledge, learning and innovation become more important to products and services, so more of us will be in at least partial control of key assets – ideas and know-how, the immaterial means of production. That in turn should allow more of us, for more of the time, to work in new, possibly post-capitalist forms of self-employment and production. Post-capitalism will not emerge through revolution but through evolution from within. It will not transform the entire system but at least create habitats that people can make their lives in, as part of the market economy but outside what Marx called capitalist relations of production. We have only just begun to educate ourselves and to see learning as a source of personal growth and self-realization on a mass scale, rather than as an imposition and obligation. Far from our culture dumbing down, as the pessimists would have it, it is just as likely that we will see a flowering of adult learning, inquiry and curiosity. Increasingly collaborative forms of entrepreneurship, in which teams get together to take risks, will give more people opportunities to join in and enjoy the sense of achievement entrepreneurship brings. More people will be able to feel they had a go, took a risk, made something happen. Firms that want to be both efficient and creative will find the only way to achieve that is by promoting a culture of authorship and self-management at work. All these developments should be seen as grounds for optimism.

I am not going to pretend that working for yourself as an independent will suit everyone. I make it work, just, because as a writer I can do so from home and I like working largely by myself a lot of the time. Nor am I going to pretend that it is nirvana. Independent work comes with anxieties about money. If you do not get off your backside and attract clients no one else will do it for you. If you do get a good client you can quickly become complacent and you are vulnerable when they decide to change strategy. I miss some aspects of working in an office, mainly the gossip, flirting and joking. I became an independent only after a long period working for large organizations such as the *Financial Times*, where I learned important skills and made contacts. I started with enough savings to get me through the first six months without earning very much.

My sense is that despite these drawbacks, more of us will spend part of our working lives as an independent. Young people value the sense of autonomy that independent work brings with it. Falling prices of computing and communications make it ever more possible for people to work for themselves, but to collaborate with others. Working for yourself is a risky business, but at least the risk is in your own hands and you will not be downsized without warning. Working for yourself as an independent has drawbacks. But the benefits, at least in my experience, are enormous. My commute to work is about five metres. I do not get memos from anyone. I do not have to attend interminable budget meetings. I do not have to pretend my boss is both brilliant and a really nice person. I do not have to endure twice-yearly 360 degree, career review meetings at the end of which I have to write down on a piece of paper my key goals for the coming six months. I get more valuable work done in an average day than I did in three days in an office. I never, ever, go to breakfast meetings. The only people who come into my room and boss me around are my kids. The person most likely to storm into my room to tell me what to do is my youngest son, who is two years old. He is one of the best managers I have had. I will leave you to decide whether or not this is post-capitalism. But it is a lot better than working for a corporation run by men in suits.

10. The Personalized Society

Imagine what it would be like if it was easy to buy a kit from somewhere such as Ikea and build, in your back garden, a reliable, small vertical take off plane. Everyone would be taking to the air to get around. The skies would be buzzing with small planes. Ground transportation, at least in cities, would become increasingly rare. Everyone would be free to take their own, direct routes to wherever they were going, to school, work or the shops, disregarding the rigidities of the earthbound road system. The scope for travel would be dramatically increased. Traffic jams would be a thing of the past. People would be able to fly around, above or below slower moving planes. Quite quickly, probably, people would develop their own codes and protocols to avoid crashing into one another. Customs from road travel, such as indicating when turning, would be adapted for city flying. Private entrepreneurs would quickly spot opportunities for plane parking lots, navigational aids and other equipment to make flying safer. But with many thousands of mini planes landing and taking off, there would be bound to be accidents. There would be a need for some kind of public regulation of low flying air space, for safety's sake at least.

That picture of the city skyscape populated by a mass of mini flying machines is roughly speaking what modern liberal societies are like. Ever more people are taking to the air on their own journeys through a potentially vast space that allows for much more diversity, exploration and individualization. But there will be no air traffic systems, no radar and landing strips. In time it would be evident that everyone would be better off with a modicum of public regulation and some shared facilities. That is the challenge we face: we have to find ways to collaborate and to some extent coordinate a multitude of different activities and aspirations, without quashing choice or extinguishing experimentation. The central challenge facing us is how diverse, market-based societies, in which people prize choice and individuality, can cohere around a sense of civic purpose and obligations to one another. That requires far more than just having efficient public services. It requires a sense of commitment, belonging and passion about civic values and public institutions – schools, hospitals, libraries, parks, museums and forums of democratic debate and decision making. That commitment is impossible unless citizens feel they have a direct stake and opportunities to participate in the life of these institutions. Renewing this civic realm of democracy and civic institutions will be vital to feed a credible sense of optimism about the future.

Optimism has to have a public and democratic dimension, not least because the supposed decline of the civic realm is such a vital ingredient in the current chronic pessimism. According to the pessimists, the sadly reduced state of democracy does not provide us with the tools for self-rule, but delivers us into the control of unscrupulous politicians and their paymasters in big business. To pessimists, politics is an increasingly vapid contest between parties that are not prepared to challenge the status quo. Political debate has been reduced to a spectacle of personality and soundbite in which debate about fundamental issues is largely sidelined. As a result, it should be no surprise that respect for politicians is in decline and with it trust in the political process. Democracy is in decline and the wider civic realm is being drained of its distinctive ethos and values by the growth of privatization, public–private partnerships and the injection of commercial values into public life. Thirty years ago public servants were looked up to even if they were not well paid. They were held in esteem for their intelligence and sense of public duty. Nowadays they seem bedraggled, trailing along in the slow lane. Most importantly, in the UK at least, critical public services seem in a dreadful state: trains often do not run at all, let alone on time; London's mass transit system is ageing; schools are falling to bits; the litany of failure goes on.

This account of the decline of democracy and civic institutions is plausible but mistaken. That is not to say that the current state of politics is perfect or even uplifting. The state of the British public sector, especially compared to continental Europe, is dispiriting. But in thirty or forty years' time we may look back and realize that we were living through a period in which the conditions for democracy around the world became far more fertile. Arguably we are not living through the death of democracy nor its silent takeover by corporations, but the flowering of a much richer democratic culture of self-expression and organization, in large part enabled by technology. As with education so it is with democracy: we have only just got started. There is a lot more to come. Even in the UK the universal suffrage is a fairly recent creation. If we look at our culture, rather than the formal institutions of official party politics, we see a far more democratic, less deferential society in which people enabled by plentiful communications are far more able to find information, express themselves, challenge power and come together to organize themselves in political activity. Of course, there are many ways in which this culture of democracy could turn sour: growing transparency could erode privacy; vested interests in government and business will attempt to control spaces for debate; direct democracy could lead to push button populism. But if we can be aware of these potential pitfalls and guard against them, there is no reason why we should not witness an expansion of democratic political activity in the first half of the twenty-first century. The case for optimism is as strong if not stronger than the case for gloom.

It is equally possible that we could witness a renewal of civic spirit and public values. Much of what gives us quality of life, especially in materially rich societies – health, a clean environment, opportunities to learn and take leisure, to enjoy culture – depends on civic spaces and public institutions. This social infrastructure will only become more important as knowledge, innovation and creativity become more important to economic growth and improving well-being. The key capabilities of the knowledge-driven economy – the ability to apply knowledge, make judgements, identify and solve complex problems, work creatively with people from diverse backgrounds – are all socially created. We develop these abilities through learning, play, work, drama and music. The knowledge economy is built on social foundations: that is why public services will remain so critical.

In this respect Britain in particular faces daunting problems. The systems of welfare provision and education, in particular, seem increasingly unable to tackle chronic problems. In 1997 when Labour came to power the social security budget was £100 billion and yet poverty was rising. A third of children were living in families earning less than half the average income. Ten million adults were living in households with an income less than half the average, including four million children, three times the number in France. About 80 per cent of children from middle-class homes go on to university, compared with only 14 per cent from working-class homes. About 36 per cent of people on state benefits cannot read and write properly. After more than a century of universal primary education more than seven million adults, a fifth of the working-age population, are functionally illiterate. Four out of ten young people who go through the New Deal training scheme cannot read well enough to understand the instructions on a medicine bottle. There is an intimate connection between poor education, poor job prospects, low earnings, dependency on benefits and likelihood of being involved in crime, at least for young men. If we want to create an economy of equal opportunity, in which most jobs are in services and most well-paid jobs are in knowledge-intensive activities, then we need a welfare and education system that attacks these chronic social problems at their root in families and communities.

That is why our ability to adapt and innovate in our public services, particularly in education, family policy, childcare and welfare, will be so vital to our future economic prospects and to create greater equality of capability and opportunity. A modernized, adaptive, problem-solving welfare state is not a drain on a modern knowledge economy but in many respects a precondition for it, as outstanding examples of successful adaptation in Holland, Sweden and Finland show. These innovative, high-tech welfare state societies are not models that can be picked up and copied elsewhere. But the evolution of their welfare and education systems, to adapt to a more globalized, service-based and technology-driven economy, does provide one important lesson. An innovative, high-tech economy, rich in the use of the Internet and mobile phones, that trades globally and creates conditions for entrepreneurship does not have to be harsh, divisive and exclusive, if its public institutions can adapt to change. The key determinant of social success then is not just the rate of innovation and entrepreneurship in the private sector but the rate of innovation and adaptation in the public sector.

The second half of this chapter sets out some of the principles which should guide public service reform, and against which the current government's mainly managerialist, target-driven strategy for renewing public services should be judged. But before doing that let us examine the prospects for expanding the space for democracy.

Votes Unlimited

The conditions for the spread of democracy are growing more promising worldwide. One of the fundamental building blocks of democracy is education. Participation in basic junior school is now near universal, apart from some regions in Africa where it runs at about 75 per cent. Between 1960 and 1995, according to UNESCO, the proportion of children allowed to attend school rose by 80 per cent around the world. Illiteracy still affects a large number of adults, as many as 700 million perhaps, but it is falling fast. About three quarters of adults born in 1926 in developing countries were illiterate. Illiteracy among those born in 1970 in those countries runs at about 25 per cent. The biggest issues in education are to do with girls and poverty. Girls make up 65 per cent of those not allowed to attend school. In many countries the poorest are the least able and least likely to gain an education because families cannot afford to do without the wage of young children or the rewards from education are too limited. Only in the last fifty years have we begun to take education seriously on a global scale. In the next fifty years it is highly likely that access to at least secondary education will become a near universal entitlement. When the spread of education is combined with low costs of acquiring, sharing and publishing information, the stage is set for a rapid spread of democratic culture.[1]

A century ago women were excluded from the suffrage and large swathes of the world were ruled by colonial empires. That is unthinkable today. The growth of global trade in goods and investment, coupled with more educated and informed populations, has made life increasingly hard for separatist dictatorships. According to the US think-tank the Freedom House, 3.5 billion people, 60 per cent of the population, live in the world's 120 democracies which have multi-party political systems and universal adult suffrage. About 2.5 billion people live in societies described as 'free', which guarantee the rule of law and open debate. When information and ideas are freely available tyrannies find it much harder to sustain themselves. The Internet will be a huge tool for democracy in the twenty-first century because it will promote self-expression and self-organization. The economist Amartya Sen has shown how vital it is to a sense of well-being that people not only have choices but also the capability to exercise them. The spread of education and democracy not only opens up choice but will help spread those capabilities. Democracy is an engine for economic development. Democracies are far more likely to trade with one another than go to war with one another. According to Sen societies that hold democratic elections and have a free press are far less likely to suffer a famine than those that lack these democratic features. Education and the free flow of information are the engines for democracy and democracy in turn helps to drive economic development. Technology will play a vital role in enabling this virtuous circle in future, expanding our horizons, giving us the opportunity to graze across vast fields of abundant information and organize ourselves to make our voices heard.

While the dot.com dream may have turned to nightmare, at least for the time being, the utopian political hopes invested in the Internet have not dimmed so much. James Fallows, the US media commentator, sums up that utopian appeal in 'He's Got Mail':

Elections will become more about 'issues' as voters can more easily investigate each candidate's position. Government will become more honest, as the role of money is exposed. People in different cultures will become more tolerant, as they build electronic contacts across traditional borders. Tyrants will lose their grip, as the people they oppress gain allies in the outside world and use the Internet to circumvent censorship. Liberal democracies will govern with a lighter hand, as information technology makes them more efficient and responsive.

Technology should be an elixir for tired democracies.

Well, not according to Cass Sunstein, a law professor at the University of Chicago and perhaps the leading pessimist about the political impact of the Internet. In *republic.com* Sunstein argued that the Internet threatened to undermine freedom of democratic debate and expression. His argument is that democracy involves three crucial ingredients. First, people have to be exposed to unplanned encounters with people who have different opinions and views, whom they might find irritating and annoying. Democracy thrives on debate between competing points of view. Second, people who hold different points of view nevertheless have to share some common frames of reference, which provide a social glue and common standards of debate. This common glue has in part been provided by mass circulation newspapers, magazines and broadcast news media. Third, democracy is about more than merely voting. It is a never ending, unfolding process of debate and deliberation, punctuated by moments when people register their views through voting. The debate that takes place around a poll is at least as important as the poll itself to the long-term health of democracy. Democracy is not just a mechanism for totting up votes to provide a snapshot of aggregated opinions. Citizens have a duty to engage in deliberative debate to sustain democracy.

Sunstein's argument is that the Internet will make it far more difficult to fulfil these conditions. Democracy will begin to unravel. People will increasingly personalize their sources of news and views: they will live in electronic echo chambers that play back to them their own prejudices. As a result they are less and less likely to confront people with different views. When it is not promoting outright solipsism and isolationism, the Internet and the wider communications revolution in television and radio will fragment our common cultural space. Increasingly, as if we did not already, we will live in electronic enclaves, talking only to people who think, dress and talk like us. The common codes on which democracy depends will fragment. Finally, super fast modern technology will not promote the thoughtful deliberation on which democracy depends, instead democracy will be reduced to push button populism as people vote capriciously and at will from their sofas using their TV remote control. The political process will be reduced to something a bit like *Pop Idol* in which contenders are eliminated by a mixture of expert jury judgement (political pundits) and popular voting (opinion polls and focus groups).

Sunstein concludes his alarmist critique of the Internet with this impeccable statement of ill-thought-through pessimism:

I have stressed the severe problems, for individuals and societies alike, that are likely to be created by the practice of self insulation, by a situation in which many of us wall ourselves off from the concerns and opinions of fellow citizens. The ideal of consumer sovereignty, well represented in the supposedly utopian vision of complete 'personalization' could produce severe risks for democracy. Rather than a utopian vision it . . . would make self government less workable. In many ways it would reduce, not increase, freedom for the individuals involved. It would create a high degree of social fragmentation. It would make mutual understanding far more difficult.

What should we make of Sunstein's alarmism? Not much. In common with pessimists in other fields Sunstein uses a hefty dose of nostalgia in his argument against the Internet.

He talks wistfully about debates on street corners and in public parks. If Sunstein loitered in one of our nearby parks he would be offered something far more interesting than a debate. His alarm that the scope and reach of general interest news has been curtailed is overdone. Not only do Yahoo, AOL and MSN provide general news portals as their basic services but we can get news, day or night, from a growing variety of television and radio channels. While it is true that the television audience is fragmenting, it is also brought together by large news events. Sunstein's worry that people will use new technology to wall themselves in stems from naively accepting overoptimistic claims made for so-called 'personalization' technologies. In truth many of these services are rudimentary: they allow you to select from a common menu, rather as you do at a restaurant. They do not allow you to make up esoteric mixes of news that no one else gets. There is no evidence that the invention of the menu led to a catastrophic fragmentation of recipes, idiosyncratic eating habits and a disintegration of social capital. In food terms Sunstein's implication is that society would be a much stronger place if we all ate from the same limited selection at McDonald's.

On the contrary, the Internet is as much a tool for socialization, collaboration and cooperation as it is for personalization. It allows people to wander, meet other people and share stuff with them. Many of the most important political movements in the last forty years, which have expanded democracy, have come from self-organizing, collective action taken outside the political system: the civil rights movement, the women's movement, anti-apartheid. The Internet will only increase this capacity for self-organization, citizens' ability to challenge authority and have their voice heard by a mass audience. It is helping to unearth previously unheard voices and amplify them. One of the features of the Internet is how quickly it allows you to discover unexpected connections, how often you can find yourself somewhere other than where you expected to be.

As Fallows puts it:

Compared with most other indoor activities, time with the Internet is less filtered, more open ended, more likely to lead to surprises. If you read a book or a magazine you usually keep reading. If you watch a video you watch. But if you start looking up information of Web sites, you almost never end up where you expected.

The truth is, and this perhaps is what really alarms Sunstein, we will be living in a markedly less deferential, more participative, more democratic culture but we will likely treat formal democratic institutions and processes with far less reverence. David Weinberger predicts in *Small Pieces, Loosely Joined* that we will be less prepared to accept a diet of three square meals a day of news and information handed down to us and we will spend more time grazing, picking up mouthfuls from here and there, more socially rather than less. Democratic culture will be more open, energetic, unpredictable perhaps, but also more amorphous, messy, noisy and difficult to control. Indeed one of the most pressing problems will not be that there is too much personalization but too little privacy and protection from intrusion.

According to Jeffrey Rosen in *The Unwanted Gaze: The Destruction of Privacy in America* the danger is that we find ourselves increasingly defined by public soundbites of information – our postcode, credit rating, employment history – and our privacy is intruded upon by marketing and media. Telephone companies can already keep a detailed record of our movements and conversations. Credit card companies can say where we shop and what for. The government and banks have massive amounts of information about our financial affairs. Soon television companies will be able to work out in great detail what we watch and when thanks to the information we give to our personal digital video recorders. All this will allow companies to measure our lives out in numbers and transactions. They will have a more complete picture of what we do and with whom than many of our friends.

Rosen argues that a private refuge is essential for us to form intimate friendships, points of view of our own and so a sense of our individuality. Milan Kundera made the same point about the indecency of communism, which through constant surveillance turned private conversations and activities into public property. The sociologist Erving Goffman argues that we all need backstage areas of our lives, where we can allow the public mask to drop and be ourselves. Rosen for one fears these backstage areas are increasingly encroached upon by intrusions by the media as much as the government. This erosion of privacy and lack of control over how data about us and generated by us is used is a far greater threat to democracy than personalization, as Sunstein maintains. That is why we need stronger personal rights to control our own data, such as electronic health records, and to find out and question what data other people hold about us and how it is used.

The evolution of the Internet will have far-reaching implications for how government is organized, how people vote, scrutinize decisions, shape policy, pay taxes and access services. The best way to sum up what all that could mean for government is that government will probably have to become more porous, responsive and networked and work increasingly through partnerships with the voluntary, community and private sectors. A far-sighted report for the Dutch government, *Contract with the Future*, published in May 2000 put the challenge this way:

Almost every individual takes part in a number of networks, often totally different, and determines what role he or she plays in this network and for how long . . . Greater individual freedom of choice ensures that social networks remain flexible and dynamic. They can continue to exist only if they cater sufficiently to the needs of individual participants. In a network society, government is more frequently one of the players and will have to cooperate with others. Government action will increasingly have to be collaborative, interactive, fast and custom-made. Society is no longer the object of policy, but helps to shape government policy.

Channels for government and citizens to engage in dispute, debate and policy making will multiply with digital television and the Internet. Relationships will be more connected and perhaps less episodic: the Swedish government, for example, plans to collect tax directly from people's bank accounts electronically. It will be increasingly difficult, the report argues, to divide society into discrete blocks determined by ideology and religion, age and occupation. People will increasingly want to define themselves, and with that their relationships with government. Citizens will make greater demands on government. They will want more custom-made services, more options, more participation and more influence. The report concludes:

Government and citizens are increasingly operating in a network society in which they are becoming more and more equal and in which the strength of government is determined by the delivery of quality and by the joint creation and sharing of policy. Indeed policy can be said to be a co-production.

This more open, democratic culture is the setting in which we need to examine the renewal and revitalization of public services. It will be difficult to feel much sustained optimism about the future in Britain unless we can upgrade the public infrastructures for transport, education, health and welfare, upon which so much of our lives depend. The public perception across a range of public services is that they are run down and often deliver poor service, in part because customers have no alternative but to accept what they are given. Public offices operate inflexible opening hours, waste too much resource on internal bureaucracy and devote too little time and money to serving users. Staff are generally poorly paid and motivated, and so often do not care about the quality of service they provide. The physical facilities of many public services are in a demoralizing state of bad repair. It is difficult to feel optimistic about life if your journey to work every day is a nightmare, your child's school seems to be falling to bits, your parents cannot get a routine hernia operation for weeks and the local authority seems incapable of efficiently organizing even basic services. How should we modernize public services for a networked society that nevertheless prizes the idea of choice and self-rule?

The Apple of Public Service

When Steve Jobs set out to create the personal computer he did not start by drawing up 100 targets to make IBM's lumbering mainframes work faster. Jobs set out to create a radically different way to distribute computing power that would meet the still emergent needs of a new generation of users. Jobs's innovation did not meet an already evident need. It allowed people to articulate an emerging need. The Apple Mac was a radical innovation because it allowed consumers and producers to explore different ways to use computers in new ways, at home and in the office, to learn, communicate, share and trade.

The Apple story sums up a vital missing ingredient in the government's approach to modernizing public services. Much of the time the government seems intent on improving the public service 'mainframe' rather than taking the more innovative course of reconfiguring how public services are organized, funded, governed and consumed. The government faces two imperatives in its approach to public services. The first is an urgent managerial imperative to improve basic services that are lagging well behind public expectations. The second is a political imperative to recuperate the role of public services and civic values, in a society that is increasingly vocal, diverse, open, fluid and part of a global market. These two imperatives do not necessarily lead in the same direction.

Labour has chosen to tackle the immediate problems of public service underperformance with managerial measures that allocate money to public services with the aim of driving them to meet centrally set targets. For government insiders, the most successful initiative of Labour's first term was the literacy and numeracy hour, a massive, centrally driven effort to get the entire primary and junior school system to address an urgent need. In relatively short order a small and committed team at the Department for Education and Employment drove the entire state education system in a different direction. It was a huge undertaking and in many ways a success. The lessons are being digested in other departments. The outcome of this managerial crusade may well be more effective and consistent public services that are less likely to fail. But the costs could be a more centralized and controlled state machinery, with less room for creativity, innovation and initiative.

The managerial tools the government is mainly using to tackle underperformance could severely compromise the strategic goal of revitalizing public services to serve the kind of network society foreseen by the Dutch government. Britain needs a new generation of public services fit for a more open, diverse society, in which people want more choice and expect more opportunities to voice their views, needs and opinions.

We need to create a new generation of public services that can serve a mobile society, in which the nuclear family is in a minority, jobs are rarely for life, most people work flexible hours in the service sector, firms compete in global markets, life expectancy is increasing, education and learning last far longer, consumers are better informed, values are more diverse and people expect a say in what is going on. If you started from scratch to design services for such a public you would not come up with the public organizations that we have today, many of which are hierarchical, command and control style, mass producers of standardized services.

We need better management to deliver better quality basic services. That might pull public services up to scratch, but it will not renew public services in the long run. To achieve that, we need a wave of civic innovation to create services that inspire pride and loyalty, which speak for and sum up the spirit of the times. By relying on management tools of targets and central direction to solve the immediate problems of poor performance, the government is in danger of compromising the larger goal of creating public services that better suit the more open, fluid and diverse society they serve.

That is where Steve Jobs comes in. Only radical innovation of the kind that Jobs engaged in will allow the government to address both needs at the same time: to create effective services which also seem attractive, flexible and innovative. Of course that is far easier said than done. Steve Jobs had a series of advantages that government lacks. He started from a blank sheet of paper: a start-up in a garage. Government starts with a heavy inheritance of ingrained practices, organizations and cultures that are extremely difficult to change. Steve Jobs was able to enter a computer market that was relatively open to new entrants. The established incumbents, IBM and the other mainframe makers, could not stop Apple setting up in business. The room for new entrants in public sector markets is very limited. Many of the computer companies that were around when Jobs launched Apple – the so called Seven Dwarves, a group of mainframe manufacturers who were smaller than IBM – subsequently merged and went out of business. Public sector organizations, almost by definition, never fail so completely that they go under. In the private sector, entrepreneurs such as Jobs have at their disposal a range of techniques to raise capital and turn ideas into products, services, businesses and jobs. Crucially, he was able to recruit and reward a team of people who were prepared to share the risks of pursuing his visionary idea. In the most dynamic parts of the private sector, capital and talent is attracted to the most promising ideas. In the public sector, capital and talent are allocated according to a relatively centralized plan. In the public sector, it is very hard to rapidly pull together teams of people, with funding to develop an idea into a new product, service or organization. That happens the whole time in the private sector, within large companies and in start-ups.

Given these constraints it is not difficult to see why the government finds reform of public services such a daunting prospect. Many aspects of public services need radical renewal. Yet that impetus for reform has to come from inside the very systems and organizations, which are often widely seen to be failing, face little competition and have few opportunities, incentives and pressures for radical new thinking. No cavalry will charge to the public sector's rescue in the form of vastly improved funding to wish away its problems. Private sector finance and management may play a useful role but it is not a miracle cure. Technology, the delivery of government services electronically, will improve services in the long run but it is not a magic panacea. The stakes are very high. People depend upon public services for critical aspects of their lives: treating illness, dealing with crime, educating their children. Innovation invites the possibility of failure. Radical attempts at public policy innovation have often gone badly wrong: the Child Support Agency, Individual Learning Accounts, the National Air Traffic System, the 'AS' level, the poll tax and Railtrack are just some recent examples.

So there are good reasons why the government has adopted a managerial approach to the modernization of public services. The electorate does not want to wait for a greatly improved train system nor a shorter queue for routine operations. The public wants high standards in basic services that other societies seem to take for granted: operations done more quickly; streets policed more visibly and effectively; trains that run on time; teachers who are well trained, enthusiastic and committed. Citizens are far more aware of how British public services compare with those abroad and of the marked differences in performance between similar public organizations within the UK.

The government's main tool has been to set clearer central targets for public sector performance. The rationale for this is very sound. Until quite recently much of the public sector operated without clear targets. Targets have helped to focus effort in large and unwieldy bureaucracies. They have helped to get more information into the hands of users, for example through league tables that compare the performance of schools and hospitals. Taxpayers, politicians, managers and users can assess performance only if there are yardsticks against which it can be measured. Public service agreements between spending departments and the Treasury have created a new framework for assessing how well money is being spent. Three-year plans for public spending allow departments to avoid an unseemly annual scramble for resources.

Target setting, however, is in danger of reaching the point of diminishing returns. There are too many conflicting and detailed targets set by a central government machine that has become more diverse and powerful. These detailed targets often make staff on the ground feel as though they are not

trusted. Often public servants feel they are simply on a production line to deliver a series of central targets. Excessively
directive instructions that appear to treat front-line staff as
unable to think for themselves, untrustworthy or, worse,
incompetent undermine the very motivation and adaptability
on which good service depends.

To make sure that targets are being met, inspectors are
appointed. The inspection industry then creates its own
bureaucracy and anxiety. The UK public sector has a far
higher proportion of measurers, checkers and inspectors of
performance than most other countries. For every person who
delivers a service there seems to be another person looking
over their shoulder to check what they are doing. This shadow
workforce of inspectors is a giant machinery for second guess-
ing those working on the ground. The public sector is the
most regulated part of the British economy.

Ministers like to fund improvements in services not by
increasing 'core' funding but by announcing 'new initiatives'
that attract attention. Each new initiative is accompanied
by some targets, to ensure the money is being well spent.
Performance against each target has to be inspected and
reported upon. Targets drive efficiency within existing departments and services but do not make them more adept at
identifying and solving complex problems that span several
different services. The target set for putting existing public
services online by 2005 does nothing to encourage innovation
to create new kinds of services, for example.

Targets for public services will not work in many key areas
of policy because, as the Dutch recognized, government is
often only one among many players who jointly create a public
good such as better public health, a cleaner environment or
safer streets. Government efforts to improve the quality of life
depend on the behaviour of third parties – local authorities,
police, judiciary, voluntary sector and private contractors,

businesses large and small, as well as citizens themselves – who may not respond in straightforward ways to legislative commands, financial incentives or instructions. You cannot renew a community, create culture or revitalize public space by issuing a set of directives.

None of this is helped by an increasingly myopic culture of accountability as everyone runs in fear of the Public Accounts Committee, which checks how public money is being spent. The current approach to auditing public spending is too focused on: processes and rules rather than outcomes; micro issues rather than strategy; administration rather than entrepreneurship and innovation.

The target culture is being taken to excess and is in danger of becoming the enemy of change. As public investment goes up, there is a danger that bureaucracy goes up as well, at the expense of front line service delivery. A government that says it is focused on 'delivery' seems to underestimate the complexity and significance of the task of delivering services. At the heart of government people seem to believe delivery should automatically and mechanistically follow from central instructions. Too many targets, tied to too many initiatives, with too little consistency and too little clarity about priorities: these are the enemies of good service. The public sector needs targets to make sure resources are devoted to services that matter to consumers, but those targets need to be about outcomes and general priorities rather than micro-details and set within a framework of trust, long-term planning and flexibility to meet local circumstances, demands and opportunities.

There is a danger of a vicious circle setting in as the government responds to the public sector's failure to meet targets, with stronger centralizing measures to drive the machine even harder. When Labour came to power it found the centre of government, particularly around the Prime Minister's Office and the Cabinet Office, relatively weak in terms of long-term

strategic thinking and driving policy delivery. The Prime
Minister would ask for something to be done and find that he
had little scope to make sure it happened. The Prime Minister's
Policy Unit was one of the few tools the PM had to chase
delivery of policies with departments. But that meant people
in the Policy Unit had little time for long-term thinking. Nor
have demands on the state reduced. People still turn to the
state to take responsibility for solving a range of issues such
as family breakdown, community decay and crises in food
production. These issues can often flare up suddenly, accompanied by a media-driven panic – foot and mouth, BSE, the
MMR controversy. They are often sorted out – foot and
mouth is a prime example – only with extreme measures and
central coordination.

In the weeks after the 2001 election the government greatly
strengthened capacity at the centre to drive the rest of the
government machine more effectively. The centre of government now comprises several overlapping spheres. Around
Number 10 Downing Street, as well as the Policy Unit and the
Cabinet Office, there are now the Strategic Communications
Unit, the Centre for Management and Policy Studies, the
Performance and Innovation Unit, the Prime Minister's Forward Strategy Unit, the Delivery Unit and the Office of Public
Service Reform. In addition the Social Exclusion Unit and
the Office of the E Envoy (the senior civil servant responsible
for the adoption of the Internet within the government) report
directly to Number 10. As government departments compete
for resources on the basis of their long-term plans most departments have internal think-tanks, policy units and strategy
teams. As a result, the Treasury has also increased its capacity
for long-term policy thinking. The Chancellor has a team of
special advisers and a council of economic advisers, akin to a
policy unit.

Many aspects of this stronger centre have certainly proved

effective, chief among them the Performance and Innovation Unit. However, the centre of government has taken on a large number of roles – crisis management, target setting, driving delivery, medium- and long-term policy thinking, communications coordination. We now have not just a stronger centre but several competing centres of power. The rest of government does not know which way to jump until they get a decision from the centre, which can be an enormous bottleneck. While the quality of strategic thinking may go up, the ability to deliver on the ground may be further jeopardized if a stronger centre strangles local initiative.

The danger is that public services improve but at the cost of the government machine becoming more centralized, regulated and target-driven. It is a mark of the lack of coherence in the government's strategy for public sector reform that it emerged from the 2001 election carrying the belief that privatization and public–private partnerships were its 'big idea'. The idea of the private sector being involved in helping to deliver public policy goals is neither new, revolutionary nor big. It is just a sensible tool, with a long track record, some good and some bad. Our children read textbooks in schools published by commercial publishers. General practitioners are independent contractors within the NHS. They prescribe drugs made by private drug companies. Many essential public services – utilities and telecommunications – are now provided by regulated private sector companies. Even the use of private finance to create public infrastructures is hardly new: many of the infrastructures of the industrial economy were first established with private capital.

The further the government goes down a managerial route to modernization, replete with a battery of targets, performance indicators and long-term plans, the further away it could be drawn from renewing civic values in society. To achieve that we need not just a well managed state machine. We need to reconfigure public services: how they are owned, funded, managed and delivered. In the long run, only radical reform will allow the government to achieve both goals at the same time: to deliver much more efficient services from organizations that are designed for the more demanding, diverse and open society we live in.

Public services embody civic values. They distribute goods and services not according to ability to pay but according to need and desert, based on political decisions made about how resources should be used. Every act of using a public service or entering a civic space should underline civic values. Public services will thrive only if the values they embody are as vital to society. The problem is that too many public service organizations appear so out of kilter with the times. They seem designed for another era (as indeed many of them were) and for a different kind of 'public': one that was far more deferential, accepting and homogenous in its tastes and needs. That is why, as well as improving services through better management, we need a larger vision of a new generation of public services. What should those services look like?

Nine principles should be at the heart of a new generation of public services:

1. Above a basic minimum, public services should provide far more choice about types of service for a far more diverse population. The most fundamental challenge is how to create a sense of civic commitment in a society which is mobile and fluid, in which people want personal autonomy to define their version of the good life. Command and control systems of allocating goods and services, whether those be language lessons or heart operations, are at odds with this desire for autonomy and choice. In the long run we need an education system which is capable of delivering the basics to everyone, a smaller core national curriculum,

but is increasingly able also to deliver individualized educational programmes tailored to the specific needs and learning styles of different children. That would be an education system that promoted equality of opportunity and high standards in the basics, but also tapped into the individual aspiration and motivation of children.

The recent experience of public service broadcasting may be a harbinger of what could be to come for other public services. Public service broadcasting was first set up, back in the 1920s, to compensate for a chronic social and market failure. Most people were poorly educated and faced lives of drudgery. Original BBC, Reithian radio was a paternalistic exercise in adult education, in which entertainment was there simply to sugar the pill. These days people are much freer, better educated, far less willing to accept paternalistic direction. Public service broadcasting of a high-minded kind could command viewers even in the late 1980s because the industry was built on scarcity of channels, in which the priesthood of channel controllers could determine what was watched. Now thanks to digital technology, deregulation and vastly changed consumer expectations, people have many more sources of entertainment and information to choose from. Public service can no longer assume it will be dominant. It has to provide a distinctive service, based on innovation and commitment to quality, amid a sea of other options. The one-size-fits-all public service is as much of an anachronism as the BBC1 of the 1970s.

2. Modern consumers do not just want more choice, they want more say. They want a voice in the governance of services and they are not averse to playing a role in contributing to the creation and delivery of services. One distinction between many public and private services is that in public services the user is invariably an essential part

of the production process, a co-producer of the service. Education is useless without avid learners. People recover from operations only by taking exercise and eating properly. The tax system increasingly works thanks to self-assessment. Neighbourhood safety depends on neighbours who look after one another. We need not just a more effective police service but a society better able to police itself. Of course some public services are not like that. Benefits, for example, might best be delivered by a highly centralized system, akin to McDonald's. But most of the services that people value require user involvement to deliver.

We should extend the scope for responsible self-government in the way that services are designed. The most impressive examples of public renewal in schools start with the parents becoming more involved. The most fruitful areas for radical reforms in education, health, crime, welfare and business life will be where the drive for better government and the urge for local self-government converge, to combine the power and resources of the state with the strengths of local self-government to embed changes at the grass roots, gather local support and ideas and allow people to have a say in how policies affect them.

If the Labour government wants to be remembered for competence it should stick to modernizing government. If it wants to change the country it needs to unlock the desire for more self-government.

3. Public goods, such as health and education, are increasingly created in society. They are not delivered to waiting citizens from a state-run production line. These public goods are created by complex, mutually adaptive systems, in which the state is just one, large and often clumsy, player among many. The public services of the future will need to work with the grain of this complexity.

After a period in which markets have been opened up to allow more individual choice we are now trying to tackle the collective consequences: traffic congestion; unacceptably high levels of material waste in the environment; the insecurity of many public spaces; the implications for children of relationship breakdown. These collective issues can no longer be channelled and resolved through old-style authoritative public institutions that rationed choice and access to resources. Nor can they be solely resolved through the market, although market mechanisms, such as emissions trading vouchers and road pricing, will play a vital role in creating public goods.

How can government persuade households to change the way they use energy and recycle their waste? How can an education system offer a more diverse, individualized service while also providing common standards and a measure of equity? How can cities tackle traffic congestion? Clinging to old models of command and control as the basis for collective action to tackle questions like this will in the end become self-defeating. The challenge is to evolve new kinds of public institutions that can influence public behaviour amid its complexity, diversity and flux. Instructions from on high will not work.

4. Complex systems that create public goods need a capacity for constant evolution, adaptation and innovation. Innovation is the public sector's Achilles heel. It swings between occasional bouts of extremely high-risk, system-wide innovation, in which all eggs are thrown in the same, very large but fragile basket, and long periods of stasis when nothing much seems to change. Innovation often comes about only in response to a sense of crisis. Instead we need an evolutionary model of innovation.

   Evolutionary innovation involves at least six main

ingredients. First, the creation of diversity. In biology this comes about through genetic mutation. In public institutions it can come only from imagination, creativity and maverick entrepreneurship. As well as a stream for the promotion of high-flying young civil servants, we need a 'mavericks programme' in the public sector, to recruit and develop civic entrepreneurs. We should make it a rule that no one can get a job in the senior civil service if they have not been involved in some kind of start-up, inside or outside the public sector. Second, the selection of more promising developments. In biology this comes about through the force of natural selection: the fittest for the environment in question survive. In public policy, we need to set aside funds to invest systematically in developing promising pilots and models, across the public sector. The public sector invests far less in research, development, innovation and entrepreneurship than the private sector. One useful target would be to benchmark public sector investment in its innovation and R & D for public services, against private investment. Third, the best new ideas need to be able to spread and reproduce. In biology sex and genetics provide the transmission mechanism for successful mutations. In public policy we need much more rigorous and effective mechanisms to spread routines and the thinking behind best practices, including franchising good ideas and allowing more successful public organizations to take over others. Fourth, the unsuccessful must be allowed to fade out. Nature's approach, the survival of the fittest, would be the wrong approach in public policy, but the public sector needs to be far more effective in unlearning routines, practices and working methods which no longer deliver. Unlearning is as important as learning. Fifth, keep it simple. The most successful adaptations in nature tend to be very simple. The more complex an innovation the less likely it is to succeed.

Sixth, innovation is impossible without spare capacity, time and space. A perfectly honed machine, in which each part has a specific job, leaves no room for innovation.

5. The public sector of the future will need to exploit the networked forms of organization being created by a mixture of business and social innovation.

Government organization is still largely dominated by hierarchical structure, centralized command and control over resources, a workforce organized around rank and a chain of command in which scope for initiative is concentrated at the top. Networked organizations turn this model on its head. They operate with simple, centrally set rules, that allow decentralized decision making over how resources should be applied on the ground to meet users' needs.

The potential of the distributed technology of the Internet and related communications networks lies in the way they allow highly decentralized, independent activities to achieve a level of coordination traditionally associated with structured organizations. These networked organizations offer the promise of greater flexibility and adaptability combined with coordination and clarity of purpose. They should be more open and responsive to shifts in user demand and more innovative because they can draw on ideas from many sources outside the organization.

Digital technologies should allow us to create new relationships between government and citizens, services and their consumers, the state and other service providers, whether those are companies or voluntary organizations.

A good example is the impact digital television may have on the way we provide health services. Digital television should be near universal by the end of the decade. Information of the kind currently available on the Internet will be available through the television: the pilot digital health service run by Telewest, the cable television operator, has 18,000 pages of information, akin to that available on NHS Direct Online. The television should deliver interactive consultations in which a patient calling into NHS Direct, for example, should be able to see a nurse on screen who will be able to advise them on their symptoms. In time the video link on this service should become two-way so that the nurse and patient will be able to see one another. People recovering from surgery at home will be able to watch related programming to help them through physiotherapy. In time telecom links will allow doctors to remotely monitor a patient's vital signs.

However, developing these more advanced, interactive services with richer content will require the NHS to form partnerships with media, technology and broadcasting companies. The platforms for digital television delivery are mainly privately owned. The skills for creating attractive television content are outside the NHS. To exploit the health potential of digital television, the NHS will increasingly have to work in partnership with private sector providers. The potential for digital television will not be exploited by the state developing its own stand-alone service.

The Internet will also play its role. In the near future patients will be able to access information to compare the performance of different NHS Trusts, hospitals and even surgeons. Patients should be able to book appointments online, review their electronically held records and get electronic prescriptions. However, the greatest potential for the Internet may be in creating networks of self-help among carers and patients. These peer-to-peer applications would build on an already thriving self-help sector. A vast informal sector of family care, largely individualized and fragmented, cares for disabled relatives, the elderly, sick children and the mentally ill. Some 5.7 million people in Britain are unpaid carers. The informal care sector provides services worth perhaps £30 billion a year. Non-profit organizations are significant providers of residential care. One estimate is that there are perhaps between 2,000 and 3,000 such self-help groups in the UK, many of them organized around particular chronic diseases and conditions where special long-term treatment at home is required.

By 2010 it should be routine for a patient leaving hospital after an operation to be given: an NHS Direct telephone number to seek advice on recovery; a website address from which they can download relevant information, either through the Internet or digital television; a list of digital television programmes relevant to their recovery; an interactive television service through which they can see a nurse who will advise them while they talk over the telephone; a list of e-mail addresses for patients in their locality who have recently been through the same operation; the Internet address for a national self-help group which will provide support and advice. Already about 80 per cent of 'health incidents' are dealt with at home and surveys show that patients want more home-based healthcare. The advent of digital technology should make it possible to take some large strides away from a hospital-based healthcare system to a home-based one.

6. Future public services should explore new forms of community and mutual ownership and involvement to bring them closer to the people they serve and to gain access to additional finance. Modernization in this area may mean recuperating older, mutual ideas of how we should organize education, welfare and health.

Britain has a rich tradition of mutual self-help and voluntary organizations, from the Salvation Army to the VSO, from Barnardos to Water Aid. Millions of people are active in organizations as diverse as the CSV and the WRVS, the Territorial Army and the Police Specials. About 80,000 people serve in residents' associations. There are 350,000 school governors.

Mutuals play a critical role in providing many public goods: childcare and care for the elderly, adult education, the Workers Education Association and community safety, as well as pensions, life assurance and mortgages. Mutuals are organized for, and to some extent by, their members, who are also usually the owners of the organization. The mutual's members come together with the shared purpose of collectively providing a service from which they all benefit. One estimate is that mutuals, from trade unions to cooperatives, development associations to credit unions, building societies to community foundations, have a combined turnover of more than £25 billion a year, more than thirty million members and 250,000 employees.

The idea of mutuality combines the promise of social cohesion and collective action with the principle of decentralized self-organizations, within a market economy. Mutuals are often outside, and at odds with, the bureaucracy of the public sector, because they stress the value of voluntary and collaborative action. Yet the mutual ethos is also at odds with the individualism of the market. Mutuals are about people banding together to help one another. The mutual movement is based upon the instinct that in your own town, your own community, the solution to immediate problems of work, finance, housing, family instability and self-respect lies within your own grasp. We have to take responsibility for ourselves, together, rather than relying on the state to do the job.

Mutuals have distinct strengths and weaknesses, which stem from the way they involve their members and the quality of the service they provide. Mutuals can become inward-looking and conservative, serving their existing members at the expense of attracting new ones. Small mutuals can lack the scale to make the most of their skills. Large mutuals often have a highly diluted sense of membership. Yet the best mutuals can call upon the know-how and involvement of their members to help produce the service they then consume: Linux programmers are also Linux users. The membership of mutuals should be a source of innovation, new ideas and effort. Mutuals are not in business to serve shareholders and so should be more trusted than corporations. People often join a mutual or club because they share an interest with its other members.

The ethic behind the political modernization of public services should be mutuality: the state helping people come together to identify and resolve shared problems.

7. A more diverse, self-governing, networked and mutual state will evolve only if there is greater devolution of political power and managerial discretion.

The central job of politicians is to articulate the outcomes people expect public services to contribute to and to ensure as far as possible that systems are in place, both inside the state and outside, to deliver those outcomes. The more these outcomes can be decided upon by an open political process, in which people feel engaged, the more likely they are to attain legitimacy. That is why further devolution of political power to regions and cities to start making their own decisions and taking responsibility for their actions will have to be part of the agenda of public service modernization. The arcane dispute between the Labour government and the government of London over the financing of the tube stems from an incomplete process of devolution. London should have the power but also the responsibility of organizing a decent transport system.

Devolution of managerial responsibility will also be vital. Politicians should set general outcomes and basic standards for education, health, policing but beyond that the centre should not prescribe in detail how budgets should be spent and services should be organized. That should be left to local discretion. While the overall objectives might be the same, the way they are achieved in Newcastle and Newquay will be different. And increasingly the electors in those cities should be allowed to vary the outcomes they seek above and beyond the national minimum.

8. Public services must become much more adept at communicating the public value they create. One reason why the private sector is widely seen as being 'ahead' of the public sector is the investment in branding the private sector has made in the last decade, to persuade people to see products and services as part of a lifestyle they aspire to lead. Although the public sector has some outstanding, if slightly worn brands – the NHS, the Inland Revenue, the BBC – very few could claim to be aspirational.

One response to this failure to communicate public value is for the public sector to invest in advertising, new logos and marketing campaigns. But the best way to communicate public value is through tangible changes to the physical environment in which people work and take leisure. New buildings and public spaces should translate into improved services, a richer public space and a stronger sense of shared, civic purpose. In the past high-quality design of public buildings and utilities was one hallmark of the standing of the public sector: the original red phone boxes and the Routemaster bus are outstanding examples. In the nineteenth century public buildings embodied the rise of new public authorities that oversaw our lives: local authorities. In the postwar era the public sector was at the forefront of modernism and design, in buildings projects and the Royal Festival Hall. Equally, poor design, particularly of public housing in the sixties and seventies, cast a long shadow over the entire public sector. Those buildings symbolize all that was wrong with the cheap, mass public sector.

A new generation of public services needs new buildings and spaces to house them. New schools, hospitals, bus stations, parks and benefit offices should embody the civic spirit of the times. The danger is that new building and design programmes will be driven by a search for efficiency and shallow comparisons with the private sector: hospitals that feel like hotels; benefit offices that look like banks; canteens that mimic McDonald's. The award-winning new Peckham library, which embodies a confident sense of civic purpose, has seen book lending rise by 400 per cent since its opening. The best way to communicate distinctive civic values is to deploy design imagination into public buildings, spaces and products, as Tate Modern, the Millennium Bridge, the Walsall Art Gallery, the Eden Project and Huddersfield Football Stadium all show. Well designed public spaces excite people.

9. Culture and outlook matter as much as structure. The culture, working methods and outlook of the senior civil service is one of the biggest obstacles to change. We need a civil service that is recruited, paid, managed and organized to respond rapidly and creatively to public need.

The civil service needs to reduce its reliance on the intelligent generalist policy analysts, and recruit a greater diversity of people, with different skills and particularly with a background in management and service delivery. Value in public services is created at the front line by staff working with clients. Resources and pay need to be shifted away from central processing and bureaucracy to those who create value.

The civil service is perhaps the most hierarchical organization in a country that is increasingly less hierarchical. Access to meetings and information is determined by a series of ranks that is unfathomable to outsiders. That hierarchy needs to be broken up, for example through promotions and rewards for younger people with bright ideas and energy. Money, responsibility and opportunity should be shifted away from rewarding rank and length of service and towards rewarding contribution.

Increasingly the government's ability to deliver public policy goals will depend on its ability to orchestrate resources and people from across many different organizations, public, private and mutual, large and small, staff and consumers. The civil service, working with politicians, should be capable of orchestrating these alliances for change. The job of politicians is to provide leadership: the clarity of purpose to mobilize people around these goals. At the moment politicians are expected and often want to be in charge of every last detail. The job of the civil service should increasingly be to act as the 'prime contractor' for public services, to draw these different ingredients together and to drive projects forward. As a prime contractor the senior civil service can afford to be smaller than many of its suppliers, whether those suppliers provide policy advice, IT or other services. The civil service needs to excel at orchestrating these resources, in and outside the public sector, rather than providing them directly.

The pessimists argue that democracy is being corrupted and diminished. New technologies such as the Internet will only fragment society, turn politics into push button populism and allow more people to live in hermetically sealed worlds that only echo their prejudices. Meanwhile the public realm is being sold off to commerce, while public services continue to decline.

This is far too gloomy a prognosis. The prospects for democracy are very strong and arguably have never been stronger. Education is the raw material of democratic culture and it is spreading around the world while educational attainments are rising. The twenty-first century will be the first in which universal access to basic education is commonplace for a majority of children in the world. Not good enough, because many poor children and girls may still be excluded. But a step in the right direction. Electorates will be better informed and more able to make use of that information for their own political purposes. It will become ever harder for tyrants to maintain power by controlling media and communications to keep populations in ignorance. It will become much more difficult for leaders to lead populations on disastrous utopian political journeys, to fascism, communism or war. Messianic leaders will emerge, but they will be kept in check. Liberal democratic governments will be more open to scrutiny and public demands. Technology will allow some people to wall themselves into their echo chambers. But the main impact of the Internet will be to enable people to self-organize politically far more easily. Self-organizing social movements, sometimes local and specific, sometimes global, will be the more dynamic, disruptive and innovative forces in politics. Political parties and governments will often seem leaden-footed in response. This capacity for political self-organization will be vital to democracy.

It is becoming increasingly clear that the market extremism of the 1980s will not work in the public realm. A successful innovation-driven economy, which relies on the generation and application of knowledge, rests on a social base of investment in education, children, families and culture. The knowledge economy requires a social base: that is why public and civic services will be so vital. Many of the most important aspects of the quality of our lives in materially rich societies –

health, the environment, education, culture – depend on civic investment. Societies that want to promote equality of opportunity and social cohesion, in the midst of innovation and globalization, will need effective, well funded but adaptive welfare states. That is why across Europe societies have begun to embark on far-reaching reforms to public services and welfare states. While these are dismantling some historic legacies of inherited systems, they are in the long run paving the way for renewal. Welfare systems which have their roots in the late nineteenth century and a wave of reforms introduced after the Second World War are now entering a further, long and uneven process of reform, not just in the UK but in Sweden, Holland and Germany as well. While the first stage of that process has involved a focus on targets and management changes, the next stage will increasingly have to be about creating a new generation of services fit for a more diverse, open and demanding society. Far from marking the end of the civic sphere, as the pessimists claim, this could mark the start of its reinvention.

Above all, what we are witnessing, perhaps, is the attempt to find a new mix between individual and collective provision. For most of the twentieth century the idea of individual choice and collective provision were at odds. The civic sphere of the twenty-first century will increasingly have to find ways of combining them creatively. That is what I mean by the 'personalized society': we have to find ways to collaborate and to some extent coordinate a multitude of different activities and aspirations, without quashing choice or extinguishing experimentation. The central challenge facing us is how diverse market-based societies, in which people prize choice and individuality, can cohere around a sense of civic purpose and obligations to one another.

11. Globalization Can Be Good

The Baltic state of Lithuania has just become the world's first privatized nation state. The state airline was acquired, by mistake, by Dale Myers, an investor from Iowa, whose computerized stock trading programme accidentally built up a controlling stake. Lithuania's main port is controlled by a US conglomerate, Orfic Midland, and the central Bank is in hock to a bank in Atlanta, Georgia, which is itself in trouble. Most of these assets are now up for sale because the US investors have made such big losses elsewhere on their portfolio. Dale Myers has already sold most of Lithuanian Airlines' fleet to an air freight company in Miami and a commuter airline in Nova Scotia. The IMF, which encouraged Lithuania to privatize large chunks of its economy, now says the country is too small to be given emergency assistance to save it from economic collapse. It is twenty-eighth on the list of needy nations: the IMF says it will be eighteen months before its officials could focus on the Lithuanian crisis. But all is not lost. An entrepreneurial politician, Gitanas Misevicius, has launched the Free Market Party Company, which is planning to use money from foreign investors to buy enough votes to win the next election, after which everything down to the pavements and sewers, will be privatized. Investors will be able to have streets and parks named after them and have their portraits hung in the National Gallery in Vilnius.

That is one aspect of Jonathan Franzen's acid account of the effects of globalization in his novel *The Corrections*: markets out of control, public assets sold to the highest bidder, politicians deeply corrupt, companies toying with the future of entire nations. Globalization is one of the most ubiquitous, controversial and least understood forces. Its works, for good but mainly for ill, can be seen everywhere and yet the nature of globalization proves very difficult to pin down. No account of the future, whether pessimistic or optimistic, can be complete without an account of globalization: what it is, how it developed and what its effects are.

One feature of globalization is that we seem to be living in a more globalized economy, in which there is more trade and investment across national borders, to the extent that vital aspects of economic performance and policy have passed out of the hands of nation states and politicians, and into the hands of transnational markets and companies. It is not just that the volume of transnational trade and transactions has gone up dramatically but that as a result the locus of control over economic life has shifted on to a global plane. Since 1950 world trade has increased fourteenfold, far faster than the growth of world GDP which has increased by a factor of six. This was driven in large part in the last two decades by a dramatic increase in foreign direct investment as companies set up international production and distribution systems. Global foreign direct investment rose from about $57 billion in 1982 to $1,271 billion in the year 2000. As a result perhaps fifty of the world's top 100 economies are now companies, rather than countries. Trade within and between these companies is the driving force for world trade and investment. Sitting on top of that are global, constantly connected financial markets, which are so integrated they operate as a single twenty-four-hour financial market. The regulation of this global economy is increasingly in the hands of bodies such as the World Trade Organization and a few of the world's central bankers at the Federal Reserve Board in Washington and the European Central Bank in Frankfurt rather than national governments. As the economy has globalized so control of it has become more concentrated in a few hands, which are beyond normal democratic controls and operate at a global level.

The extent and novelty of economic globalization since the 1970s can be overstated. As Paul Hirst and Grahame Thompson point out in *Globalisation in Question* the world economy was just as integrated in the period 1870 to 1914 under the aegis of the British Empire and the stability of the Gold Standard. Although international trade and investment has increased markedly, most of these transactions are between already developed, rich economies. They are not genuinely global in reach. Genuinely transnational companies that are footloose and rootless are relatively rare. Most multinational companies have long-standing investments in their home or adopted territories. While nation states acting on their own may have less influence than they used to over some aspects of economic policy, such as interest rates, they still have considerable discretion over the level and structure of taxation. While the last twenty years have been a period of economic internationalization, in which national borders have become blurred, they have also been a period of nation building and rebuilding after the fall of communism. Arguably, there are now more nations with national economic policies than there were when the Soviet Union was operating what little was left of an integrated planned economy. The creation of regional trade blocs in Europe, Asia and America has been as important as genuinely global trade. Clearly, globalization is neither a simple process nor the only one at work in reshaping the economy.

But globalization is not just an economic process. We are in a period when the volume and velocity of cross border exchanges of all kinds – goods, services, investment, culture, people, food, pollution, crime, terror – is going up. In 1990 about 461 million international journeys were made; in 1998 there were 668 million. An increasing number of those journeys come from poor developing countries: up sixteen million to twenty-nine million over the period. While the Internet is still a minority pastime global usage is forecast to rise from 500 million users in the late 1990s to 700 million in 2003. Half of the world's population has never made a telephone call. But falling prices for communications bandwidth and technology should see that figure dramatically reduced in the next decade.

Globalization is as much a 'cultural' phenomenon as an economic one. We are increasingly likely and able to see ourselves in global terms, through our potential to access global communications and enjoy the fruits of diverse global cultures. Globalization is felt at home, in the changing texture of cultural life in major cities, as it is felt 'out there' in the rest of the world. Increasingly consumers in rich countries and workers in developing countries, investors and environmental activists, corporate executives and terrorists, are likely to see their actions in a global as well as a local context that provides opportunities as well as constraints. Globalization is a process of interconnection, in which national and local cultures are increasingly penetrating one another, through the medium of global exchange. The prospects for this cultural globalization are controversial. Pessimists argue it will lead to a growing convergence and even homogenization of culture around American norms. American culture will increasingly provide the operating systems for our societies from music and films to the conduct of democracy and the nature of political leadership. Globalization could spell growing cultural homogenization. Another possibility is that as well as promoting common standards where these are useful, such as Internet protocols and common air traffic procedures, globalization will allow for greater diversity, in which cultures will mingle and mate to create new hybrids. In addition, of course many people will seek to protect their distinctive culture or retreat from globalization into distinct local, regional or even fundamentalist identities.

There are many different ways to react to the idea of globalization, to resist it or accommodate it. Large multinational companies and global organizations are certainly powerful players in this process, but it is not a process they can control in detail, as if they were a kind of executive committee for global capitalism. Globalization is an open, evolutionary process in which there are many players, many possible niches, habitats and strategies for survival. It is very difficult to say in detail where it might lead.

The major exception to that is the anti-globalization movement, who are already convinced they know where we are headed. One of the ironies about globalization is that its power and coherence have been articulated most powerfully by its major critics, rather than its supporters. Although the idea may have started with management theorists such as Kenichi Ohmae and pronouncements from corporate executives and financiers, who talked about economic life beyond the reach of the nation state, in the last few years globalization has become a creature and a creation of its opponents. For these opponents globalization is a bogeyman that only voracious capitalists would dare to defend. For these deeply pessimistic critics, globalization is a very real but degenerative process in which the poor are being exploited, consumers manipulated and the environment devastated. Multinational companies with the help of weak-kneed governments are homogenizing our culture, privatizing all public space, eliminating cultural diversity, ruthlessly exploiting the already wretched of the earth as well as the earth itself. Globalization is blowing a gale of disorder across the planet, withering everything in its path, spreading anxiety, alarm and poverty wherever it goes. Globalization is the new Evil Empire.

One can find anti-globalization sentiments, in part as

anti-US sentiments, wherever one goes, from Russian and Japanese nationalists to disdainful French intellectuals and angst-ridden German social democrats, from Brazilian peasant farmers to English aristocratic environmentalists. In the last few years, the most vociferous and influential exponents have been the diverse and angry voices of the anti-globalization movement that has grown mainly in Europe and North and South America. The tone of their commentary is harsh, their vision of globalization nightmarish. In his analysis of the movement, *The Protest Ethic,* John Lloyd says that these mainly Anglo-American critics see themselves as being in the 'belly of the beast' of global capitalism. Their special insight justifies their sense of morally righteous rage. Lloyd sums up the movement thus:

They have established themselves as uncompromising, even apoca-lyptic, critics of capitalist globalisation. They are diverse, but tend to agree that the effects of globalisation . . . are harmful to the poor, to the environment and to animals. The only people who gain from globalisation are, they believe, the rich overwhelmingly concen-trated in the West.

And even they are often unwittingly victims of the system.

This ragbag networked alliance of protectionist trade unions, anarchists, leftists, environmentalists, animal rights protesters and concerned citizens have multi-authored one of the great narratives of our time: globalization is bad. They have a moral cause: exposing the misery, drudgery, helpless, silent oppression of much of the world's poorest people for the sake of efficiency, shareholders and consumer brands. This is politics with moral purpose, defenceless victims, big bad enemies and exciting tactics: street demonstrations. Even rela-tively mild-mannered exponents of the movement's philos-ophy employ powerful rhetorical techniques to get across their message. They paint globalization in Orwellian terms, as a force that insidiously controls our space – the public space we live and work in, which is draped in corporate logos, and the inner space of our imaginations, which is infiltrated with corporate symbols. In the name of consumer choice we are lured into a lock step conformity. They do not shy away from using the terminology of warfare: multinational companies are waging a war on our imaginations just as they are on the rights of working people. They encourage us to see ourselves as hapless victims and to search for the enemies and culprits who are to blame. We are powerless to stop a force that will carry apocalyptic consequences for the world. Our lives are increasingly beyond our control, either because globalization is out of control left to the collective whim of financial markets or because it is controlled by a tiny handful of people who are beyond the reach of national, democratic politics.

Jay Mazur, president of the US Union of Needletrade, Industrial and Textile Workers, put it thus in *Foreign Affairs*:

Millions of workers are losing out in a global economy that disrupts traditional economies and weakens the ability of government to assist them. They are left to fend for themselves within failed states, against destitution, famine and plagues. They are forced to migrate, to offer their labour at wages below the level of subsistence, sacrifice their children, sell their natural environment and often their personal health, all in a desperate struggle to survive.[1]

These common themes run through the very different key texts of the anti-globalization movement, among them the writing of Naomi Klein, the Canadian activist journalist, John Gray, the melancholic political theorist, and Michael Hardt and Antonio Negri, who write about globalization in metaphysical and abstract terms. It is worth briefly comparing and contrasting what they have to say. It is their case against globalization that a more optimistic account will have to answer.

In *False Dawn: The Delusions of Global Capitalism* Gray argues that transnational organizations, both corporations and regulatory bodies such as the WTO are seeking to incorporate the world's diverse economies into a single global market, producing social dislocation and instability on a massive scale. For Gray, the global free market stems from the same intellectual roots – a faith in reason and science – as communism. He goes as far as to suggest that in time the utopian pursuit of the free market may come to rival communism in the scale of the suffering it inflicts upon people, forcing peasants in their millions to become migrant labourers, excluding millions from work in the advanced economies, devastating the environment and handing some societies over to the control of organized crime. He talks of the global market in Orwellian terms, putting nonconforming societies under economic siege to change their ways. This is Gray's melancholy in full swing:

We stand on the brink not of the era of plenty that free marketers project, but a tragic epoch, in which anarchic market forces and shrinking natural resources drag sovereign states into ever more dangerous rivalries . . . The likelihood must be the laissez faire regime will not be reformed. Instead it will fracture and fragment, as mounting scarcities of resources and conflicts of interest among the world's great powers make international cooperation more difficult. A deepening international anarchy is the human prospect.

The age of globalization, Gray predicts, will be remembered, presumably by the few who survive, as another turn in the history of servitude.

Naomi Klein in *No Logo* is more limited in her focus on the role of corporate brands but as unrestrained in her rhetorical denunciations of globalization. Klein's argument is that competition in the global market has become so intense that all products are in danger of becoming disposable commodities. To defend against this, consumer goods companies in the last decade have sought to invest their products with new meaning in the form of brands that seek to connect with our longing for individuality, community, fitness, calm, well-being or wilderness. These brands encroach into the nooks and crevices of our lives irresistibly. We start to live our lives through them. Increasingly we have no alternative. These brand bullies such as Starbucks, Wal-Mart and Microsoft use ruthless commercial practices to drive out smaller producers and force suppliers to toe the line. The enemies of brands are national habits, local producers and regional tastes. Klein talks of a reign of logo terror in the lives of teenagers; of big companies waging war on small economies and consumers alike; of brands stripping host cultures of all their meaning, sucking the lifeblood from them as all barriers between marketing and culture are removed, leaving no room for unmarketed time and space. Brand culture is creating an army of teen clones all marching in step into the global mall, she says. Vast apparent consumer choice is everywhere combined with Orwellian restrictions on cultural production and public space. Products are now consumed because they appear to embody ideas, ideals and values. As a result, manufacturing has become so devalued and degraded as a process that it has become dispensable. US factories are closed and jobs exported to sweatshops in the developing world. Yet as consumer goods become clothed in idealistic brand values, so in turn that has exposed the companies that make them when it transpires that these idealistic promises are being produced in the sweatshops of Sumatra or Vietnam. Exposing that vast gap between apparent promise and dreadful reality has become the goal of a new generation of activists.

Michael Hardt, a US academic specializing in literary theory, and Antonio Negri, an Italian intellectual who has spent many years in jail for his support for left-wing terrorism in the 1970s, write in very different, and at times difficult, style in *Empire*. Hardt and Negri attempt to describe a world governed by a disembodied 'logic' of global markets and communications, in which no one, not even the US is in charge. The ruling logic of the market and the information society operates at all registers of our lives, from the global rules of organizations such as the WTO to the way we eat hamburgers; at every level it frames our expectations and values. This logic is spreading not through colonialism, not even through corporate coercion, but as a kind of virus, replicating and drawing in new territories the whole time. People get sucked into the logic of Empire, because there is little alternative and because it offers to satisfy their needs. It does not destroy or even annex territories but absorbs them into the system. Hardt and Negri argue that coercion of the old-fashioned kind would not work, because so much of the work, product and services of the new economy depends upon people's goodwill and choice to make it possible. They recognize that in particular, work in the networked information economy increasingly involves people applying their minds and brains. This kind of work cannot be coerced. The US may be the original model, main protagonist and main beneficiary of globalization but it cannot control this new disembodied Empire. The US can act to defend its own interests only by painting them in the terms of universal global interest in peace, growth and trade.

The anti-globalization movement has been a huge success. As an anti movement it has been able to bring together a huge diversity of people with different agendas and backgrounds, older international charities such as Oxfam and Save the Children Fund, environmental groups such as Greenpeace and

Friends of the Earth, indigenous people and pop stars, anarchists and elements of the Catholic Church, who nevertheless seem to share a common enemy, at least some of the time. As a movement it is difficult for politicians and business to deal with because it has no hierarchy, organization or leadership. It does not draw up policies or make specific demands that can be negotiated but when it does, for example over debt relief, it can achieve much progress. The lack of an agreed programme is a huge strength because it allows the constituent parts of the movement to slide over their differences; they do not have to set priorities or fall out over the terms of messy compromises. As a result it operates on an idealist plane, taking on what little is left of the broken rhetoric of socialism, and so operating beyond the reach of everyday politicians of the left. The movement is largely leaderless. However, it does have inspirational symbolic figures – Jose Bove, the French militant farmer, and Bono, the pop singer, for example. It has none of the paraphernalia of political parties, of membership systems, branches and annual conferences. Anyone with a computer, an Internet connection and a passion can join in. The movement makes its position known through symbolic and emotive actions: trampling fields of genetically modified crops, smuggling smelly French cheese into international meetings, trashing branches of McDonald's, defacing advertising billboards. The anti-globalization movement is as much a creature and creation of global communications as the giant corporations it seeks to confront. One of the sources of the movement were the Live Aid and Band Aid concerts for Africa in the 1980s, which showed how people could be mobilized for an international cause through the media. Now the movement is organized by the Internet: it is decentralized, self-motivated and yet capable of great coordination. It is a creation of the global networked society.

But as with the green movement in its time, the anti-globalization movement cannot stand still. Its own very general arguments are increasingly exposed to scrutiny. Let us examine its key claim that giant global companies are homogenizing our culture, creating poverty and deepening inequality in a process of globalization which is covering the world in a suffocating blanket of American values.

Cultural Homogeneity

Local cultures are the victims of globalization, which drives out distinctiveness and difference. Authentic cultures survive, but only as shallow performances for the tourist industry, which are overshadowed by the spread of global brands – Nike, Calvin Klein, BMW, Ikea – which need global distribution to make profits. But surely only up to a point. There is as yet no equivalent in global culture to the ethnic core to mainly national cultures with their heroes, myths, stories and cultural representations. A global culture of brands is accessible and easy to use but shallow: it spreads precisely because it lacks the depth of attachment that local and national cultures provide. As a deeper global culture develops and with it a sense of global citizenship, these are likely to come from stories and myths of heroism and danger, in which affecting events which people care about such as September 11th and issues such as global warming are likely to play a larger role than marketing. To the extent that a global culture is being created then, political, religious and social movements are as likely to be its authors as marketing departments.

The pessimists who see the world homogenized around brands assume that brands mean the same wherever and whenever they appear: that the brand message is received in just the way that it is transmitted. This assumes that consumers have little or no capacity to interpret and make judgements for themselves about brands. Soccer is now a genuinely world sport but it is followed quite differently in countries around the world. The fact that people are playing the same sport, with the same rules, does not mean they all behave and play in exactly the same way. Global messages and standards are interpreted and used in different ways in different localities. Equally what is being spread by global markets often tends to be distinctive local and national cultural products: Australian wine, Scottish whisky, Indian curry or Japanese sushi. In the last decade sushi has become a global food. A decade ago most British consumers would probably have turned up their noses at the thought of eating raw fish. Now you can get it in Marks and Spencer's. This is just one example in which the cultural flow has been from south and east to west and north. As anthropologist Theodore Bestor points out in a *Foreign Policy* journal article on the globalization of sushi, just because you can get sushi easily in any major world city does not mean it has stopped being Japanese. On the contrary, it is seen, even when made in odd ways by chefs who are not Japanese, as a little piece of Japanese culture abroad. Our cities are increasingly patchworks of cultures from around the world. Their local flavour has not been lost but transplanted and adapted. Being different, having distinctive roots, stands for something. Having a strong local culture is vital as an entry ticket to global cultural exchange, just as having a strong science base in some areas is essential as an entry ticket into global exchange of scientific ideas. Cultures are not made strong by becoming inward looking, nostalgic and defensive. They are vibrant by being confident enough to engage with new sources of ideas and influence, borrowing from them and melding with them. Local cultures are invariably seen as victims of globalization but in many ways they are enriched and opened up by it.

In short the pessimists belittle consumers' ability to work out what they want from brands and how much they should invest in them. Watching American television programmes does not make you American, any more than watching *ER* makes you a doctor. The pessimists underestimate the critical intelligence of consumers: they see the masses as all too easily duped and manipulated to succumb to consumer culture. People are too active and too complex in their responses to cultural products for these claims of automatic manipulation to stand. The pessimists' view of the future is so nightmarish precisely because they take what companies say at face value: they give it too much respect. A media executive at a trendy advertising company might like to think an advertisement for biscuits is really selling the value of community, but consumers know it is just another ad for biscuits. The way that media messages are received and taken up is far from simple or straightforward. The pessimists assume they know what happens at the moment of cultural impact: they do not. As a result, all too easily they slip into exaggeration. Thomas Frank, for example, in *One Market Under God*, describes a television advertisement for Cisco in which children say what they hope for from the Internet in terms of Orwell's *1984*. Colonialism in the nineteenth century and twentieth-century authoritarianism used violently coercive means to achieve their ends. It does not bear comparison to put corporate jingles in the same moral category.

That is not to say that the spread of a global media culture is entirely benign. It is just that the pessimistic argument is far too sweeping and partial. A prime example of the contest between deeply pessimistic and more optimistic accounts of the cultural effects of globalization is the impact it may have on languages.

Language: Births, Deaths and Marriages

It is easy to feel pessimistic about the prospects for the world's languages. According to the most alarmist prognostications, about 90 per cent of the world's 6,700 languages could disappear within the next century. Even cautious moderates accept that perhaps half of them might be killed off. In *Vanishing Voices* Daniel Nettle and Suzanne Romaine argue that any language depends for its life on a community of users, which is large enough to sustain the language through a shared culture and possibly a distinctive way of life. That community of perhaps 100,000 users needs a supportive environment to survive, in which it makes sense culturally, politically and economically for young people to learn the language. Yet Nettle and Romaine's research shows that 90 per cent of the world's population speaks just 100 languages. More than 6,000 are spoken by less than 10 per cent of the world's population and just 4 per cent of the world's population, mainly its remaining indigenous people, speak 60 per cent of world languages. Perhaps 600 languages have more than 100,000 speakers and so might be considered 'safe'.

The coming century could well witness a catastrophic loss of linguistic diversity across the globe. Distinctive languages convey different ways of viewing the world. They attach different meanings to similar objects and experiences. They are stores of distinctive knowledge and most importantly perhaps the bearers of particular identities and communal histories. As languages die off so do entire cultures. The mass extinction of languages could parallel the extinction of endangered species. The linguistic massacre that is in prospect has come about through the expansion of a limited number of metropolitan languages used in colonization and commerce. Their growth, and in particular that of English, is threatening

a process of growing cultural homogenization and standardiz-
ation, according to the arch-pessimists, which will unfairly
advantage mother tongue speakers of English, from the US
and Britain, and people who come from developed economies
with good education systems that teach English well from an
early age. The rise of English as a global language will spread
cultural destruction and inequality hand-in-hand.

The problem is all the more pressing because the rise of
English as a global language has been so rapid and so recent.
Even in 1950 the idea that English would within decades
become a global language was treated with grave scepticism.
Yet in the last two decades of the twentieth century it became
increasingly clear that English is taking on that role. English is
now spoken fluently by between 1.2 billion and 1.5 billion
people, a quarter of the world's population, about 350 million
of them native speakers. The world's language system is in
uncharted territory. Never before has a language attained such
ascendancy, in such a short space of time. English seems to be
benefiting from the 'winner takes all' tendencies of the global
communications economy. It has become the linguistic
operating system for the global system. The more people who
use English for global exchanges, whether in culture, science,
commerce or politics, the more it makes sense for other people
to adopt this lingua franca. For the pessimists there is a huge
risk that globalization will promote, through English, a cultural
and linguistic monoculture, even though it still has a long way
to go: two thirds of the world's population do not use English.
The language has a limited presence in many parts of the
world, the former states of the Soviet Union for example.

Yet on closer inspection the story is far more complicated
and open ended than the arch-pessimists imply. First, the
pessimists regard the rise of English as an external imposition
upon native speakers of other languages, which by and large
has only downsides. Yet the case for a global language is very

powerful, to promote easier exchange and mutual intelligibility to trade, resolve conflicts, avoid wars, exchange ideas. In 1945 the United Nations had just fifty-one members. By the mid 1950s there were eighty. These days, after the collapse of the Soviet Union and the decolonization of the 1960s and 1970s, the organization has 180 member nations trying to communicate with one another about an expanding array of issues. As David Crystal puts it in *English as a Global Language*:

There has never been a time when so many nations were needing to talk to each other so much. There has never been a time when so many people wished to travel to so many places. There has never been such a strain placed on the conventional resources of translating and interpreting . . . And never has there been a more urgent need for a global language.

English is spreading mainly because, when a global language was needed, it was the most likely candidate to fit the bill. It is spreading for evolutionary reasons – it serves a vital need – rather than being imposed from outside.

Second, although the rise of English to the position of pre-eminent global language is very rapid and recent it cannot be simply reduced to an outgrowth of late twentieth-century globalization. The rise of English has been complex and protracted. Had the Normans stayed longer in England after their invasion we might well be speaking world French now. The English language developed only through a process of constant inbreeding. Between 1500 and 1700 thousands of new words entered the English language, mainly borrowed from Italy, France and Spain. English began its rise as a global language in the seventeenth and eighteenth centuries because England was the pre-eminent colonizing power. But in the nineteenth century many were drawn to use English because it was the leading language of innovation in science, technology and industry. By the late nineteenth century the main driver was America's spreading economic power. A century later television, radio, films, music and the Internet are the main forces behind its growth. But English is a global language of knowledge and culture as much as of commerce. It is the leading language in science, software, academia and medicine. Even two decades ago one study found that 85 per cent of research papers in biology and physics were written in English and 73 per cent of papers in medical journals. In the previous fifteen years the use of English as a medium for exchange of scientific know-how had risen by between 30 and 40 per cent according to the research. English is the language of safety in the air and at sea, as well as the lingua franca of diplomacy and conflict resolution in the swelling ranks of global institutions. However, English has also been a language of national emancipation, for example in parts of Africa, where it has been adopted as an 'official' neutral language to avoid elevating the language of one ethnic group in a multi-ethnic nation. Arguably English as an official and neutral language has allowed nations to come into existence, as well as being a tool of colonialization.

Third, in this process English itself has been changed markedly. There is no single standard English that is spreading around the world forcing people to speak in BBC and CNN accents. Instead as it has become a global language many varieties of English have developed as people have adapted it to their distinctive cultures and needs. Standard cut-glass English is not spreading around the world; many forms of English are. There are different versions of standard English in mother tongue countries from England, Scotland and Wales to Australia and different parts of the US. Different versions of English are used where it is an official state language, alongside other tongues used in civil society, in countries such as Ghana, Nigeria and India. In India alone there will soon be more than 50 million fluent English speakers, more than in Britain. English is different again where it is given high priority as a second language taught in school in places such as China, Russia and Germany. As English has developed its global role so it has fragmented into a lattice work of Creoles, dialects, nativized forms in East and West Africa, South-east Asia and the Caribbean. In *The English Languages* Tom McArthur estimated there are probably about eighty different major, overlapping versions of English spoken by about 700 million people. As a result the English language is no longer owned by the English. Increasingly it is a global property, a tool for global development, which different people have chosen to develop in different ways. The English happen to speak just one version of a global language.

Fourth, as a result a new division of labour seems to be developing between languages. English or near English is increasingly being used as a basic tool of commerce and global exchange, to get things done. Meanwhile, people use other languages to engage in more intimate, expressive and emotional exchanges. It seems quite likely, according to analysts such as David Crystal, that we will see the emergence of growing bilingualism, as people switch between their mother tongue and a version of English to achieve different ends. In the process English is flowing into other languages, complementing them rather than killing them off. The Japanese, for example, have a 'Made in Japan'-style English which they selectively incorporate into their language. The outcome of this process could well be the growth of new hybrid dialects and language versions, rather than a single killer language. West Indians who are comfortable using standard English nevertheless break into Creole when they are excited. They move between the two pretty seamlessly. The Nigerian novelist Chinua Achebe sums up this hybrid position in *Morning Yet on Creation Day*:

The price a world language must be prepared to pay is submission to many different kinds of use. The African writer . . . should aim at fashioning out an English which is at once universal and able to carry his peculiar experience . . . I feel that English will be able to carry the weight of my African experience. But it will have to be a new English, still in full communion with its ancestral home but altered to suit its new African surroundings.

The pessimists argue that English will be a killer language exterminating distinctive cultural strands; yet the spread and adaptation of English could create new viewpoints and allow their expression.

Fifth, the pessimists present the looming catastrophe in once-and-for-all terms, in which there will be no turning back from the prospect of world domination. In truth English has emerged as a global set of languages through a messy, complex and far from complete process that has a lot further to run yet. Previous world languages have not survived, most famously Latin, which dissolved into a set of Romance languages, now spoken by about 400 million people (more than the mother tongue speakers of English). Something similar could happen to English. As one contributor to a British Council conference on the future of English put it:

One wonders whether the varieties of English are not in danger of deviating from the commonly intelligible norms so markedly as to become unrecognisable . . . Will English assimilate the enormous cultural flux of these new literatures, and so increase its metaphoric and expressive potential? Or, on the contrary, will it be overwhelmed by this powerful stream, and prove unable to integrate the new literary voices from these distant and distinct cultures?[2]

English could crack and dissolve in the century to come. Or just as likely, the technology of speech recognition and automatic translation might develop as an alternative to English as a commercial tool. Why bother learning English when a clever piece of portable software might do the same job for you?

Far from reason for deep pessimism there seem to be strong grounds for a measure of optimism. A global language would be a huge resource for knowledge, innovation, peace, exchange and mutual intelligibility. However, language also matters as a prime source of distinctive identity. Often these two roles are in conflict. As a global language spreads to promote intelligibility, so it might erode language's role as an expression of identity. However, that is not a foregone conclusion and as Crystal and McArthur propose quite plausibly people are increasingly adapting their own hybrids of language use and dialect to cope with different circumstances, using their mother tongue for intimacy and expression and perhaps a version of English for more utilitarian ends. For the language scholar Manfred Görlach:

Electronic communication and air travel are likely to prevent the fracturing of English into mutually incomprehensible languages. Locally divergent forms of English may drift off into separate languages, but the core of English is likely to remain a varied, diversified but recognizably 'same' language.[3]

That is not to say that there are not significant problems to address, such as the protection of linguistic heritage from the ground up among indigenous peoples, investment in bilingualism (an expensive policy) and measures to ensure more equal access to the global language. But just as we might be on the verge of a catastrophic loss of linguistic diversity so we might be on the verge of the birth of a genuinely global language. As Crystal argues, the chance to create such a language might come only once and it might happen in our lifetime.

Twin Standpoints

The challenge we face of protecting our historic sense of identity, expressed through culture and language, while also engaging in more global exchange, often through the global lingua franca of a version of English, is just one example of a much larger challenge to our sense of ourselves. As the philosopher Thomas Nagel put it in *Equality and Partiality*, we are constantly torn between an elevated, impartial and ethical point of view of our actions that demands people be treated fairly and a deeply personal standpoint, rooted in commitments to our families, friends and communities, which makes us what we are and gives our lives meaning. We have no option but to see the world from where we happen to be, with our particular needs and loyalties, and yet we also feel the moral claims of a more elevated stance, that we should apply impersonal and impartial yardsticks to moral issues such as inequality, hunger and poverty. Nagel's argument is that we are always simultaneously occupying two standpoints on the world – one which reflects our particular interests and commitments and the other which reflects our belief in universal ideals and standards of morality and justice.

Indeed as globalization has advanced we have become more aware through the media of the conditions others live in. As a result people in economically advanced countries are more likely to find themselves shuttling backwards and forwards between these two views of the world. Modern western consumers with liberal views are constantly trying to reconcile their daily concerns for their standard of living with the knowledge of the scale of global poverty for which they feel some kind of responsibility. When we survey the world from the impersonal standpoint its sufferings press in upon us: the alleviation of misery, ignorance, poverty and powerlessness seems an overwhelmingly important goal. If we were to arrive from outer space as a benevolent despot and judge our world from the outside, the priority would surely be to elevate people to a minimum decent standard of living, taking many tens of millions of people out of poverty. Yet few of us can sustain a utopian, hair shirt moral standpoint all of the time. Our special concern for how our life goes, in our society, cannot be abolished or even, apart from unusual circumstances, minimized for long. Our personal, individual point of view on the world creates our own, independent sense of what is valuable to us. Many, perhaps most, of us find ourselves committed to two positions, which we find hard to combine. Everyone's life is equally important. Everyone has his own life to lead, including me.

We are searching for ways to reconcile these two moral standpoints most of us occupy at least some of the time. As globalization proceeds, as it will, we need more institutions which show how the impartial requirements of an impersonal ethical standpoint, which should lead to commitments to tackle global poverty, can be balanced against the personal commitments people have to live their lives to the full, in the society they find themselves in.

In global terms the key to this is a sustained attack on poverty and inequality. Globalization will be legitimate only if it spreads opportunity and reduces poverty. We are so accustomed to great social and economic inequality that it is easy to become dulled to it. Yet if everyone matters just as much as everyone else, it is appalling that the most effective social and economic system we have yet devised permits so many people to live in such deprivation. No matter how consuming our own lives are, it is impossible to completely extinguish the moral claim of the impersonal and impartial standpoint. Nagel's argument is that we are more able to concentrate on our own lives, and of those we specially care about, with a clear conscience, if we do so within a social order which treats people fairly and ensures all have a decent chance to make the most of their lives. He concludes:

The collective pursuit of prosperity and justice, for themselves, by the citizens of a nation remains under a shadow while it goes on in a world like ours, where a minority of nations are islands of relative decency in a sea of tyranny and crushing poverty, and the preservation of a high standard of living depends on strict controls on immigration . . . We will be able to tend our own gardens with good conscience only when this surrounding situation has improved radically and international institutions of some kind sustain a world order.

Poverty and Inequality

The pessimists' most serious charge is that globalization is spreading poverty and deepening inequality: corporate profits, Wall Street bonuses and consumer affluence are being bought at the cost of declining living standards for hundreds of millions of people who are already poor. Millions, perhaps billions of people, live on an endless plateau of poverty, disease and degradation.[4] The major moral plank of the case against globalization is that most people in the world live in abject poverty, if not outright misery, by the standards of the west. Globalization has only deepened their plight. Our standard of living in the west grows more affluent only thanks to poorly paid workers in developing countries making branded goods, often under morally unacceptable conditions. We can afford to buy new trainers so easily, to keep us on the fashion treadmill, only because the people making them are so badly paid. Put it another way: the poor are being left further and further behind, but because of modern communications and travel, they are increasingly aware of the gap. The figures on global poverty, mainly provided by the World Bank and open to much dispute, are shocking.

The poorest 20 per cent of the world population account for just 1.3 per cent of its expenditures. Half the global population, perhaps 3 billion people, live in poverty, 1.2 billion of them survive on less than $1 a day. Perhaps 1 billion people do not have secure access to clean drinking water and 2.4 billion do not have access to adequate sanitation. A quarter of a billion children work, most of them in agriculture, often ruining their lives before they reach adulthood. About 100 million children subsist on the streets. An estimated 1.3 billion people breathe in deeply polluted and unhealthy air mainly in the enormous cities of the developing world. As the world economy has become more global and more technology-driven so the gaps between rich and poor have widened. Two hundred years ago average annual global income per capita was about $650 in today's prices. The richest people were about three times richer than the poorest. By 1950 that ratio of rich to poor had risen to thirty-five to one and now it is seventy to one. About 85 per cent of the world's income goes to 20 per cent of its population and 60 per cent goes to just 6 per cent. The rich nations and people enjoy vastly superior incomes and consume vastly more resources and goods than the poor.

These figures are a source of shame and revulsion. The questions are, what can be done about them and what role has globalization played in generating poverty, compared with other factors such as war, disease, corruption, famine and technology? It is arguable that in the era of late twentieth-century globalization world poverty had been reduced more dramatically than at any time, according to World Bank figures. In 1820 about 900 million people lived on $1 a day in today's prices, about 85 per cent of the world's population. The world was more egalitarian then, in part because everyone was poorer. The number of people living on $1 a day peaked at 1.4 billion in 1980. Since then there has been a fall of 200 million in those living in absolute poverty. The proportion of the world population living in absolute poverty has fallen from 31 per cent to 20 per cent. Although the numbers living in poverty are still huge and morally unacceptable, the fall has been dramatic. The drop is mainly due to faster economic growth in the most populous developing countries, India and China. In India about 100 million people have been taken out of poverty in the last twenty years. In China, which uses a different poverty line, the number of people counted as living in absolute poverty has fallen from 250 million in 1978 to 34 million in 1999. This is not the only respect in which living conditions may have improved.

At the start of the twentieth century average life expectancy in the developing countries was thirty years; now it is about sixty-five. People in developing countries now live longer than people in rich economies did a century ago. Ninety per cent of people can expect to live beyond the age of sixty. In 1960 that was true for only 60 per cent of people in the developing countries. Agricultural food production, in part driven by technology, has dramatically reduced the regular incidence of hunger. According to the UN Food and Agriculture Organization 960 million people in the developing countries were malnourished in 1970, falling to 790 million in 1996. Thirty years ago 37 per cent of the population of the developing countries was malnourished. That is now down to 18 per cent. Global food production has doubled in the past half century and in the developing world it has tripled. Developing countries are producing 49 per cent more grain per capita than they were forty years ago, in large part because agriculture has been made more efficient. We are feeding vastly more people from the same amount of land. About 25 per cent of the world's rural population are without pure water; but a decade ago the figure was closer to 90 per cent. In India alone more than 80 per cent of the population have access to clean water. In the 1980s that was true for barely half the population.

None of this makes it acceptable that so many millions of people live in abject conditions. But it does suggest that improvements in living conditions have been made through the period of globalization, in large part through developing countries' access to trade and technology. The message seems to be that abject poverty can be dramatically reduced in populous developing countries if they can sustain economic growth. Economic development is the precondition for reducing poverty and the preconditions for economic development include: a stable and effective state; the rule of law to provide security for people and property; reasonably widespread literacy and numerary; basic health services and adequate infrastructure; a reliable financial system and macroeconomic stability; limited corruption. With those factors in place a developing country seems to be able to benefit from integration into the global economy, rather than being exploited by it. With a reasonably educated workforce and stable government, the conditions are in place not just for trade but also the transfer of technology and know-how on which development thrives. There is a huge debate about whether integration into the global economy causes economic development or whether that integration should follow only after a period of investment in education, infrastructure and know-how. However, it does seem, in the phrase of the *Financial Times* chief economic commentator Martin Wolf, that trade is the handmaiden of growth.[5] Participation in the global economy, on the right basis, does not cause poverty, on the contrary it seems to reduce it. The biggest problem is not that poor developing countries are integrated into a global economy that makes them poor. The biggest problem is that too few countries are integrated into the global economy in a way in which they can benefit.

However, even if participation in the global economy can be shown to reduce poverty, it is far less likely to have an impact on overall inequality. World incomes were far less unequal 200 years ago, but then everyone was poorer and lived shorter lives. It is possible that global inequality might fall in years to come in part because low population growth in the richest countries means that the proportion of the world's population living in high-income OECD countries is likely to fall from 32 per cent in 1950 to 13 per cent in the year 2050. Almost all the forecast 3 billion increase in population over the next fifty years is likely to come in the developing world. However, to reduce absolute inequality between the US and China, say, would require either unsustainable economic growth in China, of more than 10 per cent a year over twenty years, or implausibly high transfers of resources from the US to China.

In short, the goal of making further dramatic reductions in absolute poverty in developing countries is achievable with more successful integration of those economies into international trade and the global economy. With the right policies and approaches in these populous developing countries hundreds of millions of people could be lifted out of abject poverty in the next two decades, through globalization not despite it. It may also be possible to limit the growth of inequality in the quality of life and longevity, in education and health, if not in income. Globalization is an essential component of a poverty reduction strategy in the developing world.

Corporate Power

Many will doubt that conclusion because we are now so used to thinking of globalization as a process driven by multinational companies which switch their investments around the world in search of cheap labour and with little or no regard for the environment, to benefit their shareholders while adding no offsetting social value for anyone else. Voracious corporations are the agents of global destruction, according to the anti-globalization pessimists. About a third of world trade takes place within the global supply chains of multinational companies. These supply chains have been created in part through the growth of foreign direct investment. The United Nations estimates that the total book value of foreign investment at the end of 1998 was close to $14.6 trillion, about 150 per cent of US gross domestic product. The stock of foreign direct investment has risen by a factor of six since 1985. The argument is that these companies are setting off on a 'race to the bottom' to drive down wages in the developed world by shipping jobs overseas where they exploit poorly paid and non-unionized labour.

These investments in global production systems have been driven by the search for profits in companies which can be ruthless and morally myopic. Multinational companies, by and large, do not see themselves as agents of social change. Some engage in questionable practices. But the case that multi-national companies are engaged in a race to the bottom to cut wages is far from proven.[6] By and large investment by multinational companies in developing countries creates higher-wage jobs in those countries, increases productivity, improves international competitiveness and provides a route for technology transfer.

Employees of these companies in developing countries are

paid far less than their counterparts in the US. Ed Graham's survey for the Institute for International Economics shows that manufacturing employees of US companies in middle-income developing countries are paid 37 per cent of their counterparts' wages in the US and in low-income developing countries the figure is 18 per cent. But by local standards wages in these companies are much higher than average. US affiliates pay 1.8 times average manufacturing wages in middle-income developing economies and two times average wages in low-income companies. Arguably, multinational companies help to push up wages and productivity in developing countries, rather than reduce them. As Hirst and Thompson point out labour costs in Indonesia may be less than 2 per cent of labour costs in Germany, but as labour costs account only for at most 20 per cent of the total costs of many manufactured products, low wages on their own are unlikely to be a decisive factor in foreign investment decisions. Indeed they go so far as suggesting that the idea of the footloose multinational company is a myth:

Most international companies still only operate in a small number of countries . . . most multinational companies adapt passively to government policy rather than continually trying to undermine it. The real question to ask of multinational companies is not why they are always threatening to up and leave a country if things seem to go badly for them there, but why the vast majority of them fail to leave and continue to stay put.

Multinational companies are increasingly likely to take supplies for standard commodity products from global, outsourced supply chains. But they are by and large reluctant to uproot their own activities unless there are fundamental structural disincentives. Those disincentives for continuing manufacturing in high-cost European locations may be growing as developing countries increasingly provide not just lower-cost but well-educated workforces and world class technology. Economic development cannot be delivered by governments alone or by international aid programmes. Companies play a vital role, and in the process the best can help to spread technology, improve productivity and address social and environmental issues. To play this role to the full many companies will need to broaden their moral and social imaginations, to see themselves as actors on a larger stage than simply making profits.

A US Conspiracy

America is inescapably part of our lives. The US is not only the world's pre-eminent superpower, it also provides the platforms on which we play out our lives, from Starbucks and McDonald's, to Intel and Microsoft, Madonna and MTV. From corporate legal and financial systems to military might and trade rules, we increasingly live within frameworks which the US plays a major role in shaping. Even if America is not the architect of the logic of globalization, it is the main beneficiary. As Hardt and Negri put it, we are all to some extent, no matter how distantly, citizens in an Empire in which the US is the leading player. Some critics of globalization go much further. They see the US not just as one player in the process but as an active and often evil agent of globalization, in which it uses its power unilaterally to promote its interests. America shows little respect for difference or diversity, it has no sense of history or culture, the critics say, and it always seems to be on the wrong side of conflicts in Palestine and Chile, Nicaragua and El Salvador. US power is deployed to defend US economic and corporate interests. The playwright Harold Pinter, for example, recently described America as a fully-fledged, gold-plated monster that knows only the language of bombs and death. He went on: 'The US has exercised a sustained, systematic, remorseless and clinical manipulation of power worldwide while masquerading as a force for universal good . . . the US is the most dangerous rogue state the world has ever seen.'[7] Echoes of that sentiment, perhaps more cautiously expressed, can be heard especially in intellectual circles around the world. But this attack on America is only possible because the critics work with such a diminished and distorted idea of the US.

American cultural life is far more diverse than people think. Since the Second World War New York has been the global centre for high and fine arts, displacing Paris. The US has a lot of pap culture but it also has lots of everything: 1,700 symphony orchestras, 7.5 million opera visits a year, 500 million museum visits. Since 1945 most of the radical political ideas in the world have found their roots in America: civil rights, the women's movement, the environmental movement, gay liberation, the anti-war movement. As Fred Halliday puts it in *Two Hours That Shook the World*, the US is the most prosperous country in the world and one to which many hundreds of millions of people would wish to emigrate from developing countries (in preference to Europe). American vitality in culture, music, the arts, technology and commerce stems in part from its open and egalitarian culture of mass democracy and individual rights. Far from being a gun-toting bully, the chief characteristic of US foreign policy, according to Halliday, has been its reluctance to get involved in wars. From the Second World War through to Kosovo its allies have often complained it does far too little, too late, as much as its critics complain it throws its weight around too freely. It often has to be dragged into conflict unwillingly by allies. Some of the most recent wars it has fought, in Bosnia and Kuwait, have been on the side of, if not entirely for, the

Muslims as well as in defence of US commercial interests. To present the US as only a blundering, evil giant abroad and a social and cultural wasteland at home is to paint a woefully partial, simplistic picture.

This is not to argue that US foreign policy is benign. On the contrary in Central and South America it has been brutal and anti-democratic. The Bush administration in early 2002 was obscenely silent as Israel launched a war on Palestinians. Nor can one be relaxed about the way the US is likely to respond to the world in the wake of September 11th. Already there is an evident tendency for the US to want to engage in its global responsibilities only on its terms and for the sake of its interests. President Bush is clearly drawn to unilateralism which means the US is likely to make occasional forays into the world, to 'sort out' problem states but then withdraw from it, possibly in a sulk, when globalization does not deliver what the US wants. The Bush administration is attracted to populist economic nationalism in trade and environment policy (imposing tariffs on imported steel to protect the US industry and withdrawing from the Kyoto protocol) combined with selective military interventions to deal with rogue states abroad, almost regardless of international opinion. This mixture of interventionism, complacent neglect and wounded withdrawal could create the conditions for Europe to become divided from America and for many in the Islamic world to see the west as only an enemy. As yet there is little sign that the administration recognizes the need to build complex alliances among states and non-government pressure groups around global policies that command support beyond Washington. Under Bush the US may well be a global power but it is unlikely to be a global leader. The US wields unprecedented world power. It may not be benign but it is almost certainly a better world power than say Soviet Russia, Nazi Germany, Communist China or Imperial Japan would have been. The issue will be how effective checks and balances can be established, both within America and through international institutions, to make the exercise of US global power legitimate.

But the US is far from alone in finding it painful to understand and accommodate globalization. In *The French Challenge: Adapting to Globalisation* Philip Gordon and Sophie Meunier point out that defence of French culture against American influence and globalization is a goal shared across French politics. The rhetoric of politicians remains robustly anti-America. Yet French people are adapting. About 40 per cent of the Paris Bourse is now owned by investors outside France. Vivendi, the former water company turned media group, is now headquartered in New York. In 2001 four of the top ten films in France were French made, but 60 per cent of French cinema ticket sales were for American films. The dangers of an official posture of hostility to globalization became all too evident in the 2002 presidential elections with the success of arch far-right nationalist Jean-Marie Le Pen. Would we be happier with France as the world's superpower rather than the US?

Two centuries ago Alexis de Tocqueville realized that the spirit of initiative and expansion in American society would quickly leave more conservative European societies in its wake. That is still true today. That spirit of innovation and hope that US mass democracy and capacity for reinvention generates is a vital global cultural resource. One of the unfolding stories of globalization will be how this American spirit of optimism is blended and mixed with other more conservative and cautious cultures. When people say they want a bit of America, it is not just American products they want, but a taste of that optimism, that they can remake themselves. When people become Americans they do not forget or dispose of their cultural past; they hyphenate it.

People become Italian-Americans, or Chinese-Americans: their ethnic and cultural identity is appended to their American identity which is primarily a political notion. Michael Ignatieff, the Canadian writer, summed it up: American scripture is the power of democratic reinvention. The US is the only country that believes in itself as the creation of an act of democratic will, as faith in democracy.

The US is both the source of our most intense hopes and fears then, of utopia and dystopia. It is the home of modern, radical, egalitarian mass democracy and the world's brutal, bull-headed cop.

Globalization is a more open, complex and fluid process than the nightmarish scenarios of the arch-pessimists suggest. Globalization may be spreading some brands and media products worldwide but that is not creating a homogenized global culture. The pessimists seem to regard consumers as passive dupes, whose lives can easily be reprogrammed by advertising. They give global brands far too much respect and assume that media messages are consumed just as they are transmitted by those who send them out. Instead globalization is likely to create a mix of hybrid cultures, both local and global. The pessimists argue that globalization is draining local cultures of their meaning and value. Yet globalization is also spreading local cultures, through food, music, fashion and design to global markets. Most major cities are now patchworks of globalized versions of local and regional cultures. The cultural flows in globalization are from south and east to north and west as well as the other way around. Nowhere is this process more evident than in language. English is becoming a global language, with many variants, because it serves a useful purpose: it allows greater mutual intelligibility for people who want to exchange information, ideas, knowledge as well as goods and services. But that is the culmination of a very protracted process that has accelerated only in the last three decades. And there is also quite a lot of evidence that people are combining English with their native tongues, which they still rely on for expressions of culture, intimacy and emotion. Once again globalization is promoting new hybrids as much as a homogenized, global system.

Globalization is criticized by the pessimists for deepening global poverty and inequality. But there is just as much evidence that world poverty has declined dramatically in the last twenty years through increased economic growth in India and China which in large part was due to their deepening integration into the world economy. There is a good case for believing that world poverty would be reduced more quickly if more poor developing countries were able to take part in the circuit of world trade and investment flows more successfully. Globalization is not a panacea but international trade is vital for economic development. Poverty will not be reduced by a retreat into protectionism and nationalism.

Companies with global operations are a crucial agent in this process. However, truly global companies are very rare and global companies that operate as entirely footloose investors, switching their operations from country to country in search of cheap labour, are even rarer. Indeed, there is quite a lot of evidence that investment by international companies can push up wages and productivity in developing economies, rather than driving them down. This is not to say that global companies are saintly, social enterprises. Far from it. They are mainly driven by the search for profit. However, it is far too simplistic to paint international investment by multinational companies as essentially an evil, destructive force. In the right setting and framework, private investment and enterprise are a vital condition for economic development and poverty reduction. Multinational investment does not cause poverty in the poorest developing countries; on the contrary it could be the lack of such investment in the poorest countries that helps to prevent development.

Finally the pessimists argue that globalization is just a cloak for the smothering spread of American culture, values and corporate interests. Globalization is Americanization, they argue. In many respects they are correct. The US does provide the operating platforms for many aspects of our lives. But a blanket condemnation of American influence as dangerous and corrupting is a far-fetched, distorted and diminished account of the US. In many respects American culture of mass democracy and cultural optimism is a huge asset which has and will continue to bring enormous benefits to the rest of the world. An America turned in on itself would be far more dangerous and worrying for globalization than an America engaged with the process.

Globalization is not breeding a single, homogenous capital-ist system, as the arch-pessimists complain. Many different accommodations with globalization are possible. Several different varieties of capitalism will emerge from this process, with their own distinctive cultures, institutions and mixes of the market, social welfare, religious affiliation and state involvement. There is no single template that everyone has to fit into.

The anti-globalization movement, at its best, is a part of this process of exploring the different possible futures for globalization. Its challenge to the nature of globalization will prove useful in prompting reform and adjustment. Arguments like John Gray's that the global market is ungovernable and uncontrollable, have prompted a more active search for insti-tutions of governance, social policies and debt relief to make the global economy fairer and more stable. Arguments like Naomi Klein's force international companies to answer whether they can live up to the values laid out in their 'brand promise' to consumers, which in turn means companies have to engage in a debate about the kind of values and standards that should guide globalization. Michael Hardt and Antonio Negri argue that the global economy is developing to unlock the potential of new technologies and forms of work and organization in which communications, creativity and knowledge play a much larger role. But this knowledge economy rests on social and collaborative foundations which are at odds with the values of the market. In Hardt and Negri's own words: 'In the expression of its creative energies, immaterial labour seems to provide the potential for a kind of spontaneous and elementary communism.'[8] Each of these arguments suggests that forces unleashed in the process of globalization will in turn force the process to adjust, adapt and change.

The prospect of the creation of a global market, and even more the creation of global webs of communications, is giving rise to an intense debate about the possibilities of global citizenship and governance. The stories and myths of a global culture are starting to emerge around events such as September 11th and issues such as global warming. There is an emerging recognition among national governments that they share common problems which often can only be addressed co-operatively: terrorism, crime, environmental pollution, rules for trade, investment and debt relief. The war crimes tribunal in the Hague and the arrest of General Pinochet of Chile are the start of exploring the scope for global notions of justice. The pressure of immigration means that across the developed world societies are debating the terms of citizenship and the nature of their obligations to people from the developing world who aspire to a higher standard of living. In other words, we are actively engaged in a debate about how a global market might give rise to a sense of global citizenship, governance and society. The anti-globalization movement is one part of that debate, which is an urgent necessity. Global governance, although ramshackle, is slowly being shaped and developed to reduce poverty, promote democracy and extend basic common rights such as freedom of speech. For globalization to be seen as legitimate, world poverty has to be further reduced and dramatically; corporations will have to acknowledge their wider social responsibilities, for health, education and the environment as part of the process of economic development from which they benefit; international institutions will have to give greater voice to poorer developing nations; those nations will have to be helped by public and private investments to better equip them to take advantage of international trade; markets in the north will have to be further opened to exporters from the south. It is a big agenda but one that we are now embarked upon. The prospect is alluring, a more globally integrated, stable, fairer, environmentally sustainable world order. Far from retreating from globalization we should take it forward and deepen the process, from markets and trade to society and governance.

12. Militant Optimism

In 1918 the Russian poet Aleksandr A. Blok greeted the Russian Revolution in ecstatic terms. Its aim, he wrote, was 'to make everything over . . . to make everything different, to change our false, filthy, boring, hideous life into a just, clean, gay and beautiful life.'[1] He went on:

The sweep of the Russian Revolution which wants to engulf the whole world . . . is such that it hopes to raise a world wide cyclone, which will carry warm winds and the sweet scent of orange groves to snow covered lands, moisten the sun scorched steps of the South with cool northern rain . . . 'Peace and the brotherhood of nations' is the sign under which the Russian Revolution runs its course.

These days it seems incredible that a revolution that led to such disastrous consequences could have been greeted with such high hopes. For many on the left, in particular, the loss of the kind of hopes Blok articulated is a cause for extreme pessimism. American academic Russell Jacoby sums up this melancholy in *The End of Utopia*:

Politics has become dull . . . At worst, it is defined by economic collapse, despotism and fratricidal violence. At best, liberal regimes resist challenges by regressive religious and nationalist movements. We are increasingly asked to choose between the status quo or something worse. Other alternatives do not seem to exist. We have entered the era of acquiescence, in which we build our lives, families and careers with little expectation that the future will diverge from the present. To put this another way: A utopian spirit – a sense that the future could transcend the present – has vanished.

Among a litany of failures of imagination, Jacoby highlights what he sees as the paucity of vision about the future of work. In the past leftists and radicals would muse about the abolition of work and liberation of the working class. Now the best we can do is yearn for full employment in poorly paid jobs. No society promises a future of a world beyond work. If anything affluence now requires more work from us, Jacoby complains. While Thomas More, the originator of the modern ideal of utopia, foresaw a society without war, money, violence and inequality, latter-day futurists see only a future with war, money, violence and inequality.

Jacoby is wrong. We should not mourn the passing of grand utopian political projects but instead celebrate. The demise of political utopianism is one of the main reasons we have for hoping that the twenty-first century may be significantly better, or at least nowhere near as bad, as the twentieth. At first this might sound odd. The lack of utopian vision, especially among our political leaders, is regularly bemoaned, especially on the left. The loss of faith in utopianism is taken as grounds for pessimism, that we have no alternative but to adjust to the world around us, rather than seeking to transform it for the better. Without utopian vision politics is sadly diminished and our horizons narrowed. Utopias of the future have never had much appeal for conservatives and reactionaries. Their sense of hope rests, instead, on our ability to maintain a natural, stable, moral and social order, handed down from history. The conservative utopian vision is far more likely to be located in some mythical past of national greatness (Mrs Thatcher's Victorian Values), stable community (John Major's England of warm beer and cricket) or an Arcadian idyll of rural life (Prince Charles and the organic aristocracy).

Both kinds of utopianism proved to be hugely destructive in the twentieth century. The promise of a utopian future, combined with authoritarian politics, industrialized warfare and mass terror, created some of the worst catastrophes of the twentieth century. Some of its most glaring evils arose from populist and revolutionary movements that were exploited by ruthless authoritarian leaders in the name of distorted utopian ideals. The Nazi party began as a campaign for workers' rights before it was taken over by Hitler's genocidal anti-Semitism. The Bolsheviks emerged from political and social turmoil in Russia to take over an enfeebled state and through that the rest of the country. Mao Zedong's Great Leap Forward to collectivize and industrialize agriculture killed perhaps twenty million people. Tens of millions died in the twentieth century in pursuit of and battling against authoritarian utopian dreams. Myths in pre-modern cultures largely enforced tradition by justifying the existing social order. The dream worlds we inhabit are more often expressions of a desire to escape or radically alter the way our lives are organized. That is why they are so animating and so dangerous. Yet as Susan Buck Morss points out in *Dreamworld and Catastrophe: The Passing of Mass Utopia in East and West*, the inspiring mass utopia projects which animated the twentieth century – mass sovereignty, mass production, mass culture and consumption – have left huge problems in their wake. The dream of mass sovereignty helped to propel the world to wars about nationalism and justified revolutionary terror from the Soviet Union to Cambodia. The dream of mass production and consumer affluence created in its wake global warming. Conservative utopias have perhaps been less damaging, because they have been less systematic. Yet millions died in the twentieth century in defence of nation, tribe, land and religion. While leftist utopian visions have been vanquished, these reactionary utopias will perhaps be even more potent in the twenty-first century.

This book is an argument against the spread of a chronic, disabling pessimism in our politics and culture. Yet implicitly it is also an argument against forms of utopian optimism that can be equally dangerous. Radical utopianism of the future, which promises us a perfect society to live in, is dangerous because it focuses all energy and effort on a single goal that embraces all of society. Reactionary nostalgic utopianism of the past, which enlists us to defend history and tradition as the core of our identity and society, risks trapping us. Both radical and reactionary forms of utopianism provide us with a sense of hope based on our membership of a static, idealized society. For radicals that society will come into being in the future; for reactionaries it is largely drawn from the past. For radicals politics is about breaking through the constraints of the present, to make that utopian future possible. For reactionaries politics is about resisting the corrosion of modern culture, morals and technology, to protect the utopian core of our way of life which has been handed down from history.

We should reject both radical and reactionary utopianism. It is far more likely that we will avoid large-scale catastrophe if we avoid utopianism altogether. In this century there may well be an abundance of populist movements among the poor and dispossessed, rallied around ethnic, demonizing ideologies. Technology to provoke terror may also be plentiful. However, it is far less likely that authoritarian political leaders will be able to lead entire societies, over a long period of time, in pursuit of a violent, economically disastrous utopian dream to preserve the past or create a brave new future. The multiple checks and balances imposed by a globally integrated economy, in which multinational companies and non-government organizations play an important policing role, combined with the spread of global communications, means that all societies will be more open, less cut off and less prey to authoritarian leaders with messianic visions of the future and the past.

Such leaders will face greater challenges and constraints in the twenty-first century.

The problem that leaves, however, is how we maintain a sense of hope without the fix of a utopian dream. For while utopian visions have caused great damage, it is also true as Jacoby argues, echoing T.S. Eliot, that many people feel their lives are 'hollow' in a modernity seemingly bereft of higher vision and purpose. For all its downsides, utopian thinking is inescapable because it is so vital for us. In his essay 'The Soul of Man Under Socialism', Oscar Wilde wrote: 'A map of the world that does not include Utopia is not worth even glancing at, for it leaves out the one country at which Humanity is always landing. And when Humanity lands there, it looks out, and, seeing a better country, sets sail. Progress is the realisation of Utopias.' Casanova is reported to have put the same point slightly differently when he said the best part of making love was walking up the stairs.

So it seems we are trapped. To entertain utopianism runs the risk of endorsing calamitous experiments with possibly catastrophic consequences. To retreat from utopianism seems to leave us consigned to reality as it is with no significant hope for the future. Can we break through this impasse to generate a non-utopian source of hope and optimism? My argument is that we can if we base hope on our capacity for constant imagination and innovation. Rather than pin our hopes on a static, idealized vision of society, derived from the past or imagined in the future, we should rest our hope on our shared capability for constant innovation and change. Optimism based on our capacity for innovation is at odds with both reactionary and radical utopianism. Reactionaries and conservatives see innovation as a potential evil, uprooting tradition, heritage and history. Radical visions of utopia, though often rich in technology, are also hostile to innovation: were we to reach the perfect society, why would we want to change it?

The Utopian Urge

Utopia means nowhere, an imaginary non-place that expresses our fantasies and desires, just as dystopias reflect our fears and anxieties. Thomas More's *Utopia*, published in 1516 and the starting point for the modern literary utopian tradition, was a report of a visit to a mysterious island on which society was organized quite differently from the England More knew. Utopian ideas emerged in the sixteenth century from a new understanding of how different the world could be. The exploration of the physical world by seafarer explorers in turn bred awareness that there could be quite different kinds of society, made up of different people in different lands. Imaginary utopias emerged in an era of intense curiosity and exploration as people tested the boundaries of the world they inhabited. The real journeys propelled imaginary explorations as well as the other way round.

Utopia was a fabricated upside-down world designed to expose the shortcomings of contemporary society. In More's hands it was less a blueprint for the future than an indictment of the present. More was addressing a society that was starting to face profound choices over how it should be organized, including the appropriate roles for religion and the monarchy, as well as the emerging forces of commerce and science. More's response to these pressures was not to propose a return to an Arcadian rural idyll, nor to expect solutions to be handed down by God, through the rule of a monarch. More's *Utopia* was revolutionary because it suggested that society should organize itself, through idealized cooperation and self-governance. Utopia would require a collective leap of the imagination.

More's utopian society was rationally organized and fundamentally egalitarian, being founded on the notion of communal rather than private property and collective rather than individual self-interest. The ideal commonwealth looked after its citizens but at a cost: it was rigidly authoritarian, hierarchical and highly restrictive of personal freedoms. No one in More's utopia was homeless, hungry or unemployed. Gold, silver, gems and other material goods were valued purely for their utility in everyday life (chamber pots were made of gold). No significant human material needs were unmet. However, More's utopians were banned from debating politics outside the assembly, on pain of death. Anyone wishing to travel had to get the police's permission. Even taking a walk in the countryside was difficult.[2]

As western society developed so did the kinds of utopias it spawned. The scientist Francis Bacon's *New Atlantis*, published in 1627, provided a vision of utopia based less on travel and more on the transforming power of science, technology and knowledge (along with a heady mix of religion and magic). By the nineteenth century this scientific strain of utopianism had surfaced in H. G. Wells's fascination with time travel. The possibility of utopia rested on the power of human creativity and design to allow us to break free of the chains imposed by nature, fate or history. Utopia was increasingly an anticipation of the modern future rather than an attempt to restore a lost Arcadian past, uncorrupted by modern vanities and distractions.

By the twentieth century the journey to utopia was no longer to be made by a lone inventor or explorer, who might chance upon an ideal society as the result of a shipwreck. Utopia became a destination for all of society to travel towards, along roads designed for the task often by authoritarian fascist and communist leaders. Utopia became about re-engineering society in a headlong drive to the future in which nostalgia and tradition had to be purified for the sake of the perfect planned society. Utopianism did not just emerge in politics but also in new visions of modern and harmonious cities from architects such as Le Corbusier. Utopia became a way to imagine a unity of purpose in a world that seemed to be fraying at the edges. Utopians planned cities that would create a sense of belonging, pride and purpose among a diverse population of complete strangers. People would know their place in a much larger order, whether that be a tower block or an economic plan. Utopia offered a degree of certainty and security. Utopianism was not just political, but technocratic, the vision of an expert elite.

Yet the pursuit of utopias of the future has often been unforgiving and calamitous, for three main reasons. First, utopias have been oppressive because they are so planned. Second, utopias require a degree of transparency that destroys the line between the public and private, the affairs of the state and the life of the family. Third, utopias have been static and conservative because they are opposed to innovation.

Utopia is a self-defeating form of hope: it is liberating but only at the cost of being oppressive. The utopian promise of a world in which everything would be planned and nothing left to chance, including our characters, contained the seeds of its own destruction. Isaiah Berlin summed up the appeal and the weakness of utopian visions in *The Crooked Timber of Humanity*:

A society lives in a state of pure harmony, in which all its members live in peace, love one another, are free from physical danger, from want of any kind, from insecurity, from degrading work, from envy, frustration, experience no injustice or violence, live in perpetual, even light, in a temperate climate, in the midst of infinitely fruitful, generous nature. The main characteristic of most, perhaps all, Utopias, is the fact that they are static. Nothing in them alters, for they have reached perfection: there is no need for novelty or change, no one can wish to alter conditions in which all natural human wishes are fulfilled.

The ideal of utopia can all too easily be invoked to justify cleansing and purifying the world. That was certainly a powerful strain in modernist architecture and planning in the early twentieth century. For Le Corbusier modern city planning was the erasure of disorder, social turmoil and cultural difference: 'Sweep away the refuse with which life is soiled, clogged and encumbered. Let us undertake the tasks of a new civilisation.' In his opinion modern architecture provided a 'geometry for the spirit'.

'When man begins to draw straight lines,' Le Corbusier writes, 'he bears witness that he has gained control of himself and reached a condition of order.' Technology can deliver a perfection nature can never attain:

The machine brings shining before us disks, spheres, and cylinders of polished steel, shaped with a theoretical precision and exactitude which can never be seen in nature itself . . . There is nothing in nature that approaches the pure perfection of the humblest machine (the moon is not round; the tree trunk not straight; only very occasionally are waters as smooth as a mirror; the rainbow is a fragment; living beings, with very few exceptions, do not conform to simple geometrical shapes . . .[3]

That hubris about the power of technology and human design to create a perfectly ordered world, described largely in technical language, can be heard today. The utopianism of unlimited choice – the media cornucopia of any movie, anywhere, any time, on any device – can all too quickly shade into a menacing coercion. For many people, technological progress is not something they choose to participate in but something they adjust to. All too often new-tech advocates argue that fundamental changes to basic aspects of our lives are inescapable because technology will make it so and leave us with little choice but to accept. All too quickly the revolution that started by offering unlimited choice bases its power on the fact there will be no choice: the technology will make it inevitable, there is no point in resisting. The newer the technology, the better the solution, they claim. Old habits must be eradicated and new ones learned, however painful that may be.

The citizens of More's Utopia lived their lives in public, out in the open, where everyone could see. Utopian society is characterized by its trust and transparency: people have no need to keep secrets because public and private interests are never in conflict. This obsession with transparency and accountability sounds noble and democratic but it is made possible only by people and places being under constant communal surveillance. In utopia the boundaries between the public and the private dissolve because the wider public interest incorporates all individual interests. The eradication of private spaces is one thing that makes utopia so intolerable. As Thomas More describes it in *Utopia*: 'Nowhere is there any licence to waste time. Nowhere any pretext to avoid work, on the contrary being under the eyes of all, people are bound.'

Utopianism has a dreadful tendency towards closed, abstract, cold and unforgiving visions, in which the price of harmony and justice is purification and order. The dangers in utopian visions of sweeping social change in pursuit of perfection are inherent to the idea, waiting to be picked up by authoritarian leaders. The problems are fundamental to the nature of utopia as a fixed, sacred society that cannot be open to major change and innovation. How can we sustain hope for a better future without succumbing to these risks implicit in utopianism?

Hope without Utopia

The starting point is to understand how we move beyond the risks and weaknesses inherent in traditional utopian visions of the future.

The first problem is that utopian visions have tended to be grand and sweeping accounts of how all of society could be remade at a stroke. Arguably utopianism needs to become more everyday and domesticated. Utopian aspirations are implicit in a wide variety of political and cultural activities, from street protests and community projects, to daydreams and fairytales. Echoes of utopian hope crop up within architecture and design, fashion and film, poetry and advertising. They are not confined to political theorizing. The utopian urge, to dream and speculate about what a better future might look like, can express itself in many ways, large and small, ambitious and piecemeal. The reason popular culture is so attractive is in part because it is so laced with apparent utopian promise. These promises might be deceptive and illusory, but nevertheless they contain emancipatory moments, when the imagination is set free. So the best place to start with utopianism is not with grand plans and projects, but with everyday, down-to-earth initiatives, hopes and dreams that people want to enact now. The higher utopian visions soar the more dangerous they become; the more rooted hope is in things people can do here and now, the better.

The danger of grand utopianism was that it focused hope on the creation of a single, unifying vision of the future that everyone had to adhere to. Instead hope should be based on our ability to create many different pathways to the future. Utopianism builds on what is latent and possible in the world around us. As Ernst Bloch, the German theorist of utopia, maintained in his three-volume, 1,200-page work *The Principle of Hope*, utopian dreaming is possible only because the world is unfinished and unfurling, a set of latent possibilities and potential, whose direction and outcome is not predetermined. History, Bloch argued, is a repository of possibilities: options for future action. As a result we should enjoy a constant sense of anticipation about what might be in store. A credible utopianism must build on this sense of openness and possibility. Rather than presenting blueprints of the perfect future, hope should rest on our ability to devise many different and competing pathways to the future.

The grand utopianism of the twentieth century tended to rest on a centralization of imagination in the hands of a political or technocratic elite, of planners and architects, for example. Hope rested on their ability to devise a better, more rational and secure society for us to live in. Instead we should base our optimism for the future on expanding our capacity to engage in speculating about the future. We have to become a society of speculators, in business and finance but also in politics, culture, education, science and literature. Instead of the authoritarian closed utopian visions that proved so disastrous in the twentieth century, we should seek a participatory utopianism, which is fed by a widespread capacity for imagination and speculation. We are entering a century in which more people than ever will be able to read, write, communicate, argue, draw, film, paint, design and create. We live in a world increasingly saturated by advertising, mass media and branding. But thanks to digital technologies the tools of cultural production, publishing and distribution are increasingly passing into the hands of the people, for them to have their say, define their point of view. This distributed capacity for imagination, dispute, dissent and creativity will be the great strength of the culture of the twenty-first century. It may also make culture more raucous, unruly, cacophonous and unpredictable. It will be pandemonium. But we should count that as a blessing rather than a failing. Grand utopias appealed for their sense of rational order, with everything in its place. Instead we should welcome a sense of creative unpredictability in our lives.

Grand utopias provided a sense of reassurance that as a society we might be travelling towards a destination that would be just, settled and comfortable. Instead of reassurance we should promote utopias built on an ethic of self-reliance and self-governance, in which our decentralized and distributed capacity for imagination is vital. Grand utopias were closed and static. They became conservative because they were hostile to innovation and learning. All too easily, utopian visions can become hygienic, intolerant, closed and conservative. If utopian society is the perfect end point of history, then it cannot admit criticism. What matters is whether the horizon of possibility for our society, and particularly for the weakest and poorest, is expanding or contracting, in tangible terms of life expectancy, quality of life, education and political rights. Innovation through science and technology, but also in commerce, politics, culture and arts, is the most potent force for improvement in our lives. Technology will open up ways to transform our world far more than politics in the present century. The great attraction of innovation and creativity as sources of hope is that they have to be open to change, improvement, criticism and new ideas. Innovation is a constant process: it is never closed and finished. The appeal of innovation as a source of hope is the way it constantly throws up new possibilities and opportunities. Innovation, expressed through culture, science and technology, is the most powerful non-utopian source of hope for the future.

The Politics of Hope

What does the shift from utopianism to innovation as a source of hope mean for politics? Attitudes towards innovation, not just in science and in business, but in the arrangements of family life, political decision-making, international alliances, our currency, the monarchy, farming and art will be the central issue in politics. Political positions will be increasingly defined by attitudes towards innovation. Self-proclaimed modernizers such as Tony Blair see the role of politics, at least rhetorically, as the promotion of innovation in business and civic life. Conservatives and reactionaries are more sceptical. While innovation in business might be welcomed, innovation in morals and social life should be resisted. Innovation, for them, often represents the passing fads of the politically correct elite. Many radicals are equally suspicious that much innovation is no more than a cloak for corporate interests, to create new markets, for example for upgrades of software products and new types of genetically modified seeds. Perhaps most interesting will be those societies that manage a mature and open debate about the costs and benefits of innovation in all walks of life. These societies will invest heavily in the capacity for innovation in art and science, culture and society. They will seek to regulate innovation openly and carefully: they will not rush into wholesale experiments. They will see innovation fundamentally as a social and democratic process, one that requires public consent and legitimacy, rather than simply economic and commercial justifications. Perhaps most importantly, political leaders in these societies will recognize that as well as encouraging innovation, they need to provide people with a sense of stability and security, to help them through a period of intense change and upheaval.

The best models we have of these adaptive, inclusive and

cohesive societies are the small, mainly social democratic societies of northern Europe: Sweden, Denmark, Finland and Holland. All these societies are small in population terms. They have highly educated workforces and all have relatively effective public sectors, providing education, transport and welfare. However, they are all also quite open to international trade and exchange, in commerce and culture. They are inclusive but high-tech societies, in which Internet usage is high and mobile telephones are common. They generally welcome new technologies. The Nordic countries are home to some of the most impressive new technology companies in Europe, such as Nokia. Consumer innovation with new technologies is as advanced in the Nordic countries as it is in Silicon Valley. These societies have also experimented socially, with new approaches to public support for families, including time off for parents and national childcare facilities. They prize political consensus but they are also adaptive. Holland, for example, has overhauled much of its labour market and welfare policies in the past decade. In the mid 1980s the country had one of the worst long-term unemployment rates in Europe. Now it has one of the best. All these societies are home to a thriving private sector, including a host of new technology companies created in the past decade as well as older multinationals, such as Philips, Ericsson and Electrolux. Environmental awareness and innovation with environmental policies are highly advanced. In short these open, adaptive, well educated, largely social democratic countries, which are open to the global market and yet rely on an effective civic machinery to help people cope with change, may become some of the most promising models of the future. These societies practise inclusive and multi-dimensional politics: they value equality and community but also individuality and innovation. They seek to reconcile these different values rather than champion one at the expense of all the others. Above all, perhaps, they recognize the role of civic and public services is to help provide people with a sense of stability and inclusion in the face of the tendency of innovation and the market to produce change and widen inequality.

These adaptive social democratic societies will be just one among many possible models of innovation-based societies. There will be many others. Fundamentalist Muslim societies may reject much innovation from the west. Silicon Valley, based on venture capital, entrepreneurship, immigration and low public spending, will likely continue to be a world centre of innovation, particularly as information technology and advances in biology and genetics converge. Singapore's remarkable rise as a well educated, knowledge-based trading society may well continue, with a strong state role in guiding the economy, but only limited welfare provision. Other hybrids that will combine markets and state, religion and communal culture in different ways will emerge across Asia in the next few decades. Meanwhile cities and regions from Bilbao and Barcelona, to Munich and Cambridge, will be the centrepieces for experiments to create distinctive local cultures of innovation.

We have fewer grand utopian visions than we had in the past. That is no bad thing. Instead we could witness a multiplication of different kinds of societies, each attempting to adjust to the promise and problems of innovation, using the market and the state in different ways. We will have fewer large-scale, high-risk social experiments and perhaps a multiplication of smaller, more modest but more sustainable and useful experiments. All the successful experiments are likely to have five main ingredients. One of the principal jobs of political leadership will be to make sure these ingredients are in place.

First, innovation cannot get started, in any field, without variety and diversity. Utopianism becomes dangerous when all our yearning converges on a single, all-embracing vision that seems to offer everything, whether that be the politics of communism, the appeal of the Internet or fundamentalist religion. Societies innovate when there is a multiplicity of overlapping and competing visions of innovation and the future, jostling with one another. The richer the mix, the more likely we are to generate good ideas. Innovation starts not with the pursuit of perfection but with mutation, the conscious creation of diversity and variety. That implies a process in which the many failures are vital because they help pave the way for successes.

Second, the need for diversity and variety to drive innovation forward means that innovation thrives in systems, cultures, organizations and societies that are porous and open. Markets triumphed over state planning in the late twentieth century largely because markets are better at promoting many decentralized efforts at innovation. Markets provide a selection mechanism for the best ideas in terms of consumer choice. Markets also allow successful ideas to reproduce by extending their market, while also encouraging new entrants to come into play and forcing failures out of business. Markets have triumphed and will continue to be the central organizing instrument of the trading economy because they promote the evolutionary process of innovation. State planning concentrates the capacity for innovation in very few hands and generally defends outmoded forms of production thereby denying the ability of new entrants to come into the market. The weakness of markets is that left to their own devices they would underinvest in the social and cultural activities that are vital to promote learning and creativity in the knowledge economy. Innovation and learning thrive on social interaction. That is why markets are central to innovation but far from enough to promote it.

Societies that promote innovation in science as much as in the arts will need to stand for openness rather than closure, interdependence rather than unilateralism, globalism rather than parochialism. To seek closure is to want to retreat behind physical and cultural walls and mindsets that make us feel more secure and less threatened. One completely natural response to the bewilderment many people felt after September 11th was to want to close the world down and simplify it. Instead of making an intellectual and imaginative leap to explore and understand a world that is more complex than we thought it to be, it is tempting to put a lid on it. It is easy to see already some reactions that are defensive, security conscious and which lead to withdrawal and retreat, nostalgia and melancholy. Security in all its forms, public and private, is probably the world's fastest growing industry. Openness on the other hand means being constantly open to what the world is becoming, to diverse ideas and influences. That is one reason why a widespread capacity for creativity and cultural engagement will be increasingly important and will feed into many other walks of life. Art excels at articulating ambiguity. Information might be true or false, a one or a zero. Art refuses to be pinned down in that way. That is why art is so potent in exploring a complex and shifting world. Art is open when it uses metaphor to draw out similarities amid irreducible difference. Art makes us think outside the categories we normally use; it shocks, surprises and entices us to think afresh, in part by juxtaposing the odd and unusual. Art seeks the edge of our experience, both for pleasure and shock. Societies that are capable of addressing the future need investment not just in scientific speculation but a matching investment in artistic exploration, cultivating an open, diverse, vibrant space for artistic expression. We should be funding all sorts of expeditions into the future to explore what it might hold, expeditions by scientists and artists, corporate marketers and environmentalists.

Third, innovation prospers amid diversity and diversity

comes from growing interdependence among nations, cultures and disciplines. Innovation calls for a capacity to develop new ways of doing things, crafting and negotiating relationships, products and services, which calls for flexibility and ingenuity. Our capacity to assemble the ingredients we need to experiment with new recipes for work, culture and government expands the more interdependent we are and the faster we can learn and borrow from one another. Innovation thrives in networks that promote interdependence and collaboration. As innovation and imagination become ever more central to wealth creation and well-being, so interdependence will become indispensable.

Fourth, innovation is more likely to be successful, especially as a social activity, when it is a cumulative process, not a make-or-break event. We are always creatively making do with an historic legacy of routines and institutions, which limit our freedom of action. We have to build from the bric-à-brac left behind by previous generations. Moreover, innovation is often about finding new iterations for old successful ideas. This applies particularly to many of our social and civic institutions, of libraries and schools, hospitals and local governance. These are not institutions we can, or should, seek to sweep away but to innovate from within. Most social innovation is cumulative. Take libraries as an example.

The public library should have a prominent role in a knowledge-based society. Libraries embody civic principles and values: they are open, inclusive, democratic and egalitarian. They allow people to pursue their private curiosity and learning, in a private and social setting. Yet in many ways libraries have become stuck with old buildings, customs and practices and ways of thinking. The most ambitious library development project in the world is underway in Singapore, where the National Library Board is building about 100 libraries over an eight-year period. The NLB is innovating with 'fast food' libraries in shopping centres; libraries that hold performances of live music; libraries entirely designed for teenagers; the first ever 'do-it-yourself' libraries where electronic systems help users to put books back on the shelves in the right place, so that staff do not have to do so; arts libraries based entirely on materials linked to music, film, theatre and performing arts. The principles behind Singapore's aggressive expansion of libraries are simple. Rather than 'one-size-fits-all' the National Library Board is seeking to create many different kinds of library, each with a different market and users, and each providing new lessons about what works. The other key motto at the NLB is: one good idea, many different iterations. Having first experimented with libraries located in shopping malls, the NLB is now on to its sixth such venture.

Fifth, innovation is an evolutionary, messy process. There will be greater variety but also more failures. Thorstein Veblen, for example, the US economist and founding father of what has today become evolutionary economics, argued that progress is an unfolding, messy and chaotic process, in which people are constantly being thrown off balance. The free market search for perfect equilibrium or the communist search for a perfectly planned economic order were but different versions of the same mistake, according to Veblen.[4] Both sought to hold the world in a perfect, harmonious balance. The reality is that progress requires a constant disequilibrium. All progress depends on impurities and failures. Progress is an evolutionary process driven by the generation of variety and diversity. As we have seen throughout this book it is likely to throw up a widening array of hybrids, which mix old and new ways of doing things: public transport systems and electronic cars; telemedicine and personal consultants; lessons online and in classrooms. The old will not be swept away by the new, but often incorporated into it. New technology is often used to provide better versions of old and familiar experiences.

The implications for policy making in governments and corporations of this evolutionary and innovation-driven account of hope and progress include the following. Reigning uncertainty and incomplete knowledge make a fully rational, complete picture of the world and how it should be redesigned, impossible. All policies are fallible and so should be adaptive and to some extent provisional. Policy in all areas needs to be developed in part through a conscious process of exploration and experimentation, by launching expeditions to explore what the future of schooling, welfare, the family and immigration might be like. Good policy choices can be made only in the context of a variety of experiments and options for the future. Variety and diversity are absolutely essential to avoid closure in which systems and organizations get trapped on a single path to the future. No system, whether in culture, government, science or commerce, can adapt unless it can generate variety. Learning and adaptation, amid variety and diversity, are an open, democratic process. It is less like a dialogue between organized social partners or constituencies and ever more like a multilogue, involving a crowd of voices. There is little room for romance, excitement or hope in a world that is closed down by authoritarian government, corporate power, monopolies or religious authority. Keeping society open for imagination and innovation means keeping it open for diversity and variety, and that in turn means challenging vested interests and monopolies. In retrospect the anti-globalization movement of the last few years may come to be seen as the first voice of a new global polity that seeks to wrest the agenda of globalization out of the hands of corporations and remote supranational institutions. In that sense it could be a force for openness.

But there is a cost to living in a world in which hope rests on imagination and innovation, our constant capacity to come up with new recipes for how we organize ourselves. Constant innovation makes the world uncertain, unsettled and unpredictable. We can have hope only because society is unfinished, still developing and learning. That in turn means that we have to endure uncertainty about what might be in store. When hope is joined to certainty about the future, it produces closed utopian visions that in turn can all too easily lead to apocalyptic consequences.

Principled Despair, Unprincipled Hope

The danger is that without clear utopian values about justice, equality and democracy politics simply becomes no more than a brute clash of interests, without any higher purpose. The pessimists such as Robert Kaplan, writing in the tradition of Machiavelli, Hobbes and Lenin, see politics as no more than a bleak struggle for power. But politics has never been just that, at least in aspiration.[5] Politics is as much about how we can cooperate in governance, as about how we compete for power. The problem is that without innovation in politics and governance, our capacity for cooperation will always lag behind the sources of competition. This is most clearly the case in respect of globalization, perhaps the biggest social innovation most of us are likely to live through.

The tensions and inequalities thrown up by globalization and innovation require a political response. If we cannot innovate new institutions to govern the global economy cooperatively, to promote greater stability, more equitable development and much wider access to trade and education, then the disputes bred by globalization will inevitably feed competitive political solutions. As the Cambridge University political theorist John Dunn puts it in *The Cunning of Unreason*: 'Politics persistently lags economics, while being permanently required to sustain it.' This gap between the unresolved issues thrown up by globalization, from trade to the environment, and the capacity of political institutions, national and international, to respond, creates the breeding ground for a politics which in Dunn's view is 'irritable, reactive and myopic: endlessly saturated with ressentiment'.

Politics now faces an innovative challenge on a global scale. People struggle against one another and cooperate together, however unenthusiastically, on a far larger scale than they have ever done before. Politics affects more aspects of our lives, from childbirth to voluntary euthanasia, than it ever has before and it embraces more people because we live in a more interdependent world. It is very unlikely that we will overcome the causes of conflict in a global economy through articulating a single, unifying, utopian vision of the future. Instead we need to give more people, especially poorer states, a larger voice in influencing the process of innovation and growth which is driving globalization. We have less need of a vision of what the global economy will look like in future and more of a sense of how poorer states and peoples can acquire the means to influence the process, through education, communications, democratic development and reform to international institutions.

Radical anti-globalization pessimists are latter-day heirs to the traditions of socialism: a romantic response to a world disenchanted by capitalism and a natural world subordinated to technology. Socialism, as all radical utopian projects, offered instead the promise of an enchanted future. We should adopt a more limited, realizable and in many ways more useful goal: to make a future for ourselves and our children – and particularly for those who are worse off – which is as good or better than the present we have inherited from our ancestors. We need neither the fatalism of the pessimists nor the extreme and false voluntarism of the utopians that society can be remade from scratch. Instead we should adopt a far more evolutionary goal to promote socially inclusive innovation.

The economist Geoffrey Hodgson saw the challenge in this way in his recent book *Economics and Utopia*: 'In very general terms a challenge for the 21st century is not the construction of a fixed and final utopia but of *evotopia* – a system that can foster learning, enhance human capacities, systematically incorporate growing knowledge and adapt to changing circumstances.' The very fact that there is learning to be done and human capacities to be enhanced means that no fixed blueprint of a desired future is possible. However, for similar reasons, it is likewise impossible to remain satisfied with existing conditions. This is not a recipe for complacency. For globalization to succeed it needs to go further and become a far more equitable process. Our capacity for innovation needs to be directed towards extending the lifespan, especially in developing countries; providing everyone with decent housing, food, water and basic education; reducing the environmental impact of economic growth; spreading democratic debate and communication. The more our capacity for innovation can be guided to help resolve these very large social issues, rather than simply producing the next software upgrade, the better.

Some critics will argue that this account of hope based on our capacity for innovation, imagination and evolution is too pragmatic. I would prefer a pragmatic sense of hope for the future, rather than principled despair, the self-congratulatory air of pessimism which is so fashionable among the intelligentsia, both left and right. The chronic pessimism that has grown over the past few years is overdone and self-fulfilling. It is designed to alarm and then disable us, to make us feel that the world is beyond our control. According to Raymond Tallis in *Enemies of Hope*, his survey of anti-Enlightenment pessimism in philosophy and psychology:

If we do not believe in the possibility of a better future brought about by progressive and patient social reform and by the application of ever more effective technology, that future will surely not come about. We have a responsibility to those who otherwise will be without hope to keep alive the hope of progress.

Far from living in a lawless world of disorder, what is striking is how easy it is now to travel the world in relative safety and calm. There are sizeable parts of the world where millions of ordinary people are living lives of relative comfort and security, in conditions of reasonable justice and at least partial democracy. It is now far more common than it ever was in the past for the powerful to be held to account for their actions. Abuses of power are increasingly challenged and questioned. It is far more common for children to expect to be educated and then to live a long life. We routinely expect science and technology, often mobilized through global collaboration, to eliminate disease and provide solutions to environmental ills. We are more able than ever before to exchange ideas, goods, services, art and culture. In a growing number of societies, most of the people, most of the time, not just the well off and the powerful, are treated with at least a modicum of respect as individuals and not based on their status, rank or birth right. Infant mortality has fallen in the last half century in the developing world, while life expectancy has increased. The number of people affected by famine is still far too high, but it is lower than the number affected at the end of the nineteenth century, when the world population was far smaller. Food production in the last fifty years has regularly outstripped population growth without more land being required. The average worker can now buy more warmth, food, entertainment and pleasure with a day's wages than even thirty years ago. Things are not getting inexorably worse the whole time. In many respects they are getting better.

Environmentalists tell us that the earth's future hangs precariously in the balance. Yet as Peter Medawar pointed out thirty years ago in *The Hope of Progress*, although humans have been around for 500,000 years it is really only in the last 500 years that they have been a biological success and only in the last fifty that science and technology have become really effective. It is only in the very recent past that life has become anything more than precarious for most people and that we have been able to worry persistently about justice for all, the rights of the many, the enrichment of the poor and the empowerment of the powerless. Our world does not yet live up to standards that we have only recently been able to establish. That those are the standards we now employ is itself a sign of immense progress.

Above all, through science and technology, art and culture, education and learning our collective and distributed ability to imagine a range of different futures for ourselves has expanded immeasurably. These are classically Enlightenment values, but as they globalize and spread this century, they will diversify and cross-pollinate to create new varieties and hybrids. Just as English has become a global language, a global property, with many different branches, these Enlightenment values will adapt and change. Progress and improvement are impossible without innovation and imagination. We are becoming a society of speculators. The more we speculate about what the future might hold on a widening range of issues the better off we will be. We speculate or die.

Notes

Preface – Pessimism in Power

1. Martin Rees, 'Eternity: Why We Matter', *Prospect*, January 2000
2. Martin E. P. Seligman, *Learned Optimism*, Pocket Books, 1991
3. Lionel Tiger, *Optimism: The Biology of Hope*, Simon and Schuster, 1979

1 – The Gathering Gloom

1. See Oliver Bennett, *Cultural Pessimism*, Edinburgh University Press, 2001 for a general discussion of contemporary pessimism
2. Don DeLillo, 'In the Ruins of the Future', *Harper's Magazine*, December 2001
3. For a discussion of 'social recession' amid economic growth see David Myers, *The American Paradox*, Yale University Press, 2000
4. For a good discussion of the psychology of pessimism see among other essays Barry Schwartz, 'Pitfalls on the Road to Positive', in *The Science of Optimism and Hope*, Jane E. Gillham (ed.), Templeton Foundation Press, 2000
5. Alan Murray, *The Wealth of Choices*, Crown Business Books, 2000
6. This section draws upon Martin Seligman, 'Positive Psychology', in *The Science of Optimism and Hope*, Jane E. Gillham (ed.), Templeton Foundation Press, 2000, p. 419 for sources
7. The argument of Naomi Klein's *No Logo*, Flamingo, 1999
8. For material on links between pessimism and depression see

various articles in *The Science of Optimism and Hope*, Research
Essays in Honour of Martin E. P. Seligman, Jane E. Gillham
(ed.), Templeton Foundation Press, 2000; *Optimism and Pessimism: Implications for Theory, Research, and Practice*, Edward C.
Chang (ed.), American Psychological Association, 2001

9. See Dick Pountain and David Robins, *Cool Rules*, Reaktion
   Books, 2000

10. This section draws on Stuart Kauffman, *At Home in the Universe*,
    Penguin, 1995

11. Michael B. Arthur and Denise Rousseau (eds.), *The Boundaryless
    Career*, Oxford University Press, 1996

12. Marc Auge, *Non-Places*, Pluto, 2001

2 – The Great Escape

1. Andrew Ross, *The Celebration Chronicles*, Verso, 2000

2. Andrew Wood, 'Re Reading Disney's Celebration' in Amy
   Bingaman, Lise Sanders and Rebecca Zorach (eds.), *Embodied
   Utopias*, Routledge, 2002

3. J. Kunstler, *The Geography of Nowhere: The Rise and Decline of
   America's Man Made Landscape*, Simon and Schuster, 1993

4. Andres Duany and Elizabeth Plater Zyberk, 'The Second
   Coming of the American Small Town', Historical Preservation
   Forum, Spring 1995. See also by the same authors, 'The
   Neighborhood, the District and the Corridor' in P. Katz, *The
   New Urbanism*, New York, McGraw Hill, 1994

5. Svetlana Boym, *The Future of Nostalgia*, Basic Books, 2001

6. Stephanie Coontz, *The Way We Never Were*, Basic Books, 1992,
   2000 edition

7. Ibid.

8. David Boswell and Jessica Evans (eds.), *Representing the Nation*,
   Routledge, 1999

9. Robert Hewison, *The Heritage Industry*, Methuen, 1987

10. Raphael Samuel, *Theatres of Memory*, vol. 1 – *Past and Present in Contemporary Culture*, Verso, 1994

11. D. Lowenthal, *The Past is a Foreign Country*, Cambridge University Press, 1985

12. B. Frieden and L. Sagalyn, *Downtown Inc: How America Rebuilds Cities*, MIT Press, 1989

13. John Urry, *The Tourist Gaze*, Sage, 1990

14. David Matless, *Landscape and Englishness*, Reaktion Books, 1998

15. W. G. Hoskins, *The Making of the English Landscape*, London, 1955, quoted in Matless, *Landscape and Englishness*.

16. Ibid.

17. Andrew O'Hagan, *The End of British Farming*, Profile Books, 2001

18. Michael Paris, *Warrior Nation: Images of War in British Popular Culture 1850–2000*, Reaktion Books, 2002

19. Keith Thomas, *Man and the Natural World, Changing Attitudes in England 1500–1800*, Penguin, 1983

20. Nigel Slater, *Real Food*, Fourth Estate, 2000

3 – Death Wish Nation

1. Daniel Pick, *Faces of Degeneration, A European Disorder c1848–c1918*, Cambridge University Press, 1989

2. Quoted in Stanley Grupp (ed.), *The Positive School of Criminology, Three Lectures by Enrico Ferri*, Pittsburgh, 1968

3. Katharine Washburn and John Thornton, *Dumbing Down, Essays on the Strip Mining of American Culture*, W. W. Norton, 1996

4. Colin Trodd et al (eds.), *Victorian Culture and the Idea of the Grotesque*, Ashgate, 1999

5. Melanie Phillips, 'Sleepwalking to Tyranny', *Daily Mail*, 20 February 2002

4 – The Pessimists' Alliance

1. Noorena Hertz, *Silent Takeover*, Heinemann, 2001
2. Thomas Frank, *One Market Under God*, Secker and Warburg, 2001
3. Theodor Adorno and Max Horkheimer, *Dialectic of the Enlightenment*, translated by John Cumming, Allen Lane, 1972

5 – The Dream of Digitopia

1. This section draws on Herman Pleij, *Dreaming of Cockaigne, Medieval Fantasies of the Perfect Life*, translated by Diane Webb, Columbia University Press, 2001
2. For an excellent discussion of the romanticism attached to digital technology see Richard Coyne, *Technoromanticism: Digital Narrative, Holism and the Romance of the Real*, MIT Press, 1999. For good discussions of the meaning of utopia see Roland Schaer, Gregory Claeys and Lyman Tower Sargent (eds.), *Utopia: The Search for the Ideal Society in the Western World*, New York Public Library and Oxford University Press, 2000; and John Carey (ed.), *The Faber Book of Utopias*, Faber, 1999
3. These figures were quoted by the science writer Matt Ridley in his Duke of Edinburgh Annual Lecture at the Royal Society of Arts, April 2001
4. See Richard Lewontin, *It Ain't Necessarily So*, Granta, 2000
5. See Tom Wilkie, 'Genes "R" Us' in George Robertson et al (eds.), *Future Natural*, Routledge, 1996
6. Peter Menzel and Faith D'Alusio, *Robo Sapiens: Evolution of a New Species*, MIT Press, 2000
7. Quoted in Tiziana Terranova, 'Posthuman Unbounded: Artificial Evolution and High Tech Subcultures', in George Robertson et al (eds.), *Future Natural*, Routledge, 1996
8. This section draws on David E. Nye, *American Technological Sublime*, MIT Press, 1996

9. Edmund Burke, *A Philosophical Enquiry into the Origin of Our Ideas of the Sublime and Beautiful*, Oxford University Press, 1990, quoted in Nye, *American Technological Sublime*

10. Don DeLillo, 'In the Ruins of the Future', *Harper's Magazine*, December 2001

6 – The Terror of Technotopia

1. Mark Slouka, 'In Praise of Silence and Slow Time: Nature and Mind in a Derivative Age', in Sven Birkets (ed.), *Tolstoy's Dictaphone. Technology and the Muse*, Graywolf Press, 1996

2. Joseph Urgo, *In the Age of Distraction*, University Press of Mississippi, 2000

3. Vince Khosla, 'The Digital Age', *The New Yorker*, 27 November 2000

4. James Spohrer, 'The Digital Age', *The New Yorker*, 27 November 2000

5. Hilary Lawson, *Closure: A Story of Everything*, Routledge, 2001

8 – The Age of Self-rule

1. Benjamin R. Barber, *Jihad vs McWorld*, Ballantine Books, 1995

2. Charles Leadbeater and Kate Oakley, *The Independents*, Demos, 1999

3. Robert William Fogel, *The Fourth Great Awakening and the Future of Egalitarianism*, University of Chicago Press, 2000

9 – The End of Capitalism

1. Thomas E. Cliffe Leslie, *Essays in Political Economy*, 1888, reprinted August Kelley, 1969

2. Sze Tsung Leong, 'And Then There Was Shopping: The Last Remaining Form of Public Life', in *Harvard Design School Guide to Shopping*, Taschen, 2002

3. Daniel Goleman, *Emotional Intelligence*, Bloomsbury, 1996
4. Charles Leadbeater and Kate Oakley, *Surfing the Long Wave: The Rise of the Knowledge Entrepreneur*, Demos, 2001

10 – The Personalized Society

1. Johan Norberg, *In Defence of Global Capitalism*, AB Timbro, 2001

11 – Globalization Can Be Good

1. Jay Mazur, *Foreign Affairs*, vol. 79, no. 1, Jan–Feb 2000, Council of Foreign Relations, Washington
2. Ramón López-Ortega, British Council Conference, 1984, proceedings reprinted in English by Cambridge University Press, 1985
3. Manfred Görlach, *More Englishes: New Studies in Varieties of English 1988 to 1994*, John Benjamins, 1995
4. Harold Pinter, 'What We Think of America', *Granta*, no. 77, January 2002
5. Martin Wolf, 'A Stepping Stone from Poverty', *Financial Times*, 19 December 2001
6. Ed Graham, *Fighting the Wrong Enemy: Antiglobal Activists and Multinational Enterprises*, Institute for International Economics, Washington, 2000
7. Pinter, 'What We Think'
8. Michael Hardt and Antonio Negri, *Empire*, Harvard University Press, 2000

12 – Militant Optimism

1. Aleksandr A. Blok, 'The Intelligentsia and the Revolution', 1918 in M. Raeff (ed.), *Russian Intellectual History: An Anthology*,

New York, Harcourt Brace and World, 1966, quoted in Russell Jacoby, *The End of Utopia*, Basic Books, 1999

2. For a good account of the attractions and downsides of life in More's utopia see Elizabeth Grosz, 'The Time of Architecture' in Amy Bingaman, Lise Sanders and Rebecca Zorach (eds.), *Embodied Utopias*, Routledge, 2002

3. Le Corbusier, *Aircraft*, Foundation Le Corbusier, Paris, 1987

4. Thorstein Veblen, 'Why is Economics not an Evolutionary Science', reprinted in *The Place of Science in Modern Civilization and Other Essays*, Huebsch, 1990 with a new introduction by W. J. Samuels

5. John Dunn, *The Cunning of Unreason: Making Sense of Politics*, HarperCollins, 2000

Bibliography

Adorno, Theodor, *The Culture Industry*, Routledge, 1991

Arthur, Michael B. and Rousseau, Denise M. (eds.), *The Boundaryless Career*, Oxford University Press, 1996

Auge, Marc, trans. John Howe, *Non-Places: Introduction to an Anthropology of Supermodernity*, Pluto, 2001

Axelrod, Robert and Cohen, Michael D., *Harnessing Complexity: Organisational Implications of a Scientific Frontier*, Free Press, 1999

Ban Breathnach, Sarah, *Simple Abundance: A Daybook of Comfort and Joy*, Bantam Books, 1997

Barber, Benjamin R., *Jihad vs McWorld*, Ballantine Books, 1995

Bauman, Zygmunt, *Globalisation: The Human Consequences*, Polity Press, 1998

Benedickt, Michael, *Cyberspace: The First Steps*, MIT Press, 1991

Bennett, Oliver, *Cultural Pessimism: Narratives of Decline in the Postmodern World*, Edinburgh University Press, 2001

Berlin, Isaiah, 'The Apotheosis of the Romantic Will' in Hardy, Henry (ed.), *The Crooked Timber of Humanity*, HarperCollins, 1991

Berman, Morris, *The Twilight of American Culture*, Duckworth, 2001

Bingaman, Amy, Sanders, Lise and Zorach, Rebecca, *Embodied Utopias: Gender, Social Change and the Modern Metropolis*, Routledge, 2002

Bloch, Ernst, *The Principle of Hope*, 3 vols, MIT Press, 1995

—, *The Utopian Function of Art and Literature*, MIT Press, 1996

—, trans. A. Nassar, *The Spirit of Utopia*, Stanford University Press, 2000

Boswell, David and Evans, Jessica (eds.), *Representing the Nation: A Reader*, Routledge with the Open University Press, 1999

Boym, Svetlana, *The Future of Nostalgia*, Basic Books, 2001

Buck Morss, Susan, *Dreamworld and Catastrophe: The Passing of Mass Utopia in East and West*, MIT Press, 2000

Burke, Edmund, *A Philosophical Enquiry into the Origin of Our Ideas of the Sublime and Beautiful*, Oxford University Press, 1990

Burke, Tom, *Ten Pinches of Salt: A Reply to Bjorn Lomborg*, Green Alliance, 2002

Callenbach, Ernest, *Ecotopia*, Bantam, 1990

Canetti, Elias, *Crowds and Power*, Penguin, 1972

Carey, John (ed.), *The Faber Book of Utopias*, Faber, 1999

Castells, Manuel, *The Internet Galaxy*, Oxford University Press, 2001

Chang, Edward C. (ed.), *Optimism and Pessimism: Implications for Theory, Research and Practice*, American Psychological Association, 2000

Coontz, Stephanie, *The Way We Never Were: American Families and the Nostalgia Trap*, Basic Books, 2000

Cornoy, Martin, *Sustaining the New Economy, Working Family and Community in the Information Age*, Russell Sage Foundation, 2000

Coyle, Diane, *Paradoxes of Prosperity, Why the New Capitalism Benefits All*, Texere, 2001

Coyne, Richard, *Technoromanticism: Digital Narrative, Holism and the Romance of the Real*, MIT Press, 1999

Crystal, David, *English as a Global Language*, Canto, Cambridge University Press, 1997

Daniel, Jamie Owen and Moylan, Tom (eds.), *Not Yet: Reconsidering Ernst Bloch*, Verso, 1997

DeLillo, Don, *White Noise*, Picador, 1988

Dollimore, Jonathan, *Death, Desire and Loss in Western Culture*, Penguin, 1998

Dunn, John, *The Cunning of Unreason: Making Sense of Politics*, HarperCollins, 2000

Elgin, Duane, *Voluntary Simplicity: Toward a Way of Life that is Outwardly Simple, Inwardly Rich*, Quill, 1993

Esping-Andersen, Gosta, *Social Foundations of Postindustrial Economies*, Oxford University Press, 1999

Fallows, James, 'He's Got Mail', *New York Review of Books*, April 2002

Fogel, Robert William, *The Fourth Great Awakening and the Future of Egalitarianism*, University of Chicago Press, 2000

Frank, Thomas, *One Market Under God*, Secker and Warburg, 2001

Frieden, B. and Sagalyn, L., *Downtown Inc: How America Rebuilds Cities*, MIT Press, 1989

Friedman, Thomas, *The Lexus and the Olive Tree*, HarperCollins, 1999

Fukuyama, Francis, *The End of History and the Last Man*, Penguin, 1993

Gardner, Howard, *Intelligence Reframed: Multiple Intelligences for the 21st Century*, Basic Books, 1999

Gergen, Kenneth, *The Saturated Self: Dilemmas of Identity in Contemporary Life*, Basic Books, 1991

Gilder, George, *Telecosm*, Free Press, 2000

Gillham, Jane, E. (ed.), *The Science of Optimism and Hope: Essays in Honour of Martin E. P. Seligman*, Templeton Foundation Press, 2000

Gladwell, Malcolm, *The Tipping Point: How Little Things Can Make a Big Difference*, Little, Brown, 2000

Goleman, Daniel, *Emotional Intelligence*, Bloomsbury, 1996

Gordon, Philip and Meunier, Sophie, *The French Challenge: Adapting to Globalisation*, Brookings Institution, 2001

Gore, Al, *Earth in Balance: Ecology and the Human Spirit*, Boston, Houghton Mifflin, 1992

Görlach, Manfred, *More Englishes: New Studies in Varieties of English 1988 to 1994*, John Benjamins, 1995

Gorz, Andre, *Farewell to the Working Class*, Pluto Press, 1997

Graham, Edward M., *Fighting the Wrong Enemy: Antiglobal Activists and Multinational Enterprises*, Institute for International Economics, 2000

Graham, Gordon, *The Internet: A Philosophical Inquiry*, Routledge, 1999

Gray, John, *False Dawn: The Delusions of Global Capitalism*, Granta, 1998

Halliday, Fred, *Two Hours That Shook the World, September 11 2001: Causes and Consequences*, Saqi Books, 2002

Hardt, Michael and Negri, Antonio, *Empire*, Harvard University Press, 2000

Harvey, David, *Spaces of Hope*, Edinburgh University Press, 2000

Hertz, Noorena, *Silent Takeover*, Heinemann, 2001

Hirst, Paul and Thompson, Grahame, *Globalisation in Question*, Polity Press, 1996

Hitchens, Peter, *The Abolition of Britain*, Quartet, 2000

Hochschild, Arlie, *Time Blind*, Metropolitan, 1996

Hodgson, Geoffrey M., *Economics and Evolution*, Polity Press, 1993

—, *Economics and Utopia: Why the Learning Economy is Not the End of History*, Routledge, 1999

Horkheimer, Max and Adorno, Theodor, trans. John Cumming, *The Dialectic of the Enlightenment*, Allen Lane, The Penguin Press, 1972

Hoskins, W. G., *The Making of the English Landscape*, London, 1955

Jacoby, Russell, *The End of Utopia: Politics and Culture in an Age of Apathy*, Basic Books, 1999

Kaplan, Robert D., *The Coming Anarchy: Shattering the Dreams of the Post Cold War World*, Vintage, 2000

—, *Warrior Politics: Why Leadership Demands a Pagan Ethos*, Random House, 2002

Kauffman, Stuart, *At Home in the Universe: The Search for Laws of Self Organisation and Complexity*, Penguin, 1995

Klein, Naomi, *No Logo*, Flamingo, 2000

Kotkin, Joel, *Tribes: How Race, Religion and Identity Determine Success in the New Global Economy*, Random House, 1993

Kunstler, J., *The Geography of Nowhere: The Rise and Decline of America's Man Made Landscape*, Simon and Schuster, 1993

Lasn, Kalle, *Culture Jam: How to Reverse America's Suicidal Consumer Binge*, Quill, 1999

Lawson, Hilary, *Closure: A Story of Everything*, Routledge, 2001

Leach, William, *Country of Exiles: The Destruction of Place in American Life*, Vintage Books, 2000

Leadbeater, Charles and Oakley, Kate, *The Independents*, Demos, 1999

—, *Surfing the Long Wave: The Rise of the Knowledge Entrepreneur*, Demos, 2001

Leong, Sze Tsung, 'And Then There Was Shopping: The Last Remaining Form of Public Life, *Harvard Design School Guide to Shopping*, Taschen, 2002

Lessig, Lawrence, *Code and Other Laws of Cyberspace*, Basic Books, 1999

Levine, Rick, Locke, Christopher, Searls, Doc and Weinberger, David, *The Cluetrain Manifesto: The End of Business as Usual*, Perseus, 2000

Lewydesdorff, Loet and van den Besselaar, Peter, *Evolutionary Economics and Chaos Theory: New Directions in Technology Studies*, St Martins Press, 1994

Lifton, Robert J., *The Protean Self: Human Resilience in the Age of Fragmentation*, Basic Books, 1993

Lloyd, John, *The Protest Ethic: How the Anti Globalisation Movement Challenges Social Democracy*, Demos, 2002

Lomborg, Bjorn, *The Skeptical Environmentalist: Measuring the Real State of the World*, Cambridge University Press, 2001

Lovins, Amory and Hunter, and Hawken, Paul, *Natural Capitalism: the Next Industrial Revolution*, Earthscan, 1999

Lowenthal, D., *The Past is a Foreign Country*, Cambridge University Press, 1985

Luttwak, Edward, *Turbo Capitalism: Winners and Losers in the Global Economy*, Weidenfeld and Nicolson, 1998

McArthur, Tom, *The English Languages*, Canto, Cambridge University Press, 1998

McKelvey, Maureen, *Evolutionary Innovations*, Oxford University Press, 1996

McNeil, John, *Something New Under the Sun: An Environmental History of the Twentieth Century*, Allen Lane, The Penguin Press, 2000

Marcuse, Herbert, *One Dimensional Man*, Beacon Press, 1964

Matless, David, *Landscape and Englishness*, Reaktion Books, 1998

Menzel, Peter and D'Alusio, Faith, *Robo Sapiens: Evolution of a New Species*, MIT Press, 2000

Medawar, Peter, *The Hope of Progress*, Methuen, 1972

Mitchell, William J., *E-topia*, MIT Press, 2000

Moravec, Hans, *Mind Children: The Future of Robot and Human Intelligence*, Harvard University Press, 1988

Morris, William, *News from Nowhere*, Penguin, 1993

Murray, Alan, *The Wealth of Choices*, Crown Business Books, 2000

Myers, David G., *The American Paradox: Spiritual Hunger in an Age of Plenty*, Yale University Press, 2000

Nagel, Thomas, *Equality and Partiality*, Oxford University Press, 1991

Nettle, Daniel and Romaine, Suzanne, *Vanishing Voices: The Extinction of the World's Languages*, Oxford University Press, 2000

Norberg, Johan, *In Defence of Global Capitalism*, AB Timbro, 2001

Nordau, Max, *Degeneration*, University of Nebraska Press, 1968

Nye, David E., *American Technological Sublime*, MIT Press, 1996

O'Hagan, Andrew, *The End of British Farming*, Profile Books, 2001

Paris, Michael, *Warrior Nation: Images of War in British Popular Culture 1850–2000*, Reaktion Books, 2002

Pepperell, Robert, *The Post Human Condition*, Intellect, 1995

Pick, Daniel, *Faces of Degeneration: A European Disorder c1848–c1918*, Cambridge University Press, 1989

Piercy, Marge, *Woman on the Edge of Time*, The Women's Press, 1979

Pinter, Harold, 'What We Think of America', *Granta*, no. 77, January 2002

Pleij, Herman, trans. Diane Webb, *Dreaming of Cockaigne: Medieval Fantasies of the Perfect Life*, Columbia University Press, 2001

Porter, Michael and van der Linde, Claas, 'Towards a New Conception of the Environment–Competitiveness Relationship', *Journal of Economic Perspectives*, Fall 1995

Pountain, Dick and Robins, David, *Cool Rules: An Anatomy of an Attitude*, Reaktion Books, 2000

Putnam, Robert D., *Bowling Alone: The Collapse and Revival of American Community*, Simon and Schuster, 2000

Rifkin, Jeremy, *The Age of Access*, Penguin, 2000

Robertson, George et al (eds.), *Future Natural*, Routledge, 1996

Rorty, Richard, *Achieving Our Country*, Harvard University Press, 1998

—, *Philosophy and Social Hope*, Penguin, 1999

Rosen, Jeffrey, *The Unwanted Gaze: The Destruction of Privacy in America*, Random House, 2000

Ross, Andrew, *The Celebration Chronicles: Life, Liberty and the Pursuit of Property Value in Disney's New Town*, Verso, 2000

Samuel, Raphael, *Theatres of Memory*, vol. 1. *Past and Present in Contemporary Culture*, Verso, 1994

Schwartz, Barry, 'Pitfalls on the Road to Positive' in Gillham, Jane E. (ed.), *The Science of Optimism and Hope*, Templeton Foundation Press, 2001

Schaer, Roland, Claeys, Gregory and Sargent, Lyman Tower (eds.), *Utopia: The Search for the Ideal Society in the Western World*, New York Public Library and Oxford University Press, 2000

Scruton, Roger, *England: An Elegy*, Pimlico, 2001

Seligman, Adam B., *Modernity's Wager: Authority, the Self and Transcendence*, Princeton University Press, 2000

Seligman, Martin E. P., *Learned Optimism*, Pocket Books, 1991

—, 'Positive Psychology' in Gillham, Jane E. (ed.), *The Science of Optimism and Hope*, Templeton Foundation Press, 2000

Shapiro, Andrew L., *The Control Revolution: How the Internet is*

Putting Individuals in Charge and Changing the World We Know, The Century Foundation, 1999

Silver, Lee M., *Remaking Eden*, Weidenfeld and Nicolson, 1998

Slouka, Mark, *War of the World: Cyberspace and the High Tech Assault on Reality*, Abacus, 1995

Spengler, Oswald, *Decline of the West*, Knopf, 1926, Oxford University Press, 1991

Steiner, George, *Grammars of Creation*, Faber, 2000

Stewart, Susan, *On Longing: Narratives of the Miniature, the Gigantic, the Souvenir and the Collection*, Duke University Press, 1993

Sunstein, Cass, *republic.com*, Princeton University Press, 2001

Tainter, Joseph, *The Collapse of Complex Societies*, Cambridge University Press, 1988

Tallis, Raymond, *Enemies of Hope: A Critique of Contemporary Pessimism*, Macmillan Press, 1997

Taylor, Charles, *Sources of the Self: The Making of Modern Identity*, Cambridge University Press, 1989

Thomas, Keith, *Man and the Natural World, Changing Attitudes in England 1500–1800*, Penguin, 1983

Thompson, Damian, *The End of Time*, Sinclair Stevenson, 1996

Tiger, Lionel, *Optimism: The Biology of Hope*, Simon and Schuster, 1979

Trodd, Colin et al (eds.), *Victorian Culture and the Idea of the Grotesque*, Ashgate, 1999

Turner, Martyn and O'Connell, Brian, *The Whole World's Watching: Decarbonising the Economy and Saving the World*, John Wiley, 2001

Urgo, Joseph R., *In the Age of Distraction*, University Press of Mississippi, 2000

Urry, John, *The Tourist Gaze*, Sage, 1990

Virilio, Paul, trans. Julie Rose, *Open Sky*, Verso, 1997

—, trans. Chris Turner, *The Information Bomb*, Verso, 2000

Washburn, Katharine and Thornton, John, *Dumbing Down, Essays on the Strip Mining of American Culture*, W. W. Norton, 1996

Weinberger, David, *Small Pieces, Loosely Joined*, Perseus, 2002

Wilson, Edward O., *The Diversity of Life*, Penguin, 1993

Wood, Andrew, 'Re Reading Disney's Celebration' in Bingaman, Amy, Sanders, Lise and Zorach, Rebecca (eds.), *Embodied Utopias*, Routledge, 2002

Zachary, Pascal G., *The Global Me*, Nicholas Brearley Publishing, 2000

Zuboff, Shoshona, *In the Age of the Smart Machine*, Butterworth Heinemann, 1989